★

THE
SOVIET
REGIONAL
DILEMMA

THE SOVIET REGIONAL DILEMMA

PLANNING, PEOPLE, AND NATURAL RESOURCES

JAN ÅKE DELLENBRANT

M. E. SHARPE, INC.
ARMONK, NEW YORK
LONDON, ENGLAND

Copyright © 1986 by M. E. Sharpe, Inc.
80 Business Park Drive, Armonk, New York 10504

Translated by Michel Vale

Available in the United Kingdom and Europe from M. E. Sharpe,
Publishers, 3 Henrietta Street, London WC2E 8LU.

Library of Congress Cataloging-in-Publication Data

Dellenbrant, Jan Åke, 1946–
    The Soviet regional dilemma.

    Translation of: Sovjetunionens regionala dilemma.
    Bibliography: p.
    1. Soviet Union—Economic conditions—1976–   —Regional
disparities. 2. Regional planning—Soviet Union. I. Title.
HC336.25.D4513   1986   330.947′0854   86-13049
ISBN 0-87332-384-X

Printed in the United States of America

CONTENTS

List of Tables and Figures   vii

Foreword   3

Preface   7

1. The Problem of Regional Development   10
Regional Dualism
Regional Policy—Ends and Means

2. Theoretical Premises   23
Aims and Hypotheses
Materials and Methods

3. Regional Differences   35
The Official Soviet View
Soviet Location Rules
Western Studies
Soviet and Western Findings—A Comparison

4. The Administrative Organization   62
The Union Level
The Republic Level
Concerns and Enterprises
Territorial Production Complexes
Administrative Problems and Reforms

5. Regional Development under Debate   85
The Europeans and the Sibiriaks
Criticism of *Vedomstvennost'*
Three Development Strategies

6. Decisions on Regional Policy   98
The 1979 Economic Reform
The 1981 Republic Party Congress
The 1981 Union Party Congress
The 11th Five-year Plan
Development after the 26th Party Congress

7. Implementation and Results   132
Definition of Terms
The Problem of Implementation
Plan Targets and Plan Fulfillment

The Instruments of Regional Policy
The Effects of Regional Policy
Employment
Cultural and National Factors
A Reanalysis of Location Criteria

8. Review and Summary   176

Epilogue   182

Notes   184

Bibliography   195

Index   205

About the Author   218

LIST OF FIGURES
AND TABLES

Figures

Figure 1.1.   Favorable and Unfavorable Factors in the Three Macroregions—
Siberia, Central Asia, and Europe—with Regard to Human and
Material Resources *14*

Figure 3.1.   Data Matrix for the Study *Soviet Regional Policy* *54*

Figure 3.2.   Socioeconomic Development in the Soviet Union 1956–73 *54*

Figure 3.3.   Cyclical Regional Inequalities *57*

Figure 4.1.   Economic Planning and Administrative Organizations *78*

Figure 8.1.   Policymaking Stages in the Soviet Union *180*

Tables

Table 1.1.   Capital Investments, Billions of Rubles Per Year, and Cooperative
Enterprises (Including Kolkhozes), at Comparable Prices *15*

Table 1.2.   Population Growth between 1970 and 1980 (per Thousands of
Individuals) *16*

Table 3.1.   Socioeconomic Characteristics of the Soviet Republics *56*

Table 3.2.   National Income 1970, Rubles Per Capita at 1970 Prices *56*

Table 3.3.   The Soviet Republics Including Siberia's Economic Regions,
According to the Industrial Growth Index 1972 *60*

Table 6.1   Industrial Output and Agricultural Output: Percent Growth during the
11th Five-year Planning Period According to the Decision Taken at
the 26th Party Congress *113*

Table 6.2   Growth in Industrial Output in Percent during the Period 1981–85
According to the Decision of the 26th Party Congress and the Law on
Five-year Plans Adopted by the Supreme Soviet *122*

Table 6.3   Growth in Industrial Output in Percent of 1980 Level during the 11th
Five-year Planning Period by Year (1981–85) *123*

Table 6.4   Growth in National Income in Percent of 1980 Level during 11th Five-
year Planning Period by Year (1981–85) *124*

Table 6.5   Growth in Labor Productivity in Industry in Percent of 1980 Level
during 11th Five-year Planning Period by Year (1981–85) *124*

Table 6.6   Growth in Capital Investments in Percent of 1980 Level during 11th
Five-year Planning Period by Year (1981–85) *125*

Table 7.1   Growth in Industrial Output in Percent during 9th and 10th Five-year Plans   *137*

Table 7.2   Growth in National Income, Industrial Output, and Labor Productivity in Industry Plan Target and Plan Outcome for the Entire Soviet Union (Percent of Preceding Year)   *138*

Table 7.3   Growth in National Income, Industrial Output, and Labor Productivity in Industry—Plan Target and Plan Outcome for RSFSR (Percent of Preceding Year)   *140*

Table 7.4   Growth in National Income, Industrial Output, and Labor Productivity in Industry—Plan Target and Plan Outcome for Estonian SSR (Percent of Preceding Year)   *140*

Table 7.5   Growth in National Income, Industrial Output, and Labor Productivity in Industry—Plan Target and Plan Outcome for Latvian SSR (Percent of Preceding Year)   *140*

Table 7.6   Growth in National Income, Industrial Output, and Labor Productivity in Industry—Plan Target and Plan Outcome for Uzbek SSR (Percent of Preceding Year)   *141*

Table 7.7   Growth in National Income, Industrial Output, and Labor Productivity in Industry—Plan Target and Plan Outcome for Turkmen SSR (Percent of Preceding Year)   *141*

Table 7.8   Capital Investments in the Soviet Union in 1970, 1980, and 1982 by Region (Percent of Total Investments)   *144*

Table 7.9   Capital Investments in the Soviet Union in 1970, 1975, and 1980, by Macroregions (Percent of Total Investments), at Comparable Prices   *145*

Table 7.10   Investments in Rubles per Capita, 1970, 1980, and 1982   *146*

Table 7.11   Capital Investments in Rubles per Working Age Population (15–54 or 59 Years), 1980   *148*

Table 7.12   Transfers from Union to Republic Budgets during the 10th Five-year Plan (Millions of Rubles)   *149*

Table 7.13   Republic Budgets 1984, Absolute Figures (Millions of Rubles) and Rubles per Capita (Population January 1, 1983)   *150*

Table 7.14   Wage Coefficients for Industry in Economic Regions, about 1970   *151*

Table 7.15   National Income in Rubles Per Capita (Comparable Prices), 1970, 1980, and 1982   *153*

Table 7.16   National Income, Rubles per Individual of Working Age (15–54 or 59), 1980   *154*

Table 7.17   National Income per Individual of Working Age 1972 and 1980 (USSR = 100)   *155*

Table 7.18   Employed Population in Percent of Total Population   *156*

Table 7.19   Employment Rate for the Entire Population, the Female Population, and the Rural Population in 1979 (Percent of Total Population)   *157*

Table 7.20   Employed Population (Percent of Working Age Population 1970 and 1979)   *158*

Table 7.21   Capital Investments in the Soviet Union 1960 and 1980, by Regions (Percent of Total Investments) at Comparable Prices   *162*

Table 7.22   Population of the Soviet Union 1959 and 1979 (in Thousands and Percent of Total Population)   *163*

Table 7.23   Capital Investments per Capita 1959–60 and 1979–80 (Rubles per Capita)   *164*

Table 7.24   Native (Indigenous) Population and Russians in the Fifteen
             Republics   *164*
Table 7.25   Capital Investments and Distribution of Population among Russian
             Regions and ASSRs within the RSFSR (Percent of Total Investments
             in 1975 and Total Population in 1975)   *165*
Table 7.26   Capital Investments in the RSFSR (Percent of Total Investments
             during 8th Five-year Plan 1966–70 and during 1975)   *166*
Table 7.27   Capital Investments in Asian RSFSR (Rubles Per Capita 1975)   *168*
Table 7.28   Capital Investments in Autonomous Republics in the Asian RSFSR
             (Rubles per Capita 1965 and 1975)   *169*
Table 7.29   Population Composition in the Autonomous Republics in the Asian
             RSFSR (Percent of Total Population 1959 and 1979)   *169*

★

THE
SOVIET
REGIONAL
DILEMMA

FOREWORD

"To Moscow, to Moscow," ends the second act of Chekhov's play, "Three Sisters." The longing to get away from the periphery to the big city, to culture, to material abundance and expectations of great opportunities, is the *leitmotif* in much of classical Russian literature; even today, after almost seventy years of Soviet rule, the longing to go to the capital, the big city, westward, is still present.

Centripetal forces have always been strong in the vast Russian, now Soviet state, which seems to regard it as axiomatic that a centralization of political and hence economic power as well is necessary to hold together this immense land with its hundreds of different nationalities, and the most varying social conditions and world outlooks.

Nowhere in Europe was the contrast between the capital cities and the provinces so great as regards the material standard, services, and culture as in Tsarist Russia during the period of industrialization. As Dellenbrant shows, the Soviet state's doctrine of equal development has been able to change this situation only to a limited degree. As long as centralization remains fundamental to the political system and the latter maintains hegemony over the other facets of social life, it will probably be difficult to offset the vast implications of this circumstance, and reforms aimed at political and geographic polycentrism appear to be a long way off.

These factors notwithstanding, Dellenbrant shows how a growing debate concerning the geographic distribution of resources has been trickling forth, undoubtedly as a decision of central policy. Will bureaucratic centralism be given a chance to compete with other approaches to breaking down the ossified central administration in order to better meet the needs of a developing society, or is there now enough economic leeway to permit investment in the various regions even where such a course does not coincide with notions of how the production apparatus can best be developed? Dellenbrant's study comes up with no evidence to support this thesis. Soviet communism has traditionally been an "urban ideology": the urban population, the industrial workers and the intelligentsia, have represented the vanguard of change, while the countryside and the peasants have represented reaction and an obstacle to development. Equalization brought about an increasing concentration of housing and services: peasants too should live in multistoried buildings in "rural cities" (*agrogoroda*) and leave their huts with bad sanitary conditions (bad because of failure to allocate the necessary materials) and their private plots.

The idea of a more even development within regions as well, which has been such an important issue in the Western discussion of regional policy, has never gained a foothold in the Soviet Union, nor do we have any quantitative material to illustrate the current state and future trends in this respect, other than aggregated data on urbanization.

In the West, regional policy involves combatting market forces with correctives in recognition of the political and economic need to spread economic activity, jobs, and welfare over a country's territory.

In the Soviet Union there are no market forces to correct, and it might be thought that the instruments of regional policy are simply part of the norms governing the management of a planned economy. This would mean that whether the goals of regional policy are achieved is mainly a question of the political willingness to do so. That this is not the case can of course be partly explained by the reluctance of the Soviet system to admit to conflicts of aims even where they exist.

At the practical level, the meager results are partly attributable to the omnipresent systems and rules of thumb that replace market forces. These include the price system, which is based on the theory of surplus value, which in principle attributes no scarcity value to raw materials, and therefore can be expected to be conducive to a skewed distribution in value after processing at the microlevel (and hence in the geographic distribution of financial resources) to the detriment of the raw material regions in the East. Such a skewed distribution can probably be only partially offset at most by central allocations of investments to these regions.

But how should regional balance be measured? This problem is found even in the West, with its open access to a wealth of data. In the absence of other material, Dellenbrant must rely on quantitative data on industrial investments in some areas of Siberia, while the effects of these investments on the employment and welfare of the regional population can be evaluated only on the basis of periodical articles reporting on individual cases.

Scandinavian experience has shown how limited and indirect the effects of large industrial capital investments (especially after the installation phase) can be for a local population in the remote countryside without an industrial tradition (compare, for example, the employment calculations for the Swedish 1980 Steel Mill Project). Not only capital, but also a specialized work force, must be recruited from elsewhere, with considerable cost for moving, a marginal infrastructure, and a sliding wage scale, while the indigenous population is only indirectly benefitted, e.g., through the new demand for industrial maintenance work, service personnel, etc.

Dellenbrant validly asks to what extent the Iakuts benefit from the investments in the raw materials industry in Iakutia. Nor do higher wages necessarily guarantee access to welfare in a planned economy; rather it is the supply of goods and services via the regional Gossnab and local distribution apparatus, the housing standards, and the range of public services available (including culture and entertainment) that are the primary determinants.

Russian ''immigrant laborers'' can of course use their extra income and savings to purchase priority capital goods when they return to the western part of the country after several years living under the primitive conditions of Siberia, but the local population is virtually dependent on what is locally available.

There is insufficient statistical material to determine the living conditions in the Siberian regions. The units of analysis are essentially the Soviet republics, so that a study of this sort is limited from the outset.

Data from the Central Asian republics, however, confirm the Western consensus that over the short term it is easier to raise the level of consumption for a group or a region by means of transfers than to give them their own productive basis and a competitive employment for self-sustained prosperity.

The notion that the job should be moved to the worker instead of vice-versa seems to have its counterpart in the disinclination of the Central Asian population to geographic mobility. Both educational and cultural factors are at play here. The fact that a certain rapprochement (*sblizhenie*) has been achieved by raising the basic standards in Central Asia would seem to have eliminated the ''push'' effect, yet at the same time a ''pull'' effect is lacking. The willingness to move diminishes. Rises in standards, however, are not merely a tribute to the Party program, they are also a growing political necessity to offset the attraction that the self-affirmation of the Islamic traditions in the Near East since the 1970s might have had on Persian and Turkish ethnic groups within the Soviet borders.

But this policy has its challenges and weaknesses. In a region where increased production and employment should be based on local initiative and small enterprises, the Soviet system's reliance on centralized administration and large industrial complexes is of no advantage. When the state's financial resources are under strain, regional policy comes under pressure (even in Western societies). The experience of Yugoslavia indicates that patience finally wanes even in a socialist society among those groups of the population who have had to forego an improvement in their own standards to finance that of others.

The success, or lack of it, of regional policy is therefore not merely a question of geographic distribution policy in the Soviet Union. It is also a reflection of the inability of the Soviet system to keep abreast of the times, or to adapt to new priorities and aspirations among the population in the various parts of the country, independently of the "nationality problem" that has long been such a politically loaded call to action.

The lack of a political response to the calls for decentralization and to regional ambitions for development are a problem in many Western democracies. New notions of what welfare means magnify pressure for a more just regional policy even in the East. But the evidence in Dellenbrant's book and elsewhere indicates that the prognosis for the Soviet Union must be relatively pessimistic: we may expect a weaker articulation of regional aspirations and a lower priority given to demands for regional equalization for a long time to come.

ANDREAS ÅDAHL

Minister to Sweden's delegation
to UNESCO in Paris.

PREFACE

This book is concerned with regional development, regional differences, and regional policy in the Soviet Union. There is considerable regional inequality in the USSR in respect to natural resources, manpower, and other resources, which gives rise to difficult priority problems for the political leadership. The size of investments in the different regions must thus be carefully weighed, especially if some measure of regional balance is to be maintained.

However, the distribution of resources is a controversial question in the Soviet Union. Representatives of the three major regions—Siberia, Central Asia, and the European USSR—are engaged in an unending effort to augment the flow of resources to their own regions. The activities of these persons—politicians, scientists, and journalists—must be seen in light of the fact that considerable regional differences still exist in the 1980s in the level of socioeconomic development.

In an earlier book, *Soviet Regional Policy: A Quantitative Inquiry into the Social and Political Development of the Soviet Republics*, I explored regional differences in the Soviet Union and the changes they have undergone over time. One important conclusion of that study was that absolute differences between the republics remained in the main unchanged throughout the period of the study, i.e., between 1956 and 1973. In the present study, *The Soviet Regional Dilemma*, I attempt to explain why the differences persist despite the fact that according to official doctrine they should actually have been eliminated.

Chapter 1 proposes a theoretical treatment of regional differences and regional policy. In Chapter 2, the questions posed in the study are defined and the available material weighed. The official Soviet view of regional differences is presented in Chapter 3 by a systematic review of the literature on the subject, and is then compared with the results of both Western and Soviet research.

The way administrative apparatus is organized is of major importance for the implementation of Soviet policy. This is dealt with in
Chapter 4, in which various current organizational modifications, e.g.,
the territorial production complexes, are discussed.

The problem of regional development has been the subject of an
extensive debate in the Soviet press, continuing into the 1980s. This
debate is discussed in Chapter 5, with special attention given to arguments from representatives of the major regions of Siberia, Central
Asia, and the European USSR. The problem of development in the
Baltic region is also taken up.

At the 1981 Party Congresses at the republic and union levels, the
problems of regional development recurred again and again with striking frequency, and guidelines were set at the Party Congresses for
economic development during the five-year planning period 1981–85.
Political decisions concerning the 11th Five-year Plan are examined in
Chapter 6.

The implementation and the results of Soviet regional policy are
dealt with in Chapter 7. Difficulties in implementing decisions within
the Soviet organizational setting are discussed. The instruments and
effects of regional policy are studied, and national and cultural factors
are considered.

The study covers the last part of the Brezhnev period and the entire
period in which Andropov was the Soviet Union's head of state. Developments after Andropov's death have been touched upon only briefly.

Soviet regional policy has been relatively neglected by Western
scholars. Indeed the concept "regional policy" has very rarely been
applied to the Soviet Union, nor have the objectives, means, and results
of regional policy all been dealt with in one book.

That I have been able to undertake this task at all, and complete this
book on the Soviet regional dilemma, is due in large measure to my
talented colleagues on the present project. Throughout the entire period of the project, Adam Perlowski served as research assistant and was
responsible for gathering the material from the Soviet press. He also
carried out independent analyses of the data. Without Perlowski's
knowledgeable contributions, this work could have been completed
only with difficulty. Ulla Hagström, as research assistant, was responsible for administering the project and gathering Western material. Ewa
Molin was the project's secretary. Lena Wallin performed secretarial
tasks for the project in its earlier stages. Lars-Martin Åström analyzed
the statistical material. Musja Veinger and Grejnim Goldin helped the

project director with the gathering of data. A good deal of the material was obtained from the Department of Soviet and East European Studies, where Czeslaw Rozenblat has been responsible for the press archives and Stefan Michnik is responsible for the library. I wish to thank all my colleagues for their outstanding contributions.

Colleagues from a number of universities have been generous with their valuable commentary, in particular, Professors Andreas Ådahl, Daniel Tarschys, Sten Berglund, Åke Andersson, and Thorolf Rafto. Sections of the book have been discussed in a number of seminars where I obtained valuable ideas from Anders Fogelklou, Peter de Souza, Ilmari Susiluoto, Jyrki Iivonen, Mats-Olov Olsson, and Ole Nørgaard.

A good part of the work was completed at a number of research centers outside of Scandinavia. Valuable visits were made to the Kennan Institute for Advanced Russian Studies, Washington D.C., and the Russian and East European Center at the University of Illinois, Urbana-Champaign. The project director also made several stimulating visits to the Bundesinstitut für ostwissenschaftliche und internationale Studien in Cologne and the Soviet Institute in Helsinki.

Trips to the Soviet Union also yielded a good deal of valuable material for this work, in particular trips to Siberia and Soviet Central Asia. In December 1983 I visited the Institute for Economics and Industrial Organization at the Novosibirsk Section of the USSR Academy of Sciences, where Academician Abel Aganbegian and Professors Alexander Granberg and Mark Bandman kindly made parts of their own research material available to me. In April 1984 I participated in a study trip to Uzbekistan and Turkmenistan, where I obtained valuable information from Dr. Dzhuma Bairamov, director at the Economic Institute of the Gosplan of the TSSR in Ashkhabad.

But the major portion of the work on this book was done at the Department of Soviet and East European Studies at Uppsala University as part of the project Regional Planning in the Soviet Union, sponsored with generous economic support from the Bank of Sweden Tercentenary Foundation. The faculty committee for social sciences at Uppsala University, the Siamon Foundation, and the Wallenberg Foundation also made valuable contributions.

Monterey, California

1. THE PROBLEM OF REGIONAL DEVELOPMENT

Regional analyses have acquired a greater importance in international research on the Soviet Union. The inadequacy of basing a scholarly study exclusively on aggregate data for the Soviet Union as a whole has become increasingly obvious. The increased attention given to regional conditions and regional differences should lead to more concrete descriptions of Soviet society. There is no doubt that regional variations exist in many areas in the Soviet Union. Differences in climate and natural resources constitute one dimension, and differences in the level of socioeconomic development another. The vast number of nationalities—more than a hundred—is a third dimension of major importance.

One of the most important problems Soviet leaders have to face in the 1980s is, according to the American Soviet studies scholar Seweryn Bialer, the distribution of capital investments and other economic resources among the different regions. This distribution of resources with the view toward creating a desirable balance among the regions is done through the existing planning system. But the economic system is beset by a variety of problems that make changes in the regional balance relatively impossible.[1]

Soviet leaders have developed a cautious attitude in the recent period with regard to changes in the planning system. Reforms have often been carried out as experiments, and moreover on a very limited scale. Results have therefore often been unsatisfactory and the leaders have returned to traditional methods of economic control. According to Bialer *"It is the political mechanism which explains the inherent stability of the traditional economic system and the inherent instability of reform efforts in the Soviet Union.* Piecemeal and well-intentioned partial reforms, instead of transforming the traditional economic system, are absorbed and changed by this system."[2]

The Soviet leaders' reticence about introducing changes into the system of economic planning and control therefore has a political explanation. The centralized planning system is instrumental in maintaining a strong central political control over the Soviet Union's various regions.

Bialer's interpretation is also relevant to a study of regional development in the Soviet Union. Even if political leaders should undertake measures to reduce regional differences, the mechanisms described by Bialer may very well lead in quite another direction.

The huge Soviet bureaucracy is another important factor in the implementation of social change in the Soviet Union. A number of scholars regard this factor as crucial to an understanding of the way the Soviet political system functions.

Regional Dualism

Regional development problems are found in a number of countries. They are generally summed up in terms such as the "north-south problem" and "regional dualism." Initially the north-south problem referred to Italy, where the northern part of the country went through a long period of manifest economic and industrial expansion while the economy in southern Italy, the *Mezzogiorno*, in the main stagnated. Other countries as well, such as Belgium and Great Britain, have been plagued by the vexing problem of regional dualism. Sweden and Finland also have their north-south problems. A number of scholars claim that all countries, especially the market economies, have regions with widely varying income levels.[3]

The general presumption is that related causes can be discerned behind these phenomena. One theory on the north-south problem has been formulated by Gunnar Myrdal. According to Myrdal, tendencies toward regional economic inequality are to be found in all societies. These regional differences are further increased by the play of market forces.

"If things were left to market forces unhampered by any policy interferences, industrial production, commerce, banking, insurance, shipping and, indeed, almost all those economic activities which in a developing economy tend to give a bigger than average return—and, in addition, science, art, literature, education and higher culture generally—would cluster in certain localities and regions, leaving the rest of the country more or less in a backwater."[4]

Myrdal's theory refers to market societies and certain developing countries in particular. But it is also interesting to apply Myrdal's theory to a centrally planned society such as the Soviet Union and investigate whether there as well some regions find themselves left behind because of rapid development elsewhere. The Soviet Union to a certain extent has pursued a pattern of regional development inherited from Tsarist times. Myrdal's theory might also shed light on this pattern.

Myrdal claims further that expansion within a region gives rise to "backwash effects" on other regions. Often economic activity spreads from one region to another, which then also experiences economic growth. On the other hand, a third region might find itself cut off from expansion and therefore stagnate. Regional inequality is then heightened.[5]

If Myrdal's theory is found to be applicable to the Soviet Union and its economic development, this means that the situation there is not fundamentally different from that in the Western world as regards regional development. If on the other hand the contagion and backwash effects described by Myrdal are not to be found in the Soviet Union, then the organizational structures specific to that country, such as the centralized planning system and centralized economic decisionmaking, may be said to have had a positive effect on regional balance. If this is the case, state measures with regard to investments, stimulating employment, etc., i.e., the *developmental strategies*, as it were, for the various regions have had an equalizing effect.

A number of theoreticians have, like Myrdal, attached importance to imbalances in regional development. Albert O. Hirschman claims that some regional differences in the level of development can on the whole be good for economic growth, serving in general to stimulate it.[6] Other theoreticians, however, have pointed out that in many systems regional differences tend to increase with time. The *center versus periphery* relationship has been used to describe regional differences, with the periphery marked by continued economic stagnation and the center normally enjoying continuous growth.[7]

Regional dualism has been observed in most economic systems, but opinions vary on whether these differences are necessary to economic growth. There are also differences of opinion on development over time and the possibilities of eliminating regional imbalance.

There can be no doubt that the Soviet Union also has its north-south problem. The northern European part of the country is marked by a relatively high level of social and economic development while the southern part, Central Asia, has a relatively lower level. But the situation in the Soviet Union is further complicated by the existence of a third region, Siberia, which also must be taken into account in evaluating the regional problem.

The Soviet Union's resources are distributed in a *triangular pattern* with the various kinds of resources situated at great geographic distances from one another. Thus, fuels and raw materials are found in abundant quantities in the Asiatic parts of the RSFSR, while growth in the work force is in the main concentrated in Central Asia. Finally, the majority of the population and the most developed industries are found in the European part of the Soviet Union.

All three macroregions, i.e., Siberia, Central Asia, and Europe,[8] are in need of more capital investments. Problems arise in deciding on priorities among the regions, compounded by the fact that the growth rate in total investments has declined during the most recent five-year planning periods. The three macroregions are huge areas with for the most part uniform social and economic conditions. Each region tends to have characteristic and uniform problems, which may be the reverse of problems found in the other regions. For example, there is a shortage of labor in the European region while in Central Asia there is a surplus.

The problems of regional development in the Soviet Union are further complicated by the fact that within the three major regions— Siberia (in which for simplicity's sake the Far East is also included here) Central Asia, and Europe—certain resources are found in abundance, while others, just as important, are lacking. Figure 1.1 illustrates this anomaly.

Figure 1.1 is based on the figures of a few Western scholars, but analogous data may be readily gleaned from official Soviet publications and statistics.[9] The division into positive and negative factors is of course a simplification of a more complicated picture, but it does convey the gist of the problem.

Regional development has a bearing on other key social problems in the Soviet Union as well. Development of the different Soviet regions is closely interlinked with the general way the planning system functions. If for various reasons the planning system functions ineffectively— which is presumably the case in the Soviet Union—it will of course be more difficult to effect changes in the balance between the different regions.

Regional development planning in the Soviet Union is now having to cope with a declining economic growth. The Soviet Union has not been

Factors / Regions	Favorable	Unfavorable
Siberia	Very good resources of fuels and raw materials	Labor shortage; harsh climatic conditions; undeveloped infrastructure; long distances for transportation
Central Asia	Good labor resources; rapid growth of manpower; fuel and raw materials resources	Relatively poorly trained and immobile labor force; poorly developed infrastructure; lack of industrial tradition
Europe	Well-developed existing industry; established industrial tradition; skilled labor force	Labor shortage; scarce resources in fuels and raw materials

Figure 1.1 Favorable and Unfavorable Factors in the Three Macroregions—Siberia, Central Asia, and Europe—with Regard to Human and Material Resources.

Sources: Seweryn Bialer, *Stalin's Successors*, p. 291; Douglas Whitehouse and David Kamerling, *Asiatic RSFSR*, p. 235.

immune to economic problems in a period when most of the countries of the world are experiencing grave problems of their own. The causes of the problems in the Soviet Union lie both within and without Soviet society. Investments have recently shown a declining growth rate, indicating a relative slowdown in the Soviet economy (Table 1.1).

Absolute growth of investments has decreased since the mid-1970s. During the period 1965–70 the increase was 24.6 billion rubles while for the period 1970–75 it was 32.3 billion rubles. In 1975–80 (roughly the period covered by the 10th Five-year Plan) growth was lower, i.e., 20.6 billion rubles. Absolute growth declined, although some growth did occur, and relative growth suffered an even greater decline.

The constellation of regional problems is also intimately tied in with Soviet nationality problems. Strikingly often, it is the non-Russian nationalities who inhabit the regions with the lowest level of socioeconomic development, while regions in which the Great Russian population predominates are normally more highly developed. The relationship among the different nationalities in the Soviet Union has been an issue of major political significance since the very first days of Soviet power.

In this study regional policy is regarded as subordinate to economic policy and also as having some points of intersection with nationality policy, although the latter is usually more broadly conceived than regional policy, comprising aspects having to do with language and culture, demographic development, and national rights and self-deter-

Table 1.1

Capital Investments, Billions of Rubles Per Year, in Cooperative Enterprises (Including Kolkhozes), at Comparable Prices

Year	Investments
1965	56.0
1970	80.6
1975	112.9
1976	118.0
1977	122.3
1978	129.7
1979	130.6
1980	133.5
1981	138.8
1982	143.7

Sources: Narodnoe khoziaistvo 1980, p. 333; *Nar. khoz. 1982*, p. 335.

mination.[10] The purpose of nationality policy as the Soviets see it is in the first instance to eliminate inequalities between national groups such as often occur in the capitalist system. The formation and subsequent development of the Soviet Union made it possible to eliminate differences among the various ethnic groups.[11]

Regional policy and nationality are very intimately related in one respect, namely, with regard to the question of whether economic equality between the different regions and nations is a worthwhile aim. The most salient difference between regional policy and nationality policy is that regional policy focuses mainly on geographical regions, e.g., the production potential in Azerbaidzhan, while nationality policy focuses on individuals and national groups.

Still, the ethnic issue is of major significance for regional policy. It is quite likely that a national group or groups inhabiting a specific region will react negatively if resources are directed to other regions. It is therefore important to take into account the ethnic question in attempting to explain decisions on regional policy.

When priorities among the regions are set (within the framework for Soviet regional policy, which will be described in more detail later on), Soviet leaders are compelled to give consideration to one further factor of crucial importance. Population growth is to a large extent a social problem in the Soviet Union. The fifteen Soviet republics are the units of analysis in the present study. As is evident from Table 1.2, regional

Table 1.2

Population Growth between 1970 and 1980 (per Thousands of Individuals)

	1970	1980	% increase
RSFSR	130,079	138,365	6.4
Estonia	1,356	1,474	8.7
Latvia	2,364	2,259	7.0
Lithuania	3,128	3,420	9.3
Ukraine	47,126	49,953	6.0
Belorussia	9,002	9,611	6.8
Moldavia	3,569	3,968	11.2
Georgia	4,686	5,041	7.6
Armenia	2,492	3,074	23.4
Azerbaidzhan	5,117	6,112	19.4
Kazakhstan	13,009	14,858	14.2
Uzbekistan	11,799	15,765	33.6
Tadzhikistan	2,900	3,901	34.5
Kirghizia	2,934	3,588	22.3
Turkmenistan	2,159	2,827	30.9
USSR	241,720	264,486	9.4

Source: *Nar. khoz 1979*, p. 10f.
Note: The republics are grouped by geographical region, which also in the main corresponds to differences in level of socioeconomic development. See Chapter 3.

variations in population growth are considerable.

The extremely rapid population growth in the Central Asian republics magnifies the problems of regional balance, as suggested earlier on. The work force is growing, and there are signs that underemployment is increasing. But at the same time, a large segment of the population has not yet reached working age, and this must surely place a strain on the economies of the various republics. An increased demand for transfers from central funds to the republics may therefore be expected. This problem is dealt with in more detail in the chapter on implementation and results (Chapter 7).

The slow population growth in most European republics and in the RSFSR has hamstrung economic growth in these regions considerably. The problems mentioned earlier have also grown more acute, and the ethnic and cultural balance is undergoing a change: e.g., the proportion of the population from the traditional Moslem regions has increased sharply.

It is thus clear that several important Soviet social problems have a regional dimension. In Western societies action is geared to dealing with social problems having regional dimensions within the broader framework of what is called "regional policy," although the term is used rather vaguely in the Western academic and political debate. What is more, regional development has also become a controversial political issue in several Western societies, and not least because of the regional balance problem, referred to as the north-south problem or regional dualism.

Regional Policy—Ends and Means

Regional policy, generally speaking, refers to a policy practiced by the state with regard to different regions. Thus the state and its bodies are the acting subject, and the regions are the objects to which regional policy is then applied. This policy has to do primarily with measures designed to affect income level, employment, social services, etc., by means of the transfer of capital or creation of new capital.[12]

Location policy usually refers to a more limited phenomenon than regional policy. In most European countries a precursor of regional policy, it involves short-term measures designed to directly influence the location of enterprises.[13]

In most cases, the aim of regional policy is to create a reasonable balance among regions with regard to standard of living, employment, etc. In principle, one potential aim of regional policy might be to reduce the size of certain regions. In Sweden, the following objectives of regional policy have been the subject of timely debate:

1. Location of economic activity such that capital and labor are utilized to the fullest and that rapid economic growth is promoted.

2. Distribution of the social wealth in such a way that people in the different parts of the country are all offered an acceptable level of social and cultural amenities.

3. Location of economic activity with a view toward facilitating the country's defense.[14]

The Swedish state's financial situation in the 1970s changed the conditions of Swedish regional policy. The goals of the welfare state have receded into the distance, and demands to preserve jobs in the more vulnerable regions have become the primary concern.[15]

Research in regional policy and regional development has empha-sized different aspects. Economists have stressed the importance of efficiency as a goal in regional policy; geographers have studied the relationship between population centers and their surrounding areas. Relatively few researchers have devoted attention to relations between different administrative levels (national, regional, and local), although they should be quite important in the investigation of regional policy.[16]

The question is whether there exists a regional policy in the Soviet Union as well. The situation there is of course different from that in the West; after all it is a centrally planned economy and the state decides on practically every aspect of economic growth. There is also less margin in the Soviet Union than in Western countries for various groups to influence the political leadership.

Yet problems of regional balance doubtless exist in the Soviet Union. Priorities must be set that directly influence development in the differ-ent regions. In the official Soviet view, regional policy exists to elimi-nate existing regional differences. Resources are redistributed among the regions in various ways, e.g., through the five-year planning sys-tem.

In the sense, therefore, that problems of regional balance exist, and measures are taken to influence regional development, a Soviet region-al policy may be said also to exist. It is another question whether regional policy is effective or whether it is secondary to other objec-tives of economic policy.

A special difficulty in studying regional policy is to isolate the regional component. A social measure may influence regional develop-ment, although it may actually be aimed at the economy as a whole. The problem of course cannot be fully resolved, although one fruitful ap-proach might be to measure the explicitly stated objectives of regional policy against the actual results and to compare development in the different regions.

Sven Godlund pointed out that "practically all economic and social policy may be said to have an influence on the spatial distribution of economic activity and the distribution of the population."[17] It is hardly surprising therefore that there is no generally accepted definition and hence generally defined scope of the term regional policy.[18]

Elisabeth Lauschmann distinguishes two major conceptions of the scope of regional policy in her book *Grundlagen einer Theorie der Regionalpolitik*. According to one, regional policy embraces state measures aimed at influencing regions economically, socioculturally, and ecologically. Regional policy is then seen as paralleling economic policy.[19]

In the other view, which Lauschmann herself espouses, regional policy is subordinate to economic policy. Regional policy is that part of economic policy aimed at influencing economic development in its spatial dimension.[20] This definition is more restricted and seems to be the most fitting for the present study. An analysis of the regional problem in its totality, including social, cultural, and ecological development, would be too far-ranging a task for this study.

An argument similar to Lauschmann's has been put forth by the Soviet scientist B. S. Khorev, who says that regional policy should aim at resolving problems of economic steering at the territorial level. Together with sectoral policy, regional policy is an element of state economic policy.[21]

The purpose of *sectoral policy*, by analogy with regional policy, is to deal with steering problems in the various sectors or branches of the economy. In practice, there is an interplay between regional and sectoral policies. This is especially true in a country such as the Soviet Union where the planning system is in the main organized on the sectoral principle.[22]

The structure of regional policy varies. According to Khorev one may differentiate among the economic, social, demographic, and ecological aspects.[23] But, as indicated earlier, this study will concentrate on the economic aspects.

It is important that the term regional policy has came into use in Soviet terminology as well. It is difficult to perceive any basic difference between Lauschmann's and Khorev's view of regional policy.

Both general economic policy, which for the Soviet Union is primarily sectoral policy, and regional policy have regional effects, as pointed out. According to Niles Hansen, the rationale of regional policy is to be sought in its direct focus on regional effects, in order, for example, to influence the balance between expanding and contracting regions and to remedy undesired situations.[24]

There are three important aspects of regional policy that we distinguish:

—the goals of regional policy
—the instruments or means of regional policy
—the implementation and the results of regional policy.

The *goals* of regional policy are formulated by politicians. In the West, statements regarding the goals of regional policy may be found in government proclamations, draft bills and the texts of laws, economic and financial plans, and documents from national and international institutions.[25] Two principal types of regional policy with different objectives seem to be discernible. One type is nationally oriented, with priority given to national growth as a whole, while the other is regional and aims primarily at improving conditions in the various regions. The difference between ''de la région pour la nation'' and ''de la région pour la région'' should therefore be taken into account.[26]

The goals of regional policy are to be found in statements made in the Soviet Union as well; e.g., in protocols from Party Congresses and sessions of the Supreme Soviet, Party programs, and authoritative statements made by politicians and scholars. Among the goals of Soviet regional policy are, according to N. N. Nekrasov, the planned development of all regions and the reconciliation of regional and national interests. Regional policy should avoid giving undue consideration to sectoral interests, i.e., *vedomstvennost'*, or to local interests, *mestnichestvo*. Development in Siberia is especially important for Soviet regional policy.[27]

The *instruments* or *means* used to implement regional policy are of various sorts—for example, the regional development plans and measures to stimulate investment within a specific region.[28] It is considered especially important to facilitate capital expansion in areas that have abundant labor reserves. Another example are actions taken to improve the mobility of the labor force.[29] Thus the most important instruments of regional policy are:

—the transfer of capital;
—measures to enhance the mobility of the labor force.

But it should be noted that what may be an instrument of regional policy, e.g., increased investments, at one level, may at some lower level be viewed as a goal.

The *implementation* and the *results* of regional policy constitute the last step in analysis, where the results achieved may be measured against the projected aims. A study of this phase is essential to an analysis of Soviet regional policy since it is in this phase where undesired policy changes often take place in the Soviet Union.[30]

But the task is not a simple one: there are a number of problems of assessment that require resolution before a comparison of development in the different regions can be undertaken.[31] The first question is what is actually meant by regional differences. The present study deals with regional differences in the level of socioeconomic development. Urbanization, industrialization, income, and education thus become important variables for evaluating regional differences.[32] Further, it is not at all clear how regional difference should be measured; and a number of methods of measurement have therefore been developed in regional economic studies.[33]

Regional differences are in the first instance assessed on the basis of quantitative data. This of course limits the analysis to some extent, but even quantitative data on, for example, urbanization, investments, employment, etc., can provide some fair idea of a situation, especially if they are interpreted and fleshed out with information of a qualitative nature.

The American regional economist Walter Isard distinguishes between material and nonmaterial indicators of regional development. The material indicators include income, living standard, etc.; the non-material indicators are solidarity, security, respect for the individual, etc.[34] Despite the limitations imposed by an emphasis on material indicators, Isard regards this as the preferred approach since the problems of measurement of nonmaterial indicators are almost insoluble.[35]

Isard's definition of regional development also largely agrees with the view of Soviet scholars on the same problem. In an article published in 1969, A. I. Vedishchev defines the concept of level of regional economic development as follows:

> The level of economic development of a region (or republic) refers to the level of development of the productive forces in a broad sense plus the population's level of well-being. Measurement of economic levels entails a comprehensive assessment in terms of both indicators of the growth in production and the population's living standard . . . In the narrowest sense, a region's level of economic development refers to the level of development of the productive forces, especially the level of development of industry and agriculture, and finally the level of development of the regional infrastructure.[36]

In Western terminology, the level of development of productive forces corresponds to the condition and the quality of the factors of production. These constitute the basis of production in the various republics, and reflect production potential or production capacity. In Soviet usage, the living standard is in the first instance a quantitative concept and refers to the population's access to material and cultural goods and the current level of consumption.[37]

A list published by Gosplan gives an idea of those indicators that in

the official Soviet view are the most important for evaluating a republic's level of development:

1. Indicators of industrial growth (productive capital per capita, the
number of industrial workers, the relative proportion of workers in
industry)

2. Indicators of agricultural growth (output per worker, etc.)

3. Access to transportation

4. Per capita national income

5. Indicators of the utilization of labor and the population's standard of living.[38]

In evaluating regional development and regional differences in the
Soviet Union, it is essential to take into account the Soviet perception
of the problem. The above list is taken from an official document and is
in fact quite concrete. It also largely concurs with Nekrasov's view,
who stresses the importance of the labor force and national income in
an assessment of the level of economic development.[39]

As mentioned earlier on, there are several views on how the term
regional policy should be defined. *Two perspectives* on regional policy
and its goals must be distinguished. In the one, equalization as a goal is
built into regional policy. Equalization among the regions is the ultimate purpose of regional policy. In the other perspective, several goals
of regional policy are distinguished, of which equalization is one,
while maximization of the nation's economic growth is another. Both
perspectives are encountered in the academic and the political discussion. The present study employs the second, more neutral approach,
wherein regional policy may have several different goals. Which goal
is to be given priority will depend on the policymakers.

The interest of politicians in regional problems seems to have grown
in the past decades in the Soviet Union, but this does not mean that the
regional approach is on the ascendancy; planning still primarily follows the sector principle. It is true, however, that the regional or
territorial approach has grown in importance as regional problems have
grown.

2. THEORETICAL PREMISES

I shall be using Lauschmann's definition of regional policy in this study. Further, it seemed useful to draw a distinction among the goals of regional policy, its instruments, and its implementation, as proposed in the introductory chapter. Primary emphasis will be on the goals and results of regional policy, while its instruments will be dealt with somewhat more cursorily, mainly because there is simply not sufficient data available on these instruments. The more specific aims as well as the hypotheses upon which this study is based are spelled out below.

Aims and Hypotheses

The following points will be explored:

1. The situation in the 1970s and early '80s serves as a point of departure. Regional differences are defined and analyzed.

2. Political decisions on regional conditions and regional development are studied; special attention is given to how priorities are set among the regions, e.g., with regard to the allocation of investment funds.

3. An attempt is made to explain why decisions on regional development are made in the way they are in the light of several hypotheses on the distribution of power in Soviet society. Special emphasis is on the influence of decisions at the regional level on issues concerning regional policy.

4. Implementation of decisions on regional policy is explored; the results of regional development policy are also studied.

Thus the priorities set by the political leadership in respect to the different Soviet regions constitute a key aspect of the study. It is important to ascertain whether regional policy leads to a reduction or even elimination of differences in development among regions. It will be evident from the examination below of research on regional development in the Soviet Union that there is a patent tendency for regional differences to persist. Indeed, another way of stating the purpose of the study, covering elements from each of the four points described above, is as follows: Why do regional differences persist over time?

A primary focus will be on official political decisions of the 1970s and '80s, taken mainly at the central level, that affect the regions. Decisions taken at the republic level are also explored, but local opinions and perspectives on the problems of regional policy are not dealt with. This does not mean that these opinions are uninteresting, but that in my judgment centrally taken decisions have overriding importance in defining regional policy actually pursued.

The individuals mentioned belong to the official political system, i.e., the Central Committee, the Politburo, various ministries, Gosplan, and other central administrative bodies. Political leaders at the republic level and their views on regional policy are also considered, along with those of a number of influential academics.

The problem of regional priorities is seen as a political problem of central importance for social development in the Soviet Union. But I shall not be concerned with whether the decisions that are taken are the most rational, nor shall I undertake to make a complete description of raw material resources, capital investments, and employment in the different regions, although these factors are essential background variables for the study.

Decisions on regional policy in the Soviet Union include several elements. First is the identification of regional policy as a political issue. Regional development has of course been an object of concern for Soviet decisionmakers for a long time, but it is only since the late 1950s, in connection with the Sovnarkhoz reform, that regional policy can really be said to have become an issue of particular political importance for Soviet society.[1]

The next step is formal decisionmaking on issues of regional policy, based on a choice between several alternative lines of action. The decisions I shall be analyzing here were taken in the official political arena. Such decisions can result in a new or a modified regional policy, but they can also entail no policy changes. The last step in the political process is the implementation of decisions that have been taken.

I shall further attempt to explain how decisions on regional policy are shaped. The distribution of power in Soviet society is an essential factor in this respect. One of the guidelines in this study derives from theories on decisionmaking, and on the distribution and structure of power, formulated by Western theoreticians on the basis of data mainly from Western Europe and the United States. These theories can also be useful in studying political systems outside the Western world.

Western theoreticians of power are divided on the issue of how dispersed political power is. One group, primarily of a sociological cast of mind, claims that power in the United States is concentrated on a small group, a power elite. Floyd Hunter and C. Wright Mills are representatives of this view, according to which leading personages in the society are seen to be a socially and psychologically homogeneous group with power over the economy, politics, and defense.[2]

Another influential group, consisting of political scientists, reject the conclusions of the "elitists," and maintain that the leading stratum of society consists of competing political groups. In his study of power relations in an American city, New Haven, Robert Dahl found that power was distributed among many hands, judging from who actually made a number of key political decisions. For this group of theorists, the "pluralists," power means first and foremost participating in formal decisionmaking. Power can therefore be analyzed only by studying a number of specific decisions.[3]

The differences between the conclusions of the elitists and the pluralists are to a large extent ascribable to differences in their premises and in the way they design their studies. Thus, the elitists study all types of decisions, while the pluralists attempt to identify especially important decisions, "key decisions." One criticism that has been made of both the elitists and the pluralists is that they disregard "nondecisions." Those who control the political agenda can simply shelve certain issues and in this way further consolidate their power.[4]

The different views in the American discussion on power are a patent illustration of the difficulties encountered in an analysis of this phenomenon. For the present study of regional policy in the Soviet Union, I felt it important to investigate how dispersed political power is in that country. I therefore also deemed it appropriate to draw on theories developed on the basis of Soviet conditions, which I shall briefly describe below.

A group of Norwegian investigators, in particular Gudmund Hernes, has introduced some new aspects to the problem of power. According to Hernes, powerlessness should also be examined. In this condition, i.e., powerlessness, the conditions for purposeful action do not exist, as, for instance, when the actors are unclear about their interests.[5]

The distribution and spread of power has also been dealt with in Soviet research, in which two basic models have been used to describe how Soviet society functions. The *bureaucratic model* adopts an approach similar to that of Bialer, described earlier. Inertia in the administration makes it difficult to effect change in the structures of society.[6] The bureaucratic hypothesis is in part an outgrowth of organization theory developed in Western social science. Organization theorists have devoted special attention to the size and the weight carried by the Soviet bureaucracy.

The American Soviet expert Alfred G. Meyer, in a well-known article entitled "USSR Incorporated," maintains that the entire Soviet society is "a bureaucratic command structure with all of the features familiar to students of bureaucracy. The most striking of these features is perhaps the high degree of specialization of functions that has been instituted, and the consequent multiplication of agencies and jurisdictions."[7] Elsewhere, Meyer describes the Soviet society as follows:

> The USSR is best understood as a large complex bureaucracy comparable in its structure and functioning to giant corporations, armies, government agencies, and similar institutions—some people might wish to add various churches—in the West.
>
> The Soviet Union shares with such bureaucracies many principles of organization and patterns of management. It is similar to them also in its typical successes and inefficiencies, in the gratifications and frustrations it offers its constituents, in its socialization and recruitment policies, communications problems, and many other features.[8]

In the bureaucratic model the Politburo is regarded as the highest but not the only level of importance in the political system. There is reason to assume that the Politburo also consists of individuals who reflect special interests by virtue of their political and professional backgrounds.

According to the bureaucratic model, therefore, there are palpable similarities between the way the Soviet Union functions and the way large bureaucracies function in the West. Inertia and inefficiency are features that are placed in the foreground, but it is not merely negative qualities that are described. Bureaucracies are often able to accumulate power in a certain area, which then not infrequently means that problems in that area can be solved.

Meyer's description of the bureaucratic model has been adopted by several other students of the Soviet Union.[9] But the bureaucratic model can also be used as a more general model for explaining political decisionmaking. The American political scientist Graham Allison studied the Cuba crisis in 1962, utilizing several perspectives, including the "governmental" or "bureaucratic" politics model.[10]

According to Allison's bureaucratic model, political decisionmaking should be seen as a game in which several actors participate. National, organizational, and personal aims all play a role in the decisionmaking process. Different groups attempt to steer policy in different directions, and the outcome is political decisions that reflect the relative strengths of the different actors.[11]

Allison's and Meyer's theoretical approaches can be useful for explaining how Soviet regional policy is shaped. In the bureaucratic model, different groups in the Soviet bureaucracy compete with one another. Decisionmakers are encountered at diverse levels throughout the system. The outcome of the policy pursued will then depend on the relative strengths of the different groups. If regional differences persist over time, this may be explained by certain groups opposing an equalization—for instance, because they regard other objectives as more important.

I shall be using this bureaucratic model in the more detailed analysis of Soviet regional policy, although an alternative model will also be presented. Originally the bureaucratic model was devised as a polemical weapon against an older view that we may call the *totalitarian model*, which regarded Soviet society as having a number of features that distinguished it from most other systems. In contrast to all previous dictatorial systems, a totalitarian dictatorship requires the active support of the subjugated. A disciplined party and modern technology are its tools, with which it can penetrate the whole of society. Hannah Arendt was one of the early proponents of the totalitarian model.[12]

A basic assumption of the advocates of the totalitarian hypothesis is that communist and fascist dictatorships share various features in common. The American scholars Carl Friedrich and Zbigniew Brzezinski, two of the most influential proponents of the totalitarian hypothesis, argue that totalitarian dictatorships bear the following features:

1. An official ideology that contains rules for all aspects of human behavior and that in its general contours may be presumed to embrace all citizens

2. A single, hierarchically organized political party, usually led by

one man, a dictator, and comprising a minority of the population, whose members are devoted upholders of the official ideology

3. An omnipresent police control which exercises terror against arbitrarily selected groups of the population

4. Central management and regulation of the economy.[13]
Friedrich and Brzezinski noted these features in both nazi Germany and communist Soviet Union. However, totalitarian control was not total. Islands of separateness, e.g., the family, the church, the university, and the military establishment, are deemed to be relatively unaffected by the totalitarian regime.[14]

If Soviet regional policy is to be studied from the standpoint of the totalitarian hypothesis, it is clear that regional development in its entirety will be determined by the central political decisionmakers. Power is concentrated in the Party's Politburo, and in particular, in the General Secretary. The Politburo's notion of optimal regional development is decisive. In the totalitarian hypothesis, a centrally established regional policy may be expected to be loyally implemented by the Party's representatives in the republics. Further, in the totalitarian hypothesis, regional differences can be explained in terms of the preferences of central policymakers.

The bureaucratic and totalitarian models describe Soviet society at a relatively high level of abstraction; both models are general in character. For the present study of the Soviet regional question I therefore deemed it more suitable to draw on more specific statements about power relationships in the Soviet Union. A number of scholars have formulated hypotheses on the distribution of power in the Soviet Union on the basis of some general notion of the nature of Soviet society. Peter Solomon has classified these researchers into four groups in his book on the role of Soviet criminologists in criminal policy decisionmaking.[15]

The first group of scholars ascribes only negligible influence or no influence at all on political decisionmaking to bureaucrats, experts, technocrats, etc., outside the political center. Persons outside the central leadership participate extremely rarely in decisions. The only exceptions to this rule are when some outsider is used in a struggle for power. This view is represented by scholars such as Robert Conquest, Sidney Ploss, Carl Linden, and Michel Tatu.[16]

The second view presumes that outside participants have some influence, but so little that in practice it is of no significance. Various specialists may participate in the decisionmaking process, but only at a very late stage and then only on special invitation from the political leaders in the Politburo and the Secretariat. Brzezinski, Meyer, Samuel Huntington, and Frederick Barghoorn are among the scholars who have put forth this view.[17]

A third group of observers maintains that outside participants really do have possibilities to influence decisionmaking. Specialists and bureaucrats of various kinds may participate in decisionmaking but their influence is bound by certain restrictions. They must present various policy alternatives to the leaders, who then take the final decisions. Donald Barry, Peter Juviler, Loren Graham, and Philip Stewart are among the writers who have taken this position.[18]

A fourth group parallels the third in its main features, differing only in considering it normal for all political systems to impose certain restrictions on outside participants in the decisionmaking process. Jerry Hough may be taken as a typical representative of this view.[19]

These different views on the distribution of political power in the Soviet Union may be regarded as four hypotheses about power relations in the Soviet Union. They all have their origins in more generally defined models, but they are more specific than the latter, and deal primarily with only one aspect, namely participation in the Soviet decisionmaking process.[20] These hypotheses can be used advantageously to illuminate decisionmaking in regional policy, and the question is whether one of the hypotheses is better suited than the others for explaining decisionmaking in regional policy. If any conclusions can be drawn in this respect, they would constitute a not unimportant contribution to theory and to political science research on the Soviet Union.

The views presented above differ with regard to their evaluation of the possibilities of outside participants (for example, experts and bureaucrats at the central level) to influence decisionmaking by the central political body. In the present study, I shall also examine the possibilities existing at *lower administrative levels*—politicians, specialists, etc., mostly at the republic level—to influence decisionmaking. Studies on the importance of the republic level in central political decisionmaking are very rare in the scientific literature.

But one other factor must be considered in this context. The four hypotheses here presented concern first and foremost the input side of policy. The problem is to what extent persons outside the top leadership (in the present study representatives of the republic level will be examined specially) can participate in the decisionmaking process. But policy also has an output side. Once a decision is made, it must be implemented by persons outside the top leadership. The regional and local administrative levels play a major role in the implementation of political decisions. According to implementation research, as it is called, the implementation of political decisions may be affected by *policy shifts*, e.g., a change in the real content, and by *resistance*, which means active effort against a particular decision.[21] This problem must also be taken into account in assessing Soviet regional policy. Finally, we shall also attempt to *evaluate* regional policy, comparing the result of the policy pursued with the original objectives.[22]

The analysis of regional policy will thus begin with a study of the situation in the 1970s and 1980s, with special attention given to regional differences. I then investigate what decisions of importance for regional policy are made by political agencies in the context of the formal organization of planning. Then the hypotheses are tested as part of a study of the discussion of Soviet regional policy and of decisions on regional policy. Finally, implementation and the results of policy are examined.

Materials and Methods

In large measure, the present study continues research that was done at the Department of Soviet and Eastern European Studies of Uppsala University. In my book *Soviet Regional Policy* I call attention to persistent regional differences in the Soviet Union.[23] As was made clear there, and in other studies (which I shall take up further later on), the Soviet republics can be subdivided into clusters representing different levels of socioeconomic development within proximate areas. These clusters tend to remain intact over time. One of the aims of this study is, as I mentioned earlier, to investigate the reasons why this pattern does not change.

The study is based in the first instance on Soviet material, of which official documents constitute a major part; these materials are from Party Congresses at the republic and union levels and refer to decisions taken by the Central Committee and other political bodies at the union level. A large part of the study is based on an analysis of documents from five-year plans for both the union and the republics.

Soviet statistics have also been used inasmuch as they contain a lot of material on regional development. The data have been gleaned from central statistical annuals, such as *Narodnoe Khoziaistvo SSSR*. Valuable information has been taken from Soviet censuses of 1959, 1970, and 1979. Statistical data from the republics have also been used. Statistical material from the yearbooks of all fifteen republics has been consulted. Altogether, this material constitutes a comprehensive data base on the Soviet regional situation.

I have also used other Soviet primary sources, such as the Soviet press, which has been an invaluable source of information. Daily newspapers, e.g. *Pravda* and *Izvestiia*, have been perused systematically over the last few years. The same applies to periodicals such as *Voprosy Ekonomiki*, *Vestnik Statistiki*, *Sotsiologicheskie Issledovaniia*, *Ekonomika i Matematicheskie Metody*, and *Planovoe Khoziaistvo*. Newspapers and periodicals from the republics have also been used, but these were almost exclusively Russian language publications. Questions of regional policy are often taken up in the press, and the problem of regional development has sometimes been discussed quite openly, with criticism directed against the central ministries and the planning bodies.

Soviet approaches have also been used, especially in the areas of geography and economics. Direct contacts were established with Soviet scholars who offered their opinions on the findings.

Soviet ideas have been complemented by material from the West, especially from the United States, regarding, for instance, interpretations of Soviet statistics. Among geographers, economists, and other specialists in this field are I. S. Koropeckyj and Gertrude E. Schroeder, who have studied regional economic conditions in the Soviet Union.

The present study differs from these earlier ones in that more attention is devoted to the political institutions and their decisions. In addition, the level problem, i.e., the relationship between different administrative levels, is studied in more detail.

Thus rather extensive material was available, although its quality varied. The Soviet press is rich in information on regional conditions, but the data have often been on isolated phenomena or on particular regions. A wealth of data has been gleaned from official Soviet statistics, but difficulties were created by the fact that there was no information at all on a number of areas. Further, the basis for statistical calculations occasionally varies.

The strategy I followed was to pool data from different sources. By comparing and contrasting information about a republic from the press with data from statistical publications, interesting results were often obtained. Material from different periodicals was also used to shed light on developments. Sometimes, findings of scientific studies were able to add depth.

I have made comparisons with Western studies wherever possible, in the hope that by surveying various Soviet sources and then comparing them with the results of Western research we will arrive at a satisfactory picture of development.

But this does not mean that all problems have been solved. The use of Soviet material gives rise to certain *problems of validity*. There are quite a number of flaws in Soviet statistics, as in all statistics, and some data are probably misleading. Sometimes important information is omitted. It is more than likely that the flaws in Soviet statistics are greater than in their Western counterpart, but the problem should not be exaggerated. Soviet scholars also make considerable use of official statistics. An effective strategy might be to pool statistical information with information from other sources. It is especially interesting to compare the republics and the regions with one another; a routine assumption that will then be made is that the flaws and distortions in the statistics are roughly of the same magnitude for all regions. Hence, the flaws will have relatively little effect on the results.[24]

But nonstatistical material also causes problems. Often Soviet conceptions are of a normative character: regional policy is described as it should be and not as it is. Therefore, a rigorous and critical evaluation of sources is essential if these problems are to be coped with satisfactorily.

This study of Soviet regional policy is based on both a *textual analysis* and a *statistical analysis*. The qualitative and quantitative data together round out the picture. In the textual analysis, current criteria for evaluating sources are used, although it is sometimes difficult to determine the exact worth of each source. The statistical analysis is relatively uncomplicated. Quite interesting results can be obtained from per capita calculations, relatively simple correlational analyses, etc., hence I elected to forgo methods such as regression analysis in the present case.

The study focuses primarily on Soviet industrial growth, dealing to a lesser extent with agriculture. The reason for this is that the objectives and the consequences of regional policy are more readily discernible in industry than in agriculture, which to a great extent is influenced by external climatic factors. Industry has also been a higher-priority area than agriculture and is therefore regulated to a greater degree by the instruments of regional policy.

I shall be exploring a number of Soviet regions in this study. There are various definitions of the term "region" in the social sciences. The following definition was found in a Soviet text dealing with regional economic development:

> A region is an integral economic unit which has emerged and has developed on the basis of the natural resources and labor reserves, actual or potential, concentrated within a geographically circumscribed area. [25]

This definition, by Minakir, is focused primarily on the economic function of the region, and political, ethnic, historical, and other aspects are disregarded. But for practical purposes, these aspects should also be included.

The three macroregions, Siberia, Central Asia, and the European USSR, as well as the fifteen Soviet republics, are the units upon which analysis concentrated. The three macroregions are of especial interest in regard to the problem of regional priorities. The republics are also important to regional policy, but one problem in this respect is that the RSFSR is considerably larger than any other republic. Where possible, therefore, this republic has been divided into two parts, Europe and Siberia, with Siberia including the economic regions of Western Siberia, Eastern Siberia, and the Far East.

There are several reasons why using the Soviet republics as units of analysis is of advantage. The republics are juridically recognized units that have specific powers, stipulated in the law. They are circumscribed areas, marked by varying levels of development and a variegated range of economic and social conditions. Further, using the republics permits the issue of nationalities to be broached. Although it is not a main theme of this study, the nationality problem is nevertheless of major importance for a correct evaluation of Soviet regional policy. According to the Soviet view, national rights should be guaranteed within each of the fifteen Soviet republics. [26]

Another very important reason for choosing the republics as units of analysis is that the Soviet material is most often related to the republic level. Indeed this is not just true of statistical material; other material as well is often based on information from an individual republic. Thus if Soviet material is to be used—and this should be one of the conditions for carrying out the study—the republics must constitute the foundation for analysis.

But the study is not exclusively focused on an analysis of regions and republics. A major part explores the interplay between the union and republic levels in decisionmaking and in the implementation of regional policy. The relations between these two administrative levels often develop into a tug of war over resources, as will be evident from the analysis later on.

The variables used in the study are what Isard calls material indicators of regional development. The parameters most frequently used are investment and employment.

Thus the study focuses on two types of relations: horizontal and vertical. The *horizontal* concerns priorities among regions and how regional balance is maintained. The *vertical* refers to relations between central and republic administrative levels.

3. REGIONAL DIFFERENCES

A first step in the analysis of Soviet regional policy is to assess the existing levels of socioeconomic development in the regions. How great are regional differences? Have they grown or diminished in the recent period? Or have they been totally eliminated?

The official Soviet picture of regional differences is clear: differences existed earlier, especially in Tsarist times, but they have now been largely eliminated through deliberate policy. The principles applied in locating Soviet industry help to clarify further the foundations of Soviet regional policy: the requirement of regional equality is combined with other requirements, such as maximizing economic effectiveness.

According to the Western literature there is reason to believe that regional differences in the Soviet Union have not been eliminated. The findings of a number of studies indicate the opposite of the official Soviet view. But it would be incorrect to compare empirical studies with official normative statements. As will become evident, it is in fact possible to demonstrate variations in level of development among the Soviet Union's regions using Soviet statistics.

The present chapter is concerned with the official view of regional development and equalization, rounded out with an analysis of the location principles as described by a number of Soviet scholars. The Soviet material is contrasted with results of Western research, which gives a somewhat different picture of the situation. Finally, the Soviet statistics and Western interpretations of them are used to provide a summary description of regional variations in the level of development in the Soviet Union.

The Official Soviet View

On the 50th anniversary celebration of the birth of the Soviet Union in 1972, Leonid Brezhnev proclaimed that the goal of evening out regional differences had in principle been achieved. Similar statements were made during the 60th anniversary celebration in 1982,[1] which provided an occasion for devoting increased attention to the union republics and their inhabitants in official political contexts in the Soviet Union. Thus, the Central Committee's guidelines on how the 60th anniversary was to be celebrated noted that the Soviet republics could look back upon a rich and successful development. The Soviet Union was built up from the outset, the Central Committee tells us, in accordance with the "principles of Leninist national policy," the purport of which is that the right to national self-determination was upheld in the Soviet Union through, for instance, the country's federal structure.

All the Soviet republics are said to have enjoyed a rapid economic growth. The Central Committee's guidelines also said that "the task of equalizing the level of economic development of the various Soviet republics has in the main been resolved." Both *de jure* and *de facto* equality among the nationalities had also been achieved. A new "historical community of people, the Soviet people" has been achieved.[2]

The official Soviet view, as articulated by its political leaders, is that regional differences in the Soviet Union have disappeared. This means that an objective that had already been of central importance during the earlier stages of the Soviet period is said to have been realized.

Regional equalization as a goal of Soviet policy can be inferred from Lenin's nationality theory, which proposed that nationalism should be utilized as a political force to overthrow the Tsarist autocracy. It also posed the right of national self-determination, which meant that each nationality should itself decide whether it wished to be part of the Russian empire. The theory was of especial importance in the light of the multinational character of the Russian state system. A practical consequence of policies based on the theory was that several nationalities chose to leave the Russian state.[3]

The Communist Party program of 1919 reaffirmed the right of national self-determination even if this meant that some nations would actually leave Russia. The Party program also takes up relations between nationalities, and promises "full equality among nations."[4]

Thus the Communist Party had committed itself quite early to regional equality, although of course other objectives have also played a role. Regional equality and equality among nationalities are reiterated as goals with conspicuous frequency in official Soviet statements.

The 1961 Party program also dealt with regional issues, and called for a steadily accelerating economic growth in the Soviet Union to build the material and technical basis for communism. But this growth had to give due consideration to regional equality:

> The complete construction of communism requires a more rational *geographic distribution* of industry with a view toward a more economic use of social labor. . . , to eliminating overpopulation in the large cities, facilitating the abolishment of differences between the city and countryside, and further reducing the differences in economic development among the different parts of the country.[5]

The Party program thus acknowledged that some regional differences in level of development still existed, and the Party's task was therefore to carry the process of equalization among the regions further.

The documents for the Soviet five-year plans indicate that the problem of regional differences is considered resolved. The methodological guidelines for the five-year plans, which are worked out prior to every planning period primarily as an aid to planning bodies at the different levels, had earlier stated that equalization was an important goal of economic development. The methodological guidelines for the 9th Five-year Plan for 1971–75 stated that "The gradual equalization of the level of economic development among the Soviet republics and the economic regions" was a key task of a territorially oriented planning.[6] The guidelines for the 10th Five-year Plan, 1976–80, on the other hand, said nothing about regional equalization,[7] and the same applies to the 11th Five-year Plan.[8] The statements in the methodological guidelines accord quite well with Brezhnev's pronouncement in 1972 that regional differences had been abolished.

According to the official Soviet view differences between nationalities are also in the process of disappearing. The Soviet nationalities have been brought together in a new unity, *the Soviet people*. Brezhnev described the genesis and formation of the Soviet people as "an important feature of developed socialism in our country, a testimony to the increased homogeneity of Soviet society, and a victory for the nationality policy of the CPSU."[9]

Brezhnev thus attached considerable importance to the formation of the Soviet people, and at the celebration of the 100th anniversary of Lenin's birth in 1970 the following definition of the new community was given: "The Soviet people are a fundamentally new international community of people, a socialist union of all workers of the USSR, constituting a social basis for the multinational state of all the people."[10]

The new people differ quite significantly from other types of people: they are an international union of people, formed on a socialistic basis.

Views differ in the Soviet Union on when this formation of Soviet people actually occurred—some say as early as the 1930s, while others say that it first put in its appearance in the 1960s. Most present-day Soviet observers seem to share the latter view.[11]

The first important attribute that according to official doctrine identifies the Soviet people is that they are socialist and hence have no direct continuity or contiguity with former peoples. The Soviet people emerged as a result of the revolutionary social and economic changes in the Soviet Union and comprise two nonantagonistic classes, workers and peasants.[12]

According to the Marxist-Leninist analytic paradigm, material changes have direct consequences for people and their way of life. But no details are given on how the life of a socialist human being should differ from that of a nonsocialist person.

Another important identifying feature of the Soviet people is their international character; this designation comprises more than one hundred nationalities and ethnic groups.[13]

Thus the earlier nationalities remain even though the Soviet people has been formed. The group has both universal features and nationality-related differences.

The Soviet people may be seen as a transitional form, a step on the way toward the universal communist man. Under communism, people have neither class differences nor national differences.[14]

The introduction of the concept of the Soviet people could well be a step on the way toward the abolishment of the Soviet republics and national rights. A single uniform Soviet people should reduce the need for a federal structure based primarily on ethnic differences.

It is also clear that by definition a single Soviet people cannot have different levels of social, economic, and cultural development, and if Soviet doctrine here is to be consistent, equality between nations and regions is also required.

For a long time, the traditional view of the development of nationalities was that they had to go through various stages on the way to communist society. According to doctrine, the national cultures are marked first by a flourishing (*rastsvet*), after which the cultures gradually become more and more similar (*sblizhenie*), until ultimately they merge (*sliianie*) in the third and last stage of development. But in the 1970s the term *sliianie* disappeared from general usage and was replaced by unity (*edinstvo*), which less strongly suggests the total assimilation of nationalities. Western experts have interpreted the introduction of the new term *edinstvo* as a concession to those who had been critical of the idea of total assimilation.[15]

In the last years of the Brezhnev period, the term *sliianie* was hardly used at all. It aroused considerable attention therefore when the General Secretary Andropov spoke about the integration of nationalities at the 60th anniversary celebration in 1982: "Our ultimate objective is clear. To use Lenin's words, 'not only a coming together, but also a merger of nations.'"[16] Andropov thus once again used the word *sliianie*. It is clear from the text that he viewed merger as an ultimate, though distant, political goal.

Andropov never again took up the question of union in later speeches; hence, it seems as if the details in the new policy on this issue had not yet been fully worked out. Later official statements contain the term *sliianie*, but say that the ultimate goal is a long way away. The matter is described as follows in an editorial in the periodical *Kommunist*: "National differences will continue to exist for a much longer time than class differences. It is inappropriate to move too quickly and attempt to accelerate the merger of nations artificially, but we must avoid artificially hindering it as well."[17]

Thus the official view is that the different nations will be unified in one single nation at some time in the future. But this is a long-term process, as is underscored again and again. That ultimate union had been a controversial issue is evident in an article by the editor-in-chief of *Kommunist*, R. I. Kosolapov, in which he stated that the ultimate goal was a merger of nationalities. He lamented that some scholars were still "irritated" about the idea of *sliianie*. According to Kosolapov, some linguistic and cultural differences may remain even after *sliianie*.[18]

The doctrine of the "Soviet people" has a counterpart in the economy. Now, according to the official view, the Soviet economy is a *single social economic complex* (*edinyi narodno-khoziaistevnnyi kompleks*). In the period of developed socialism, i.e. the period through which according to doctrine Soviet society is currently passing, a single economic complex has emerged. This type of economy is marked by a high level of development.

> This complex is not merely the sum of the economies of the individual republics and regions, but a unitary whole, a dynamic organism, marked by an unprecedented growth of scientific and industrial potential and ever deeper and more intricate links among economic regions . . . [19]

The single economic complex features large, highly developed production units that make use of the latest technological achievements. The organization of the economy is also well developed and meets the demands of a socialist economy. The single complex is comparable with a single factory with ten million workers, a metaphor that Lenin once used to describe the production system under socialism.[20]

Altogether, the doctrine of the Soviet people and the doctrine of the single social economic complex mean that conformity is strongly stressed in Soviet society. The claim that regional differences have been fully or almost fully eliminated accords quite well with these doctrines. But it must be borne firmly in mind that the unity of Soviet society is to a large extent a normative unity, and one of the purposes of this study is to look behind official doctrine in this area.

The Soviet view is not to be gleaned exclusively from official statements. A more nuanced view of the problem may be obtained from a study of location rules.

Soviet Location Rules

The basic rules that according to the official view guide the location of Soviet economic activity are of a varying nature. Sometimes the rules are called laws, and sometimes they are called lawful regularities or principles for the location of Soviet industry.[21] According to the Soviet geographer Saushkin, these rules do indeed represent really existing phenomena, although various authors differ in how they formulate these rules.[22]

The origin of the Soviet locational principles—which seems to be the most used term—is to be found in Marxist-Leninist ideology. There are frequent references to Engels's *Anti-Dühring*, where in one place he says that under socialism industry will no longer need to be located near raw materials. Location can therefore be in the most suitable places, and in this way contribute to evening out differences between the city and the countryside.[23] Further, the location of industry is of course also governed by the transformation of society in general from capitalism to socialism and then to communism.

But contemporary Soviet location theory can only to a limited extent be derived from the early Marxist classics, and actually Lenin is a more important source for it. In his plan for scientific and technical work which he developed in 1918, Lenin affirms the necessity of reorganizing Soviet industry. Lenin said that industry should be located near raw materials so as to minimize transport costs.[24] Engels's and Lenin's views may seem to be contradictory, especially if they are applied to a country with uneven distribution of natural resources such as the Soviet Union. Both views reappear in later versions of Soviet location theory, which thus to a certain extent contains an internal contradiction.

Soviet location theory was further refined in the Communist Party Congresses in the 1920s and 1930s. At the 10th Party Congress in 1921, the uneven distribution of industrial development and regional differences in living standards received special attention. One of the revolution's foremost objectives was, so it was stated at this Congress, to eliminate all forms of regional and national inequality. This was to be accomplished by moving industries near deposits of raw materials in industrially undeveloped areas. This problem was taken up again at the 12th Party Congress, and at the 14th Congress in 1925 the need for a proportional distribution of industry throughout the whole of the Soviet Union's territory was stated.[25]

The first Party Congresses devoted considerable attention to the necessity of equalization among the different regions. The rationale for decisions in this direction is to be sought first and foremost in the necessity of integrating the various nationalities into the newly formed Soviet Union.

However, by the time the centralized planning system was introduced in the late 1920s, the situation changed. Although, to be sure, the 15th Party Congress in 1927 decided that the less developed regions should receive more resources, this had to be done in accordance with the interests of the economy as a whole. In practice, the desire for rapid economic growth came to prevail instead. The interests of defense were also of major significance for the development of Soviet industry.[27]

When the five-year planning system was introduced, with its strong emphasis on quantitative economic growth, the demands for development toward regional equality fell into eclipse. By this time the Soviet

Union had also stabilized, and earlier resistance from national group-
ings to the Soviet state had subsided.

At the 16th Party Congress in 1930, the regional question was again
taken up. The Congress decided, in line with Stalin's intentions, that
industry should be developed in the Ural mountains and Siberia. This
meant a distinct shift eastward for Soviet industry as a whole. The
extraction of raw materials in the eastern region was by far the dominant industry. At the 17th Party Congress, it was decided to continue
the development of the eastern regions, and at the 18th Congress in
1939 the need for regional self-sufficiency and an industrial location
policy in line with military strategy was especially stressed.[27]

Three basic elements in Soviet location theory were already discernible in the period before World War II: the striving for economic
effectiveness, regional equality, and location in accord with military
strategy. These three elements are also present in today's Soviet location theory.

Another important change that had already been effected before
World War II was the beginning development of the eastern regions,
i.e., the Urals, Siberia and the Far East. It is likely that this development was not in the first instance conditioned by regional policy or the
development of nationalities. There were very few people living in
Siberia at that time, and a good number of them were, moreover, of
Russian origin. Rather, the decision to develop the eastern regions was
more likely taken with a view toward accelerating economic growth,
although considerations of military strategy—creation of a second industrial base in the Urals in preparation for war—also played a major
role.

Thus, although Soviet location theory may ultimately be derivable
from Engels and Lenin, the Party Congresses in the 1920s and 1930s
also gave more specific directions on how and where industry was to be
located.

But to complete the picture of Soviet location theory, a non-Marxist
theoretician, Alfred Weber, must also be mentioned. Weber was one of
the first true location theoreticians and his work entitled *Über den
Standort der Industrien*, published in 1909, became a standard text. It
was translated into Russian during the 1920s, and so exerted a definite
influence on Soviet economists. Weber premised his argument on a
given state of production, and using various location factors attempted
to determine where industry should be located. These location factors
amounted to advantages to be gained from location in a particular

place, and, more precisely, economic advantages such as minimizing of material costs, the costs of wages and the costs of transport.[28]

Weber's theories were regarded as quite useful in the 1920s and 1930s for building up the Soviet economy, especially with regard to the geographic distribution of enterprises in a situation where capital was extremely scarce.[29] But Weber's theories were also subject to criticism from Soviet economists, whose objections were directed primarily against the fact that Weber's theory concerned an individual enterprise's choice of location, and gave little consideration to the interests of the economy as a whole.[30]

Weber's location theory was ultimately replaced by a Soviet theory that was a blend of theoretical fragments from Marx, Engels, and Lenin, as well as from decisions taken at the Party Congresses during the '20s and '30s.

As noted earlier, the rules that according to the Soviet view govern an enterprise's choice of location go by various designations, of which the three primary ones are: laws, principles, and patterns. Laws (*zakonomernosti*) refer to objectively existing phenomena that are independent of human consciousness, e.g., the law of the territorial concentration of production (in areas rich in raw materials or in traditional industrial centers). Patterns (*risunki*) refer to the result of a choice of location, when a choice of location has been made several times. We shall be concentrating mainly on principles (*printsipy*) which are presumed to guide Soviet policymakers and planners in their choice of a location.[31]

As stated earlier, the movement eastward in the Soviet economy had begun already in the '20s, and the 3rd Five-year Plan provided for extensive investment in the eastern regions. In the Great Patriotic War (i.e., World War II), 1941–45, the movement eastward accelerated and many enterprises were moved to western Siberia away from the German advance, although eastern Siberia also received some new industries.[32] Developments during the war may of course be taken as an explicit instance where considerations of military strategy directly influenced the location of enterprises. But the country was at war with Germany and relocation was the result of a state of war, rather than one location principle being given priority over others. The fact remains that a relocation of industry eastward took place on a large scale during this period, and that industry remained in Siberia when the war was over.

After Stalin's death, Soviet location principles were formulated in more concentrated form by economists and geographers, for example, Feigin, Lavrishchev, Probst, and A. T. Khrushchev. Three major types of principles may be distinguished.

1. *Economic principles*: Industrial enterprises should be moved closer to raw materials deposits and to consumers to minimize transport costs. Further, the individual regions should be planned and developed in such a way that specialized industries are located near raw materials deposits. But it is also important that every region strive toward a maximum of economic self-sufficiency. Economic activity should be distributed evenly over the country in order to make effective use of available human and material resources. Differences between city and countryside must also be abolished. But all these principles are subordinate to the requirement of maximizing production throughout the country.

2. *Social principles*: The growth of underdeveloped regions should be stimulated, especially those inhabited by non-Russian nationalities. They must be brought up to the same level as regions where Russians are in the majority. Thus, the per capita industrial output of the non-Russian nationalities must be increased substantially, an effect of which will be to improve national growth.

3. *Political principles*: The question of location must be subordinate to military strategy. Thus industry should be located in such a way as to facilitate defense, i.e., in military protected areas.[33]

Some location principles clearly conflict with others. For instance, the principle that enterprises should be moved closer to raw materials will clash with the principle of equal distribution of industry throughout the whole of the Soviet Union's territory. Economic and social principles may also be at variance. It is by no means clear that an intensification of economic activity in underdeveloped regions is necessarily the most effective way to increase economic growth. On the contrary, following the dictates of regional policy may mean higher production costs. Finally, political or military principles may require that an enterprise be located in a place that in strictly economic terms is disadvantageous.

But the differences should not be overemphasized. In practice, it is presumably possible to reconcile several principles that might at bottom be contradictory.

To take one example, an industry may be located in a region inhabited by a non-Russian nationality where there is also access to the requisite raw materials. Or an industry may also be located giving due consideration to economic interests as well as to the interests of military defense.

Of special importance for this study are the social location principles, which also have major political implications, considering the Soviet Union's ethnic pluralism. These principles, which call for regional equalization, are encountered in various contexts, and of course are also in concord with the ideas of equality that distinguish Marxism-Leninism.

But despite their importance, social principles must share their influence on Soviet economic development with other factors. Economic effectiveness has often been a guiding light for economic policy. According to Koropeckyj, strategical considerations of military defense have been the sole deciding factor in determining the location of industry in the Soviet Union.[34]

Koropeckyj found that social principles were the least important in determining the location of industry in the Ukraine during the period between the Wars.[35] It is not clear, however, if his conclusions included the whole of the 1920s and 1930s. There is much evidence indicating that social principles played an important role at an earlier stage just after the Soviet Union had been formed, when the aim was to integrate the various nationalities with one another, but that these principles diminished in importance once rapid industrialization was inaugurated. Later, as the risk of international conflict grew, military considerations most probably began to play a greater role.

The question is whether location principles directly reflect the explicit aims of Soviet economic policy. They certainly describe a number of desired effects of economic activity, such as maximum growth, regional equalization, and military defensibility. Clearly, these aims are given different priorities by the political leadership, which in turn may vary over time.

The above classification of location principles, informed to a large extent by I. S. Koropeckyj's research, is a distillation of certain general lines of thought among Soviet theoreticians. Different theoreticians will, of course, give different emphasis to different principles. A presentation of location principles typical for contemporary Soviet economic geographers may be found in Ia. G. Feigin:

1. Systematic distribution of production over the entire country with the view toward maximizing economic growth and involving all the regions of the country in socialist production.

2. Raising economic and cultural development of the republics to

the same level as that of the leading regions of the country in harmony with the interests of the country as a whole as well as of the individual republics.

3. Location of industry near raw material deposits and consumers to reduce long and inefficient transport distances.

4. Systematic distribution of labor among the economic regions and republics, specialization and comprehensive development of the economic regions.

5. Planned integration between industry and agriculture, and between the cities and countryside, by a rational location of industry and agriculture relative to one another.

6. An international division of labor within the socialist camp on the basis of mutual cooperation.

7. Location of the forces of production in such a way as to strengthen defense.[36]

As stated earlier, location principles could be viewed as the aims of Soviet policy. But it is important to bear in mind that priorities will vary depending on the conjunctural circumstances. Nor is it necessarily true that stated aims and real aims coincide. The principles for the location of industry are normative principles. They say how things should be. Actual location decisions may be based on fundamentally different considerations.[37]

It would therefore be a mistake to confuse location principles with the location policy actually pursued, although their importance must certainly not be underestimated. Location principles serve as a guideline for decisionmakers, and they recur in several different contexts. The principle of regional economic equality has been proclaimed especially often.

Nor should the value of location principles be overstressed, but if they are combined with certain official texts and statements, such as the Party programs and the instructions for the 60th anniversary of the creation of the Soviet Union, a clear idea may be obtained of how important the central decisionmakers consider the principles actually to be. In their statements, decisionmakers have made pledges of actual considerable consequences, especially with regard to the principles of regional equality. In the official view, regional inequality has been abolished, and this claim will accordingly serve as a point of departure for the following discussion on Soviet regional policy.

Western Studies

Quite a number of Western students of the Soviet Union have been fascinated with the question of whether regional differences exist in the Soviet Union. Some assume the Marxist ideal of equality as a starting premise with the corollary that a country such as the Soviet Union, which has officially proclaimed the victory of socialism, should display a high degree of equality in all areas. It is essentially correct to speak of the Marxist ideal of equality, but it is highly doubtful whether it is explicitly stated anywhere in Marxist-Leninist ideology that full equality should be achieved under socialism. True equality will be achieved only in the final stage of development, communism.

But it would be a reasonable assumption that differences in a socialist society should diminish with time. It is therefore not unwarranted to study regional variations in the level of development if Marxist-Leninist ideology is taken as a premise. Moreover, as pointed out earlier, it is the officially proclaimed view in the Soviet Union that regional differences are in the process of being eliminated, or have been eliminated already.

But that regional differences exist in the Soviet Union should occasion no surprise. The country is the largest in the world and embraces several different climatic zones. In addition, it is inhabited by over one hundred different nationalities each with its own specific cultural characteristics; several different religions are represented in the Soviet Union; and raw materials and population are unevenly distributed over the country's territory.

It is hardly the most important contribution of Western scholars that they have been able to demonstrate the existence of regional variations. More important is to define the extent and magnitude of these differences more exactly. The longitudinal dimension is also extremely important: have regional differences increased or diminished over time?

The American economist Gertrude E. Schroeder has made several analyses of regional inequalities in the Soviet Union, and finds that a study of regional differences is essential not only with regard to the question of equality, but also for an assessment of the Soviet Union's ability to solve its manpower problems. Regional differences in income and living standard influence the work force's tendency or willingness to move from one region to another.[38]

Schroeder's principal conclusion is that regional differences exist and are even growing in many key areas. The wage reforms of the 1970s thus increased the wage differential between the different regions. On the other hand, it seems that the differential between industrial workers' and agricultural workers' incomes decreased during the 1960s and '70s for the union as a whole as well as in several of the republics. But differences in living standard between the urban and rural population on the whole still exist, one of the reasons being that shortages are relatively greater in the countryside than in the cities.[39]

Living standard also varies widely among the republics. Schroeder measured living standard in terms of several indicators: individual per capita income, services and retail trade, republic expenditures for health care, education, and culture, and size of dwelling units in square meters per capita for the urban population. In terms of these parameters, the republics may be divided into four distinct groups with regard to living standard:

1. *High living standard.* The three Baltic republics, Estonia, Latvia, and Lithuania, have the highest living standard.

2. *Average living standard.* Two republics, the RSFSR and the Ukraine, have a standard just over or equal to the national average.

3. *Living standard just under the average.* Three republics, Moldavia, Georgia, and Kazakhstan, have a standard 10% below the average.

4. *Low living standard.* Belorussia, Armenia, and Turkmenistan have a living standard 15–20% lower than the national average.

5. *Very low living standard.* The three remaining Central Asian republics, Uzbekistan, Tadzhikistan, and Kirghizia, as well as Azerbaidzhan, have a living standard that is 75% of the national average or lower.[40]

Schroeder's calculations were made on the basis of data from the 1950s and 1960s, when the tendency was rather toward a growth than a diminution in regional differences. Schroeder's grouping of the republics seems to correspond well to the industrial and economic level of development the republics could be expected to have. But it is somewhat surprising that Belorussia has a relatively low living standard despite its proximity to the Soviet Union's industrial center in European Russia.

Later studies by Schroeder in the main confirm the earlier findings. Consumption of goods and services is an important measure of living standard. According to Schroeder's calculations of per capita consumption, the three Baltic republics had by far the highest standards, followed by the RSFSR, and then the remaining western republics, the Ukraine, Belorussia, and Moldavia. The Central Asian republics and Azerbaidzhan had the lowest per capita consumption.[41]

The general pattern that emerges suggests that cultural tradition may in fact play a major role in determining living standard. The republics in which a Moslem tradition had been dominant have a lower standard, whereas the more Western-oriented parts of the Soviet Union enjoy a higher standard of living. The role of cultural tradition and experience with and orientation toward industrial occupations will be dealt with later on in this study.

Ivan Koropeckyj also studied regional differences in the socialist countries, comparing the Soviet Union and the Eastern European CMEA countries plus Yugoslavia with regard to regional development. Koropeckyj's studies were based on interregional differences in per capita industrial output and employment in industry. He found that regional inequality declined for all countries studied in the 1950s and 1960s.[42] A slight increase in regional differences was noted in the Soviet Union during the period when the national economic councils (Sovnarkhozes) existed. During this period, from 1957 to 1965, there was a shift of formal decisionmaking on planning to the regional level.[43]

Koropeckyj's analysis is premised on the assumption that equality is a socialist ideal, but he points out that the goal of equality conflicts with another important goal of the socialist countries, namely maximum economic growth. A third objective of economic policy, which according to Koropeckyj is the most important for the Soviet leaders, is to increase the country's defense capacity.[44]

Although Koropeckyj's studies of regional differences in the Soviet Union are based on a relatively small amount of data, they nonetheless lend themselves to some interesting conclusions. It is noteworthy that regional differences increased during the Sovnarkhoz period, i.e., when regional interests tended to carry more weight. During this period, plans were able to give broader consideration to the interests of the particular regions with which they were concerned, so that a region's premises for economic growth assumed a greater relevance in planning. Since both natural resources and labor are unequally distributed, it is hardly surprising that regional variations increased during this period.

Koropeckyj also pointed out that economic policy pursued several objectives. Economic growth, regional equalization, and improved defense capacities are the three most important aims, but it is highly likely that they come into conflict in actual policymaking. The various goals are formulated more specifically in the criteria employed in locating Soviet industry, which will be dealt with later on.

A number of geographers have also been attracted to the study of regional differences in the Soviet Union. Roland J. Fuchs and George J. Demko studied regional differences in the industrially advanced socialist countries of Eastern Europe, i.e, the Soviet Union, Poland, Hungary, the GDR, and Czechoslovakia, on the basis of available Western and Eastern European literature in a polemic against radical geographers in the United States who claimed that a socialist system promotes regional equality.[45]

Fuchs and Demko pointed out that several studies supported the conclusion that the Soviet Union is marked by extreme differences in productivity per capita and in living standard, and that these differences are also tending to become greater as a consequence of the rapid population growth in Central Asia.[46] Similar patterns are evident in the other Eastern European countries, although the geographic differences in Czechoslovakia and the GDR seem to be somewhat less.[47]

According to Fuchs and Demko the existence of regional differences may be explained in various ways. First, geographic variations may be the result of historical patterns that the socialist states have not yet been able to change. But this explanation seems to be less convincing with regard to the Soviet Union, where the political leadership has had almost seventy years to effect change in this regard.[48]

Another explanation of the variations is that economic policy has been more geared to maximum growth than to regional equalization, despite the fact that the regional dimension is officially claimed to be highly important. Another dimension to the problem is that the leaders in the socialist states have favored investments in productive sectors of the economy rather than in the infrastructure, i.e., housing, roads, etc., which has meant that those areas where the infrastructure was already developed were in a more advantageous position.[49]

A fourth explanation of persisting differences is that large-scale organization has often been a necessity to achieve full social services.

Smaller cities and communities cannot provide the same services in health care, education, culture, etc. as large population centers. A fifth explanation, according to Fuchs and Demko, is differences in income distribution between different occupational categories. If certain high-wage groups are concentrated in a specific geographic region, the latter will of course show a relatively higher living standard.[50]

Thus it is beyond doubt that there are significant regional differences in the Soviet Union and Eastern Europe, according to Fuchs and Demko. Moreover, such inequalities often tend to be perpetuated. For the Soviet Union, the problem is especially vexing in Central Asia, where the population is to a high degree immobile. Furthermore, regional differences are not amenable to quick solutions, and almost always entail problems that require long-term measures to achieve a solution.[51]

But not all scholars agree that all types of regional differences will in fact continue to exist as time goes on. An unpublished doctoral dissertation by Ann Littmann Rappoport contains data on aspects of the living standard indicating that a certain process of equalization is taking place.[52]

Rappoport criticized a number of earlier studies on regional differentiation and pointed out that their results were based on simple statistical measurements that involved ranking the republics and studying the average.[53] Instead, Rappoport advocated using Theil's entropy measure, which states the extent to which a statistical material can be divided into subgroups, and also Lieberson's differentiation index, which measures the heterogeneity of data.[54]

These statistical parameters, which according to Rappoport give better results than simpler counterparts, were used to study various aspects of the policy of the central leadership toward the republics. With regard to economic policy, she makes use of a range of indicators such as national income, total republic budget expenditures, investments, communications, and health care.[55]

Rappoport's conclusion is that differences among the regions of the Soviet Union have been eliminated in several areas, especially as regards the distribution of living standard. Those indicators that suggest persisting differences are related to levels of development within the infrastructure, e.g., communications and production potential.[56]

These results are somewhat different from those of Schroeder, Koropeckyj, and other scholars. The question is whether differences in the findings are, as Rappoport claims, due to the fact that some scholars have used less sophisticated statistical parameters for their studies.

Rappoport's thesis is borne out in part by a study done by Martin C. Spechler, who investigated variations among the republics with regard to productivity, income, and consumption, and investments during the period 1958–78, and found that the differences among the republics are growing as regards productivity indicators. On the other hand, differences in income and other variables of well-being are not increasing, indicating that there is a considerable transfer of wealth from the relatively rich to the relatively poor republics.[57]

Spechler's analysis helps to explain the aforementioned differences in the findings of different authors. Available data indicate that the differences between the republics are greater with regard to production and industrial development than with regard to the indicators of living standard. Differences in the latter kept stable over time through budget transfers. Transfers must in practice go to the Central Asian republics, all of which have low parameters for socioeconomic development. Thus, not only are resources of various types taken from the Central Asian republics, as Western observers of Soviet Central Asia have pointed out; income transfers also go to these republics. Spechler calls this phenomenon "welfare colonialism."[58]

James W. Gillula points out that transfer takes place to the "southern belt," i.e., the Central Asian republics, yet despite these transfers differences in level of development still persist between the southern republics and the others.[59]

Regional differences can also be investigated directly on the basis of the union and the republic budgets, which reflect the priorities assigned by the political leadership to the different regions. A study by Donna Lynn Bahry indicates that the distribution of funds by way of the budget shows a very stable pattern over time, so that budget policy can have very little impact on the regional balance.[60]

Stability in budget policy seems, however, to apply first and foremost to the social domain. As Jack Bielasiak has shown, budget allocations to industry display another pattern in which economic and military considerations are paramount.[61]

The distinction brought out by Bielasiak, i.e., between industrial development and living standard, is important to bear in mind in evaluating regional differences. As we have seen, it is much simpler to find evidence of differences in industrial development than in living standard, and it is therefore highly likely that transfers of funds take place to the more poorly industrially developed republics.

Another important distinction, namely between *outputs* and *outcomes* in policy, complicates the picture further. Because inertia in various forms in the Soviet administrative system often influences the content of decisions after they have been made, the outcomes can differ considerably from the intentions of policymakers.[62]

The realization that outcomes do not give a correct picture of the intentions of decisionmakers has various implications for the study of the problem. For instance, outputs might be analyzed more attentively, in which case it would be especially interesting to explore the regional distribution of capital investments. If the investments were larger in the most poorly developed areas, this would support a compensation theory of sorts, according to which the most poorly developed areas are compensated for their relative backwardness by receiving more capital investments. Another possibility would be to explore to what extent there is a redistribution of resources from the richer to the poorer areas.[63]

All Western students of regional differences in the Soviet Union agree that these differences exist. They are easiest to discover in production, where differences have without a doubt persisted. The picture with regard to living standard is more complicated: although clear differences do exist, they are reduced by transfers from the union budget to the budgets of some of the republics. The data suggest that differences in this area are stable or diminishing; no Western student of the question claims that differences in living standard have been eliminated completely.

In another study, mentioned above, the present author was able to qualify some of the findings of other scholars on the basis of relatively extensive data covering urbanization, education, production potential, living standard, and communications, and a comparison was made between these data on socioeconomic factors and data on political recruitment for the period 1956–73.[64] The material may be visualized in a data matrix (Figure 3.1).

It is easy to see that the level of socioeconomic development underwent a rapid growth during the period covered by the study, and that this growth also occurred in the relatively undeveloped republics in the southern part of the Soviet Union. There was also an interesting correlation between socioeconomic and political variables: it appears that the Communist Party recruits more members in those parts of the Soviet Union with a high level of socioeconomic development. The Party may be assumed to have particularly broad tasks with regard to control and supervision of the advanced production sector.[65]

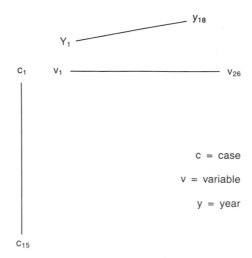

Figure 3.1 Data Matrix for the Study *Soviet Regional Policy.*

Urbanization, education, etc., were measured using a large number of variables, 26 in all. The study included all fifteen republics over a period of fifteen years. The total number of observations was 6,552. The quantity of data was reduced by factoral analysis and the different variable groups were correlated with one another with various statistical techniques such as regression analysis.[66]

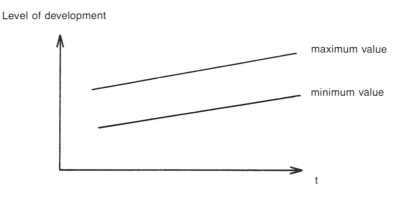

Figure 3.2 Socioeconomic Development in the Soviet Union 1956–73.[67]

Thus the analysis of the extensive data gathered in *Soviet Regional Policy* also yielded clear indications that regional differences existed, bearing out the findings of other earlier studies. But it is interesting to note that the differences between the most and least developed republics were of roughly the same magnitude in 1956 and in 1973, and that regional differences therefore persisted over time. This pattern is shown in Figure 3.2.

The fifteen republics also show different patterns in level of socio-economic development, and a number of clusters of republics with similar situations may be distinguished (Table 3.1).

In some cases, Azerbaidzhan tended to group in the same cluster as the Central Asian republics. Tadzhikistan often ranked quite far down. The variable per capita national income displayed a relatively typical distribution between the most and least developed republics. This indicator, which represents newly created value within the various sectors of material production, gives a relatively accurate measure of socioeconomic development (Table 3.2).

While the findings in *Soviet Regional Policy* concurred relatively well with Schroeder's findings in her study on the living standard, in the former study several variables were studied over a longer period of time. In particular, both output and outcome data were analyzed. The main trend evident in this multivariate material was for differences to persist over time in all areas, although they were most distinct in industrial production. In general the findings concurred with those of most other studies of the question, although of course agreement was poorer with studies that used only one variable or focused exclusively on, say, the budget question.

Thus, the clear conclusion is that lasting differences exist, notwithstanding the considerable growth that has taken place in all the republics, but the question that then arises is why they continue to exist. Is it because regional equalization is not a real aim of Soviet regional policy? Or has it been impossible to eliminate the differences despite all the efforts that have been made?

The existence of regional differences in the Soviet Union at its present stage of economic development concurs with observations made in other countries as well. On the basis of an analysis of a wide range of countries, economists and economic geographers have proposed a cyclic theory of regional differences. As a society moves from economic underdevelopment to a higher level of industrialization it passes through various stages of regional inequality. Before industrialization, regional differences are small, but as industrialization proceeds and the society becomes more centralized, they increase. But then, when the economy has reached a certain degree of maturity, the drawbacks of centralization become more conspicuous and measures

Table 3.1

Socioeconomic Characteristics of the Soviet Republics[68]

Clusters	Characteristics
RSFSR, Estonia, Latvia, and Lithuania	High level of development
Ukraine, Belorussia, and Moldavia	Low/medium level of development Rapid growth
Armenia, Georgia, Azerbaidzhan, Kazakhstan	Medium level of development
Uzbekistan, Turkmenia, Kirghizia, Tadzhikistan	Low level of development Declining growth

Table 3.2

National Income 1970, Rubles Per Capita at 1970 Prices

Republic	National income	Rank 1–15
RSFSR	1,558	3
Estonia	1,834	1
Latvia	1,796	2
Lithuania	1,535	4
Ukraine	1,334	6
Belorussia	1,382	5
Moldavia	1,087	8
Georgia	942	11
Armenia	1,025	9
Azerbaidzhan	815	13
Kazakhstan	1,120	7
Uzbekistan	805	14
Tadzhikistan	701	15
Kirghizia	839	12
Turkmenistan	947	10
USSR	1,382	—

Source: Dellenbrant, *Soviet Regional Policy*, p. 164.

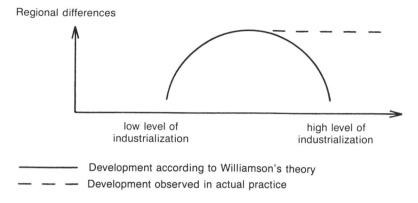

Regional differences

low level of
industrialization

high level of
industrialization

——————— Development according to Williamson's theory
— — — Development observed in actual practice

Figure 3.3 Cyclical Regional Inequalities.

are taken to decentralize, thereby reducing regional differences. However, according to one of the proponents of this theory, J. G. Williamson, in practice the differences rarely diminish in the third stage of development.[69] Figure 3.3 gives an illustration of Williamson's theory.

This theory also fits the Soviet case. Regional differences were accentuated by the rapid industrialization in the Soviet Union, and it was first around 1960, when the problem of overcentralization was discovered, that the problems of regional development began to receive more attention. The experiment with the Sovnarkhozes in 1957–64 was one attempt to resolve these problems.[70]

Thus if the theory of cyclical regional inequality is valid, regional differences should exist in the Soviet Union, and this is in fact the principal finding of some of the Western studies examined earlier. But they are merely empirical generalizations and not explanations of how these differences came to exist.

Soviet and Western Findings—A Comparison

The view of regional differentiation that may be gleaned from official Soviet doctrine and Soviet location theories is to a large extent normative. The main purpose of these theories is to postulate a desideratum for regional differences.

Regional policy and regional differences have also been explored by Soviet economists and sociologists, although it is not a well-developed area of research in Soviet scholarship. Only a few experts have confronted the question, as is evident from a paper on measuring the level of regional development, published by the Economic Institute of the

Academy of Sciences in 1971.[71] On the whole Soviet scholars and Western scholars agree in their assessment of regional development in the Soviet Union, as we will see later on.

First, however, I will describe in more detail the official Soviet view on persisting regional differences, and the distinction that is drawn between approximate and total equalization.

> It is characteristic of the stage of developed socialism that *all republics and national regions have achieved approximately the same level of economic development*, although certain differences and specific features have been retained. What is of fundamental importance in this context is that the continued equalization of the level of development of all the regions, involving a more rational deployment of production forces in accordance with the location of sources of raw materials and labor reserves, and the promotion of all sectors of the economy and all industries into the front ranks of scientific and technical progress, is a qualitatively different problem than the historical task of overcoming economic backwardness in a number of territories and among whole peoples. . . .[72]

Thus the main task of raising the level of development in the formerly very backward areas at the country's periphery has been accomplished; this is what had been regarded as the historical task, and all areas are now seen to have achieved a kind of minimal level of development.

The process of equalization among the different regions will continue on the basis of a more rational location of enterprises, and a better use of available energy and labor.[73] Although of course this objective is important as well, it should be distinguished from the historically more important task of achieving a minimal level of equality among formerly backward areas.

Thus, from this perspective as well, certain regional differences still exist, and, moreover, according to the official Soviet view it is not even desirable that all differences be eliminated.

> Differences may be due to objective factors (national customs and traditions, the population's demographic structure, etc.), or subjective factors (insufficient attention given to some social problem in the republic or, on the contrary, an overhastiness in dealing with it).[74]

If one considers this more precise statement of the Soviet view, which indeed it is possible to piece together from articles in the periodical *Kommunist*, differences from the conclusions of Western scholars prove to be much smaller; and agreement is even greater if the analyses of Soviet scholars are studied.

L. N. Telepko was one of the first to study inequalities in the level of development of the different regions of the Soviet Union. He found that all Soviet economic regions had industries ranked among the fifteen most important sectors of the economy, and hence that a certain degree of equalization could be said to exist.[75]

On the other hand, there were importance differences in other important indicators. According to Telepko, the productivity of labor varied from one region to another. Central Russia and the areas around Leningrad and the Volga River had the highest productivity, and other regions with a high productivity were the Baltic, Belorussia, the Ukraine, and western Siberia. The Caucasus and Central Asia fared poorly in this respect in Telepko's studies, which were based on data from the 1960s.[76]

Telepko's findings were later confirmed by other scholars such as A. I. Notkin[77] and A. I. Vedishchev.[78] A. K. Zakumbaev at the Economic Institute of the Kazak Academy of Sciences made a very thorough study of economic development in the republics, and one of his most interesting results was his ranking of the republics on the basis of an industrial development index (Table 3.3).

This industrial development index is the national income produced in industry per employee in the economy as a whole. The average for the Soviet Union is 100, and the value assumed by the index shows divergences from the national average.

Zakumbaev's analysis of regional differences in the Soviet Union differs little from that of Western scholars. The Baltic and the RSFSR are the most highly developed areas, while the Central Asian republics show the lowest indexes.

Zakumbaev found a distinct negative correlation between the industrial development index and the birthrate in the different republics,[79] and a positive correlation between the level of industrial development and employment.[80]

Other Soviet scholars have been concerned with similar problems. M. N. Rutkevich investigated equalization in social structures among the nationalities and republics, and found differences still existing in several important areas, including occupational training. The proportion of occupationally trained labor and of engineers and technicans in the total employed population was lower in some republics than others.[81]

While certain findings of Soviet scholars indicate that regional differences have persisted or have diminished, other Soviet data indicate that regional differences are increasing in some cases. In an

Table 3.3

The Soviet Republics Including Siberia's Economic Regions, According to the Industrial Growth Index 1972

Republics Regions	Index
RSFSR	108
Western Siberia	113
Eastern Siberia	96
Far East	93
Estonia	146
Latvia	131
Lithuania	127
Ukraine	96
Belorussia	94
Moldavia	69
Georgia	75
Armenia	78
Azerbaidzhan	72
Kazakhstan	98
Uzbekistan	65
Tadzikistan	55
Kirghizia	68
Turkmenistan	68
USSR	100

Source: A. K. Zakumbaev, *Ekonomicheskoe razvitie soiuznykh respublik i raionov*, p. 10.

analysis of the equalization process, E. B. Alaev and S. I. Khvatov found that the absolute differences among the republics increased in the period 1971–80 with regard to dwelling surface area per urban inhabitant and the number of hospital beds per capita population.[82] These indicators are often used as a measure of the standard of living, and growing differences in this area may be a sign that transfers from the budget have diminished.

Another area in which Alaev and Khvatov have noted serious problems is the housing standard in Siberia, where housing construction has lagged, with a resultant severe shortage and inferior quality of housing.[83]

According to Alaev and Khvatov, the solution to the continuing regional problems lies in placing greater emphasis on territorially oriented planning. Regional aspects must be given more attention. The present orientation of planning, i.e., with primary focus on sectoral interests, makes any further regional equalization impossible.[84]

One source of regional problems is in fact that an effective regional policy is lacking. Soviet economists say that sectoral interests come first, and the territorial aspects of economic development are hence relatively neglected. Most Western students of the regional development problem in the Soviet Union would share this attitude, putting them largely in agreement with their Soviet colleagues.

Both Western and Soviet scholars find that considerable economic progress has been made in all Soviet regions, although distinct regional differences still exist; Western scholars tend to ascribe more importance to these differences than their Soviet colleagues.

Organizational factors are often seen to exert a major influence on the way regional development problems are approached, especially in the Soviet Union, considering the difficulties that have been encountered in combining sectoral planning with territorial planning. The next chapter provides an overview of the organization of Soviet planning and administration.

4. THE ADMINISTRATIVE ORGANIZATION

Decisionmaking on issues of regional policy in the Soviet Union takes place within a complex administrative structure. Party organs, state institutions at various administrative levels, and scientific research institutes are all involved in the planning and administration of the Soviet economy. In this chapter I shall examine the existing planning and administrative bodies, as well as how decisionmaking powers are distributed among the various bodies and administrative levels. How decisions are made and implemented in regional policy will also be examined.

The study will concentrate mainly on the 1980s, with but one historical digression, to the Sovnarkhoz reform. During the period between 1957 and 1965, regional organization was fundamentally different from what it is today. The administration of the economy was concentrated in the hands of a number of Sovnarkhozes, or economic councils (initially about a hundred of them, although their number dwindled).

The main emphasis will be on the bodies of most relevance for regional policy, in particular those at the central (union) and regional (republic) levels. A peculiarity of the Soviet administrative structure is its *dual organization*. The regular administrative bodies are not the only agencies active in steering the economy; the Communist Party is also much involved. In theory, the Party, whose structure parallels that of the administrative bodies, is supposed to act no more than as a guiding hand for the society, but in practice it is involved conspicuously often in detailed issues concerning the economy. The frequent Party intervention in administrative activity, called *podmena*[1] in Soviet terminology, is often the object of criticism in the Soviet press.

Party organs definitely play a major role in regional policy, so that including them in this chapter on organization is by no means inappropriate. But as the actual Party organization *per se* has been analyzed in detail by other authors, the present discussion will be mainly concerned with those aspects that are of direct relevance to regional policy.

The Union Level

The most important decisions on regional development are unquestionably made at the central or union level, where decisions on political and economic matters are made for all important areas of Soviet society. These decisions then become laws or decrees in state bodies and are implemented by the state bureaucracy, which is under the constant surveillance of the parallel Party hierarchy.

The *Party Congress*, according to the Party statutes, is charged with setting Party line in domestic and foreign policy issues, but it also makes crucial decisions in economic policy. In practice, this is usually within the context of decisions regarding the five-year plans. The Party Congresses are now scheduled synchronously with the five-year economic plans. Thus, the 26th Party Congress in 1981 charged the Council of Ministers with the task of compiling the draft version of the five-year plan for the period 1981–85 in accordance with the "fundamental guidelines for economic and social development in the Soviet Union for the years 1981–85," which had been approved by the Congress.[2]

The *Central Committee* (CC), which normally meets twice yearly, often deals with problems of economic policy. It adopted the food program in 1982. The Central Committee also drew up the guidelines for the economic reform in 1965 at its meeting in September of that year. Central Committee members are appointed primarily on the basis of the positions they hold in Soviet society, i.e., key posts within the Party, positions in the Politburo and Secretariat and in the state administration, as well as top positions in the ministries and the committees of the Council of Ministers. Representatives of the republics and the more important local organizations are also appointed, along with outstanding enterprise managers, military figures, scientists, scholars, etc. Industrial and collective farm workers are of course also represented.[3]

But the body that is most important in real terms for shaping Party and state policy is of course the *Politburo*. The number of members is small enough for the Politburo to function as a genuine policymaking body. Final decisions on the more important issues of regional policy unquestionably rest with the Politburo.

The *Secretariat* plays an important role in determining the details of policy. It prepares the Politburo's agenda and sees to it that Party decisions are carried out. Perhaps the most important circumstance giving the Secretariat such a major influence is the number of subdepartments under its authority, i.e., the Central Committee apparatus, which comprises several thousand persons and deals with issues of foreign policy, industry, ideology, etc.

Thus a distinction must be drawn between the *Secretariat*, i.e., the secretaries selected by the Central Committee, and the *apparatus*, those who are employed to carry out the vast and far-ranging tasks of the Secretariat. The CC's various departments have the task of providing the secretariat with relevant material and supervising the ministries, state committees, and other state institutions. According to available information, they include the Administration of Affairs and the Administrative Organs department, as well as departments for agriculture, the chemical industry, construction, culture, the defense industry, heavy industry, light industry and food industry, machine industry, foreign cadres, international relations, Party organizational work, planning and banking, political administration in the Ministry of Defense, propaganda, science and education, socialist countries, trade and consumer issues, and communications.[4]

Each CC department often supervises several ministries, and every secretary may be assumed to be responsible for several departments, although formally they are headed by their own chiefs. The Secretariat and the CC apparatus show broad similarities with the organizational structure of the state administration; specifically, the Secretariat corresponds to the Council of Ministers, while the apparatus corresponds to the various departments of the ministries.

Western scholars do not have complete knowledge of the relationship between the CC departments and the various ministries, but it is most probably more complicated than a simple relationship of subordination. Indeed several studies have pointed up the occurrence of conflicts between the Party apparatus and state bodies.[5] It is unclear where exactly decisions are made.

Thus the Communist Party has an administrative and investigative apparatus at the central level. Some scholars claim that these are the real governing bodies.[6] But there would seem to be considerable risk of administrative inefficiency in a dual organization of this sort.

In the central state government the *Supreme Soviet* is formally the most important body. Its functions include approving the state budget and the economic plans. The most important body for regional policy is effectively the *Council of Ministers* and its Presidium. The Council of Ministers comprises union and union-republic ministers, the chairmen of state committees, and the fifteen chairmen of the Councils of Ministers of the fifteen Soviet republics.

Ministries and committees of the Council of Ministers at the union level are also located at the top of the Soviet administrative pyramid. The ministries are of two types, union and union-republic. The union ministries operate only at the union level, while the union-republic ministries function in part at the union level, part at the republic level. The union-republic ministries have a *dual subordination* (*dvoinoe podchinenie*). They are responsible to the ministries at the union level, as well as to the particular republic's Council of Ministers. In 1984 the following *union ministries* existed:[7]

Automotive Industry
Aviation Industry
Chemical Industry
Chemical and Petroleum Machine Building
Civil Aviation
Communications Equipment Industry
Construction for the Far East and Trans-Baikal Area
Construction of Petroleum and Gas Industry Enterprises
Construction, Road and Municipal Machine Building
Defense
Defense Industry
Electrical Equipment Industry
Electronics Industry
Foreign Trade
Gas Industry
General Machine Building
Heavy and Transport Machine Building
Instrument Making, Automation Equipment and Control Systems
Machine Building
Machine Building for Animal Husbandry and Fodder Production
Machine Building for Light and Food Industry and Household Appliances
Machine Tool and Tool Building Industry
Maritime Fleet
Medical Industry

Medium Machine Building
Petroleum Industry
Power Machine Building
Production of Mineral Fertilizers
Radio Industry
Railways
Shipbuilding Industry
Tractor and Agricultural Machine Building
Transport Construction

The following are the *union-republic ministries*:[8]

Agriculture
Coal Industry
Communications
Construction
Construction of Heavy Industry Enterprises
Construction Materials Industry
Culture
Education
Ferrous Metallurgy
Finance
Fish industry
Food industry
Foreign Affairs
Fruits and Vegetables
Geology
Health
Higher and Secondary Specialized Education
Industrial Construction
Installation and Special Construction Work
Internal Affairs
Justice
Land Reclamation and Water Resources
Light Industry
Meat and Dairy Industry
Nonferrous Metallurgy
Petroleum Refining and Petrochemical Industry
Power and Electrification
Timber, Pulp and Paper, and Wood Processing Industry
Trade

The union ministries, which administer the work of units under them without any direct collaboration from soviets on lower levels, pursue their activities in administrative areas that function integrally for the union as a whole, e.g., the Ministry of Foreign Trade. Union ministries also include those in which the organization of production and technical development warrant a tight network of production units, e.g., the ministries for technically advanced production, such as aircraft, automobiles, and electrical engineering. Obviously, security factors also play a role in the ministries for defense and the defense industry.

The union-republic ministries are often concerned with local natural resources, e.g., the ministries for the forestry industry, water resources, petroleum refining, and the coal industry. They are also concerned with local economic circumstances, e.g., the ministries for agriculture, trade, and finance. Finally, they may deal with national matters, e.g., the ministries for culture and education.[9]

About 44% of total production turnover falls under the jurisdiction of the union ministries, 50% is under the union-republic ministries, and about 6% of production is the responsibility of the republic ministries. These figures refer specifically to the Turkmen SSR, but may be regarded as typical for all republics.[10]

In addition to the ministries there are also a number of *state committees* under the Council of Ministers. Formally, these committees are a subordinate form of ministry, but in practice some of them have authority over the ministries insofar as they issue orders that are binding for the latter. There are both union and union-republic state committees, among which is the State Committee for Science and Technology (GKNT). Among the union-republic committees there are at least two that are especially important for regional development, namely the State Planning Committee (Gosplan) and the State Committee for Material and Technical Supply (Gossnab). It is Gosplan's responsibility to work out the five-year plans and the annual plans and to coordinate the planning activities of the individual ministries. Gossnab organizes the exchange of raw materials and semifinished materials among enterprises.

Gosplan bears prime responsibility for both long-term and short-term planning and a good deal of its activity has to do with drafting plans in cooperation with the ministries. The task of Gosplan is thus to consolidate the demands of the ministries. Its organization is huge—hardly surprising considering the importance of its tasks. It also has sectoral departments that work together with the planning departments of the ministry for the particular sector and with departments that deal with the principal aspects of the economy, i.e., investments, introduction of technology, and territorial planning.[11]

There are also a number of research institutes involved in planning and economic policy. The most important of these institutes, which are subordinated to the Academy of Sciences of the USSR, study how the economy and the planning system functions. There are, for example, the Central Economic-Mathematical Institute in Moscow and the Institute of the Economics and Organization of Industrial Production in Novosibirsk. But Gosplan also has research institutes linked directly to it, e.g., the Council for the Study of Productive Forces.[12]

Scientists influence economic policy in various ways, e.g., by participating in discussions and conferences on regional development, or by gathering and preparing data and research results for subsequent use by decisionmaking bodies. Scientists have been especially active on regional development programs, in, for example, analyzing a region's possibilities for economic development, and working out plans for future expansion.[13]

The most detailed regional development program drafted thus far by Soviet scholars was for Siberia, or the "Sibir" superprogram. This program discussed in detail the prerequisites for the continued exploitation of Siberia's natural resources. There have been also other large-scale scientific programs, e.g., the program for bringing water to Central Asia.[14]

The purpose of this chapter has not been to give an exhaustive description of the Party and the administrative bodies at the central level, but rather to identify briefly those agencies at the union level that have influenced regional policy. In the next section, their counterparts at the republic level are described.

The Republic Level

The next administrative level below the union level is comprised of the fifteen Soviet republics, which in a number of respects duplicate the organizational structure of the union. At the republic level as well there are Party Congresses, Supreme Soviets, Gosplans, etc.; in fact, a good portion of this book concerns the relationship between these two levels, the union and the republic.

The principle of the leading role of the Party of course holds at both the union and the republic levels. What this means is that the Party sets the main direction for economic development[15] through its formal center of power at the republic level, the republic Party Congress, which normally convenes just before the union Party Congress. The republic Congresses examine and approve proposals for the republic five-year plans. However, the largest republic, the RSFSR, does not have its own Party organization; hence political activities at this level are the domain of the union Party organization.

The highest Party bodies, the Central Committee and the Secretariat, also exist at the republic level. The republic Politburo is referred to as the Bureau of the Central Committee. The Party organizations of the republics are not independent parties, but sections of the Communist Party of the Soviet Union.[16]

The tasks of the Supreme Soviets and the Councils of Ministers of the republics correspond to those of the union Supreme Soviet and Council of Ministers, although their authority is clearly limited. For example, the union government can revoke a decision taken by a republic Council of Ministers. In addition, the republic Party leadership maintains effective control.

A number of important issues fall outside the decisionmaking authority of the republics. These regard first and foremost the activities of union ministries and state committees in republic matters. In addition, the union-republic ministries are, as was said, doubly subordinated: to the union Council of Ministers and to the republic Council of Ministers. Normally, the organizational links with the union level set the tone, although in practice there are probably extensive consultations between representatives of all-union matters and the republic Councils of Ministers. Here, too, the central level may be presumed to dominate.

Only the *republic ministries*, the third type of ministry, are controlled by the Councils of Ministers of the Soviet republics. Their relationship is one of simple subordination. This category includes ministries with strong local links or ministries that exist in only one or a few republics.[17]

The union-republic state committees at the republic level are under the dominant authority of the All-Union Council of Ministers, as are the several republic Gosplans, whose tasks at this level match those of the Gosplan of the USSR. The republic Gosplans draft the one-year and five-year plans for the republic and coordinate the ministries' planning activities.[18] Desires to strengthen Gosplan at the republic level have been voiced in the press.[19]

Research institutes and other scientific institutions also play an important role in the political decisionmaking process at the regional level, and scientists from a specific region will make an appeal for increased resources to the particularly area of their involvement. Regional development programs are also fashioned at the republic level, as well as lower levels. Estonia, the Ukraine, Belorussia, and Moldavia are said to have progressed the furthest in this area, although still not on a scale comparable to the Sibir superprogram.[20]

The Soviet Union's vast geographic expanse has meant that its sectorally oriented administration must be combined with a territorial administration. The fifteen Soviet republics vary considerably in size, population, culture, and history.

The *Russian Socialist Federated Soviet Republic*[21] is by far the largest of the republics, covering 76% of the territory of the Soviet Union, and embracing 52% of its population. The RSFSR has two of the industrially most highly developed regions of the country, around Moscow and Leningrad, as well as Siberia, which is currently undergoing a rapid economic expansion.

The European part of the RSFSR comprises the core of old Russia and is the country's center in several respects. It has remained the most developed region of the country despite efforts to develop other areas. Moscow is, of course, the country's decisionmaking center.

There has been no stinting on effort to stimulate economic growth in the RSFSR, and oil and gas extraction in western Siberia is the country's largest industrial project. Other parts of Siberia, especially the regions around the Angara river and the Baikal-Amur railway, are also undergoing expansion. The industries of western Russia, developed at an earlier period, are being modernized and revamped in a number of ambitious projects.

The Russian republic is ethnically relatively homogeneous, with 82% of its population of Russian origin. Population growth is slow, and the labor shortage is severe.

The three Baltic republics, Estonia, Latvia and Lithuania, annexed by the Soviet Union in 1940, are the smallest in the union, but are also (especially Estonia) among the industrially most highly developed areas, with their populations enjoying a high living standard compared with the rest of the country.

Estonia and Latvia can boast of a highly skilled labor force, and many technologically advanced products are manufactured in these republics. The machinery and metallurgy industries are among the most important sectors. Lithuania has undergone a rapid industrialization in recent decades as well, with emphasis on light industry and the food industry.

Numerous products of importance for the Soviet Union as a whole are manufactured in the Baltic region, and rather considerable capital investments have therefore been made here in the recent period. But economic growth has been hindered by a severe labor shortage, compounded by a slow population growth. Earlier there had been a large immigration of Russians and other national groups, but since 1970 that has fallen off. The relative size of the native population has still decreased perceptibly in Estonia and Lithuania.

The other European republics, the Ukrainian SSR, the Belorussian SSR, and the Moldavian SSR, differ rather broadly from one another. The Ukraine is a very large republic with over 50 million inhabitants, and has long been one of the Soviet Union's most important industrial regions, with most industrial sectors represented, although mining and heavy industry are especially well developed.

In Belorussia, industry is concentrated on agriculture and light industry. Farm machinery is produced on a large scale in this republic, which also has some working oil fields.

The Ukrainian and Belorussian nationalities, together with Russians, are the largest population group. Population growth is relatively slow. In Moldavia, on the other hand, the population is growing very rapidly, with Moldavians making up about 64% of the total population; Ukrainians and Russians are the other major population groups.

The Caucasian republics are three: the Georgian SSR, the Armenian SSR, and the Azerbaidzhan SSR. The Georgian economy is concentrated on agricultural products, with tea, tobacco, fruit, and wine heading the list; the private sector is very extensive. But industrial development has by no means been lacking, with steel production, the tool industry, and the chemical industry the most important sectors.

Armenia is relatively highly industrialized; metallurgy is the most important sector, but the chemical industry and machinery manufacture are also expanding. High-tech industry, e.g., computers and electronic instruments, is also represented, and the food industry is also significant.

The petroleum and petroleum processing industry has traditionally been dominant in Azerbaidzhan, although since 1950 it has stagnated severely. Attempts have been made to develop other sectors, e.g., the mining industry, but progress has been slow.

Georgia and Armenia have a Christian tradition, while Azerbaidzhan is Moslem. Population growth is relatively rapid in all three republics, but particularly in Azerbaidzhan.

The Kazakh SSR is the second largest Soviet republic, equal in area to Western Europe. Production has concentrated on energy and metals, with particular emphasis on metalworking and chemical products. Agriculture is quite extensive, and a huge land reclamation project was completed during the Khrushchev period.

Kazakhs comprise about 30% of the population, and Russians about 40%. Thus the native population is in a minority. The Kazakhs are Moslem by tradition, and population growth is relatively rapid.

The Central Asian republics, i.e., the Uzbek SSR, the Kirghiz SSR, the Tadzhik SSR, and the Turkmen SSR have many features in common: all have basically agrarian economies despite considerable industrial development in the recent period; cotton growing is an important sector especially in Uzbekistan; the level of socioeconomic development is lower than elsewhere in the Soviet Union; Islam is the dominant religious tradition; and population growth is extremely rapid.

Below the republic administrative level, there is a *local level*, comprising autonomous republics (ASSR), krais, and oblasts, as well as administrative bodies at the raion level and below.* The republic ministries operate at these levels, along with planning bodies attached to executive committees, e.g., the Oblplan, the Kraiplan, the planning commissions, etc.[22] Local administration has little say in setting the priorities that define regional policy, but this does not mean that local soviets do not have significance.[23]

The administrative structure in the Soviet Union is based in the first instance on the various nationalities. This is certainly true of the Soviet republics, but ethnically defined administrative units are also found at a lower level alongside the regular oblasts, etc. But such a structure is poorly adapted to the needs of economic planning, given that the Soviet republics vary so appreciably in size. The population of the RSFSR is several hundred times greater than that of Estonia, while the area of the RSFSR is more than five hundred times larger than Moldavia. A number of economic regions have been established to do away with

---

*ASSRs, krais, oblasts, and raions are territorial subdivisions of the USSR which function as administrative units. ASSRs and krais also serve as national homelands. Oblasts and raions roughly correspond to provinces and counties, respectively.

these disadvantages.

The economic regions have a long history. Very early, in 1920, the GOELRO (State Commission for Electrification of Russia) proposed dividing the country into regions, and in 1921 the newly formed Gosplan proposed a similar division into economic regions that differed substantially from the political and administrative division. Later, in the 1930s and '40s, several divisions were undertaken, resulting in fifteen large regions. In the Sovnarkhoz period, 1957–65, still another division was undertaken, this time into smaller regions.[24] At present there are twenty, as follows:

1. Northwest
2. North
3. Central
4. Volga-Viatka
5. Central Chernozem
6. Volga
7. Northern Caucasus
8. Urals
9. Western Siberia
10. Eastern Siberia
11. Far East
12. Donets-Dnepr
13. Southwest
14. South
15. Baltic
16. Caucasus
17. Kazakh
18. Central Asia
19. Belorussia
20. Moldavia

Eleven of the economic regions are in the RSFSR, three are in the Ukraine, three overlap several republics: Baltic, the Caucasus, and Central Asia, and two regions (Belorussia and Kazakhstan are) are congruent with a Soviet republic. Moldavia is not formally part of any economic region; its economic development is planned by the republic's own planning body.[25] There had been only eighteen economic regions, but in 1983 the northern region was separated from the northwest region, while a number of border alterations between the regions were made at the same time.[26]

The economic regions have no planning bodies of their own. They are merely units created to facilitate territorial planning, which is done centrally, and among those tasks facilitated are regional specialization, the utilization of natural resources, etc.[27]

Lacking administrative bodies of their own, the economic regions play a minor role in regional policy decisions. But the relationship between the administrative center and the republics seems to be the prime determinant of regional policy. There seems to be some conflict between the central and regional levels with regard to the allocation and distribution of investment funds, and the resolution of this conflict is rendered more difficult by the existence of two types of planning organizations, the sectorally oriented ministries and the territorially based planning and administrative bodies. These problems will be dealt with further, but first a few words about organizational at lower levels.

Industrial Associations and Enterprises

As already mentioned, economic activity in the Soviet Union is governed by a number of ministries, each of which is primarily responsible for one sector. The number of ministries has grown steadily during the time the ministerial system has been in operation, i.e., before 1957 and after 1965. In one period in the 1940s there were approximately thirty sectoral ministries.[28]

The planning work of the ministries grew progressively more complicated. Economic productivity advanced to a higher technical level, and the number of enterprises grew. A new organizational level, the *glavki* or *head administrations*, was set up in the ministries in the 1950s to take care of the details of planning. The *glavki* were revived after the 1965 economic reform, and accumulated a number of skillful administrators and planners.[29]

The intention of the political leadership in the next major reform was to bring about a radical change in the organization of the economy. The reform, ratified in April 1973, abolished the *glavki,* which had had an extremely important position in the old system, and replaced them with sectoral associations at union and republic levels.[30]

The official reason for the reform was to increase concentration and cooperation. Associations of enterprises, *ob"edineniia*, were formed to effect these changes. They were to cooperate in technology, education, etc., and in addition concentrate their activities within more circumscribed areas (a traditional problem of Soviet enterprises had been the excessive number of different items produced).[31]

Had the reform been fully implemented, the influence of the ministries would have been substantively weakened. First, they would have lost the *glavki,* which employed a large number of persons with expert knowledge. Secondly, the level below the ministerial level would have been strengthened; merging smaller enterprises into associations would have given them a common spokesman, often with considerable economic expertise. Thus, if the new structure had been fully built up, the position of the central political leadership and of Gosplan would have been strengthened considerably relative to that of the ministries. It is quite plausible that one nonofficial reason for the reform was to reduce the influence of the ministries, which indeed have often been charged with obstructing change in the Soviet economy.

But, like most other Soviet reforms, implementation has been slow. New *ob"edineniia* are still being formed even in the 1980s, and the slowness of implementation was commented upon at the time of the 1979 economic reform.[32] As the situation stands, therefore, the 1973 reform has failed to effect a shift of power away from the ministries, and in fact, as becomes clear from the debate in the specialized economic literature in the 1980s, officials at the local and regional levels still find that too much decisionmaking power is concentrated in the ministries.[33]

The 1973 reform provided for a number of ways to form *ob"edineniia,* including (for those involved in material production):[34]

1. Large enterprises or combines may be transformed directly into associations.

2. A large enterprise may incorporate several smaller enterprises, or *filialy,* to form an association.

3. Several smaller enterprises may be combined into an association.

The other type of associations are administrative associations, and like the ministries and state committees, they may also be organized at several levels:

1. All-union associations responsible for production within an area of national importance

2. Republic associations dealing with production within a republic, and subordinated to a republic ministry or an all-union association.

3. Local associations, responsible for production in a limited geographical area.

Industrial associations involved in material production or enterprises of the older type are often subordinated to these administrative associations.

Thus various types of organization are possible depending on the particular sectoral structure, and the following principal types may be distinguished:

1. Two-level organization: industrial associations are subordinate to an all-union or republic ministry. Combines and smaller enterprises may also be directly subordinate to ministries.

2. Three-level organization: industrial associations are subordinate to an all-union concern, which is accountable to an all-union ministry. Alternatively, an industrial association may be subordinate to a republic association or a republic ministry. Combines and enterprises may also be included in this type of organization.

The 1973 reform obviously entails an extremely complicated system or organization. Other variations of the two-level, three-level, and perhaps even four-level organization may be introduced, but the old system continues to exist as new associations are established.

The 1973 reform entailed a number of major modifications in regional policy. The intention of the reform was to strengthen decision-making at the administrative level under the ministries, and this was in turn to strengthen the influence of the republic and local levels. A number of new associations were also established at the republic level under the republic Councils of Ministers. However, because of the slowness of implementation of the reforms, these measures have not been significant.

The basic unit in the former organizational structure of the Soviet economy was the enterprise, the *predpriiatie*. It continued to exist after the 1973 reform, although it is now normally part of the various types of associations. The executive manager of an enterprise is typically in a strong position. Soviet enterprises are managed on the one-person leadership principle (*edinonachalie*), in which the executive manager is alone accountable to his superiors. His influence is limited in some areas, e.g., the hiring and firing of personnel, where the trade unions are strong. Since 1983 workers' organizations have had broader powers to influence the management of enterprises.[35]

Enterprises must follow the plan decided on by the central authorities. They receive information on a number of *plan indicators*, which aggregately describe the enterprise's finished output, and are expressed in physical magnitudes, in monetary terms, or as a combination of various other indicators. Soviet planners have found it difficult to find a well-functioning system of indicators, and indeed some of the economic reforms have been exclusively concerned with changes in the indicator system.

In the foregoing I have attempted to provide a frame of reference for the ensuing discussion of the debates and decisions concerning regional policy, which in fact have often touched upon organizational questions. The organizational complexity of the Soviet administrative system is evident enough, and it, together with the obstacles it creates to change, are discussed in Chapter 7.

Figure 4.1, taken from a Soviet textbook on economic planning, gives a general overview of the organization in the Soviet Union, without of course any claims of completeness. The diagram shows the formal organizational structure, but actual decisionmaking in planning issues probably takes place primarily at the highest levels. Proposals for change presented by the lower levels usually concern less important aspects of the plan. The Party agencies have also been left out of the diagram, although it may be taken as given that the overriding decisions on, for instance, the five-year plans are taken by the central Party authorities. The Party Congress ratifies plan proposals after which formal decisions are taken in the soviets at various levels.

Territorial Production Complexes

From the examination of the organization of administration at the union and republic levels it will be evident that a large number of agencies extending over different levels are involved in administration in which, of course, the Party organizations are also involved, creating all in all a rather fragmented system.

But the Soviet leaders are also aware of this fragmentation, and the territorial production complexes (TPCs) signalled among other things an attempt to come to terms with this problem. TPCs have been established mainly in Siberia, northern Russia, and in a few other regions, and entailed considerable industrial investments. A major aim in establishing TPCs was to enable economic activity to proceed without the administrative obstructions experienced under the sectoral and ministerial system. Several types of industries function in unison in a TPC, often grouped around an energy source or a deposit of raw materials.

There are three main types of TPCs:

1. TPCs of major union importance, which extend over an entire region. Examples of these huge complexes are the western Siberian

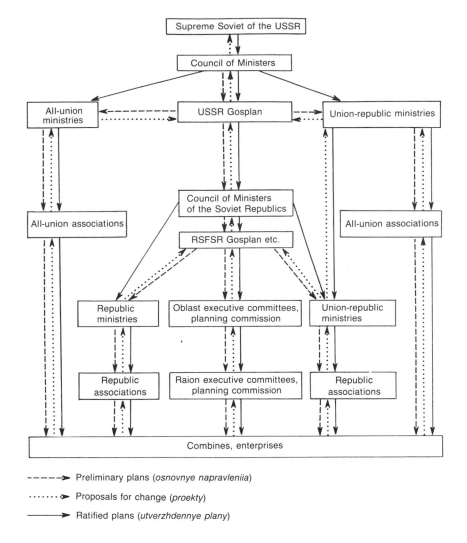

Figure 4.1 Economic Planning and Administrative Organizations.

Source: *Planirovanie narodnogo khoziaistva SSSR*, p. 73.

TPCs and the area round the Baikal-Amur railway.

2. TPCs within a more limited area, embracing several sectors. The TPCs along the Angara and Ienisei rivers are examples of this type.

3. Locally based TPCs, i.e., industrial nodal points with various sectors represented.[36]

The exact definition of a TPC is not clear, and a debate is going on among Soviet scholars on what is in fact intended with TPCs. However, it is clear that a TPC concentrates on the production of goods and services and that it draws on the resources available within a region, both personal and material. The activity of a TPC is often geared to union needs.[37]

The Soviet scholar Barabasheva defines TPCs as follows:

> A TPC is a group of industries in various sectors within a circum-scribed geographical area, united for the purpose of all-round develop-ment and joint use of this area and its natural and labor resources in the interests of the nation's economy, and of the joint efficient use of the economic and social infrastructure. The following elements are part of the basic structure of a TPC: natural resources, material production, economic and social infrastructure, and the work force.[38]

Thus what is special about a TPC is that the economic activity is carried on within a circumscribed area containing energy, natural resources, and a working population. Normally, therefore, all that is needed for industrial production is found within that area.

Other scholars would like to ascribe other more advanced tasks to TPCs. For example:

> The regrouping of industrial enterprises into a TPC makes it possi-ble to deal on a sound scientific basis with problems having to do with technological cooperation; the effective utilization of fuel and industrial wastes; the creation of central bases for storage, maintenance and repair, and common communications and transport systems; and the harmonious development of the nonproductive sphere.[39]

According to the author of these words, E. Azarov from the Executive Committee of the Pavlodar oblast, the formation of a TPC could contribute to a solution of the difficult coordination problems that plague the Soviet Union.

TPCs are especially important for the economic development of Siberia, and several of the new industrial construction projects in Sibe-ria are organized as TPCs: to wit, the western Siberia TPC (mentioned earlier on), the TPC in the Angara-Ienisei region, the Baikal-Amur railway TPC, as well as other important complexes such as the south-ern Iakut TPC and the TPCs in Saian and Kansk-Achinsk.[40]

One of the aims in creating the TPCs was to eliminate the sectoral barriers that normally describe the organization of the Soviet economy. The TPCs permit broader coordination than the former ministerial principle of management. This aim has to some extent been fulfilled, and several TPCs are now of quite considerable importance for the Soviet economy. But the better coordination that was supposed to have been achieved within the TPCs has not lived entirely up to expectations, and a number of management problems still persist.[41]

One particular problem affecting the management of TPCs is that responsibility is shared among several different bodies and the number of managerial bodies is not stable. When a new TPC is formed, a special commission attached to Gosplan, or to the Council of Ministers, is often created. The legal status of these commissions is, however, not clearly defined, and in practice it is often the Party that assumes concrete responsibility.[42]

The real coordination problems begin after a TPC has been completed. At that juncture management devolves to a different ministry than initially, and often even a large number of ministries and state committees are involved; for instance, more than twenty ministries and state committees are responsible for the management of enterprises in the TPC in the Saian region.[43]

Thus the TPC has not brought any solution to the problem of *sectoral barriers* that has plagued the Soviet economy for a long time. Each ministry tends to give priority to its own sector, often directly disregarding not only the interests of other sectors, but also those specific to the different regions.

The evidence indicates that the problems attendant on sectoral barriers (*vedomstvennye bar'ery*) in many instances still persist even after the formation of a TPC. In many TPCs, none of the ministries involved has assumed responsibility for the social infrastructure, i.e., the construction of housing, schools, day nurseries, etc. Social infrastructural problems have made it difficult to recruit sufficient labor.[44]

But there is no doubt that TPCs will continue to play an important role into the future as the Soviet economy expands further.[45] Action will certainly be undertaken in an effort to come to terms with the coordination problems that have beset the complexes from their very inception.

Special intersectoral agencies have been created to cope with these coordination problems, and a special commission attached to the Council of Ministers was formed to manage oil and gas extraction in western Siberia. In addition, the Gosplan has set up a territorial commission in Tiumen' in an effort to improve coordination among the various industrial sectors.[46]

A number of regional intersectoral complexes have also been formed, comprising enterprises within a smaller geographical region, most often an oblast, a krai, or an autonomous republic. Their activities replicate to a large extent the activities of TPCs, although on a smaller scale. Their coordination problems also seem to be more manageable since they embrace a more circumscribed area.[47]

The territorial aspects of the economy have recently been receiving more attention than formerly, if the formation of TPCs and intersectoral commissions may be taken as examples. Representatives of the various republics have also voiced their demands for a further strengthening of territorial planning. Their arguments will be dealt with later on.

Administration Problems and Reforms

The Soviet administrative apparatus is marked by a high degree of fragmentation. Bodies dealing with questions concerning administration and planning are spread over various levels. The organizational duplication between the Party and state is of direct practical significance: the Party has its own investigative and administrative apparatus and often exercises direct influence on enterprise management.

As regards the distribution of authority between the union and republic levels, however, the union level is in a particularly strong position. The republics have very few powers with regard to enterprise management and planning. Some of the most important sectors are under national ministries over which the republics have very little influence. The union-republic ministries are in principle subject to dual authority, but in practice the union level is dominant. The same seems to apply to planning authorities. The Gosplan of the USSR occupies a very powerful position, with the functions and responsibilities of the republic Gosplans being commensurately less important. There is however one countervailing factor to this central decisionmaking structure: the republics also have representatives at the union level, e.g., in the Council of Ministers and in the Gosplan of the USSR. But there is evidence that conflicts of interest exist between the union and republic levels in the planning and management of the economy, as has, indeed, been reflected to some extent in the ongoing Soviet debate on regional policy.

An examination of the administrative apparatus reveals a similar conflict of interests between sectoral and territorial planning. Each ministry tends to give priority to its own interests within its specific sector, and republic views concerning economic issues are often neglected. In planning as well, republic interests seem often to be forced into the back seat, something that has also been brought out in the debate on regional policy (which will be dealt with in a later chapter).

While decisionmaking appears on analysis to be concentrated at the central level, the lower levels seem to be more involved in implementing economic policy. This fragmented structure creates inertia within the system, permitting the lower administrative levels some opportunity to influence the economy.

During the Sovnarkhoz period 1957–64 an attempt was made to solve the problem with territorially based planning. The industrial ministries were abolished and economic councils assumed the roles of management and planning. There were initially 105 of these councils, but their number was gradually reduced to about fifty. Unfortunately, the experience with the economic councils was mostly negative. The councils' leadership tended to exaggerate the interests of their own region and disregard the fact that other regions might also have a need for goods produced within a particular council's territory. Central influence was thus gradually increased, and in 1965 a system based on industrial ministries was reintroduced.[48]

The reasons behind the Sovnarkhoz reform may be sought in a number of problems that have characterized the Soviet economy for some time.

Ministerial control down to the last detail over enterprise operations was a grave obstacle to enterprise functioning. The division of the economy into sectors made cooperation between enterprises in different sectors almost impossible even though they might be within the same geographic area. Ministerial activity tended to expand as time went on as a natural consequence of their detailed regulation of the economy.[49]

The Soviet press has also dwelled to some extent on the problem of economic management, and there has been sharp criticism of the existing system. In July 1957, when the ministries were abolished and Sovnarkhozes established, the day-to-day management of enterprises was transferred to the latter; the Gosplan USSR was responsible for the planning of the whole, and the respective republic Gosplans were responsible for planning and coordination at the republic level.[50]

The Sovnarkhoz reform also gave the republics broader powers. Sectoral ministries were reestablished at the republic level, and republic authorities were also granted greater powers with regard to budget allocations, the regulation of retail trade, etc. For a short time, a special *Gosekonomkomissiia* [State Economic Commission] functioned under the House of Nationalities of the Supreme Soviet with the task of safeguarding republic rights.[51]

There can be no doubt that the Sovnarkhoz reform brought improvements, especially in enterprise management, but the lack of coordination between the economic councils necessitated a number of administrative changes that reestablished the system's tendency toward centralization.[52]

The Sovnarkhoz reform is not often discussed in the professional economic literature, although the negative experiences with the economic councils are often mentioned. V. M. Manokhin has ventured a more positive assessment of the Sovnarkhozes, and although he is also aware of the problems, he clearly feels that "at the level of day-to-day operations the Sovnarkhozes had a number of considerable advantages over the ministerial system."[53]

The problems with sectoral barriers, which in their time had served as a major incentive for the Sovnarkhoz reform, still exist today.[54] The intersectoral commissions are evidence that the territorial principle of organization has not lost any of its relevance. In addition, a number of proposals have been made that the territorial approach should be further extended, e.g., to cotton growing in Uzbekistan.[55]

During Andropov's brief time in power, the question of economic reform was broached on several occasions. In his first major speech on the political and economic situation to the Central Committee meeting in November 1982, Andropov called for concrete action.

"There has in the recent period been much talk of the necessity of increasing the independence of concerns and enterprises, and state farms and collective farms. It would seem that the time has come to deal with this problem in practice."[56]

But even Andropov was unable to come up with a patent recipe, although he did say that it was essential to take into account the experiences of the East European "fraternal countries" in this area.[57]

The CMEA countries' experience with economic reform was to be scrutinized by a special *intersectoral committee*, under the direction of the Gosplan chairman Nikolai Baibakov, which would in particular explore the possibility of introducing new steering mechanisms of the type that now exist in certain CMEA countries, although of course the Soviet economy is considerably larger than that of any of the CMEA countries.[58]

Andropov's statement and the creation of the intersectoral committee bear directly on the issues with which the present study is principally concerned. Many of the changes and reform proposals presented are aimed at increasing the influence of lower-level administrative bodies, however slow such changes may be.

That changes should take such a long time is difficult to explain in view of the fact that there seems to be a general realization even among central political decisionmakers that a decentralization of the economic planning and management system is necessary; moreover, the problems attendant on sectoral barriers and *vedomstvennost'* have been dealt with in a number of centrally issued publications. Presumably, political factors, e.g., the risk of the central leadership's losing control of regional development, lie behind the cautiousness manifested with regard to decentralizing reforms.

In the Introduction mention was made of the importance of the Soviet bureaucracy, and hence of taking it into account in a study of political change. It is obvious that inertia and entropy are built into the Soviet administrative apparatus, and indeed organizational replication in certain administrative bodies is evidence enough to support this claim. Administrative bodies may therefore be expected to play a major role in the implementation of political decisions and it should hardly be surprising that policy should suffer distortions when implemented within such a complex and fragmented organization.

But the very fact that an extensive administrative and planning apparatus does exist at the regional and local levels indicates that these bodies do indeed have at least a potential influence. Of course most important decisions are centrally made, although under certain circumstances, e.g., when knowledge of local conditions is important, the role of the regional administrative apparatus may be magnified. If this reasoning is correct, it should support hypotheses 3 and 4 presented in Chapter 2, "Theoretical Premises."

Organizational issues are of major importance for how the Soviet economy functions. Any future economic reform will probably in some way provide for a strengthening of territorial planning. In the debate on regional development, strong criticism was levied against present planning and management and how it is organized, and in particular, the behavior of the industrial ministries. There are two major questions to be considered: how efficient the present organization structure actually is, and the role of the planning bureaucracy within the economic system. To judge from the complicated organizational structure, it will probably be difficult to implement changes in this respect as well. These and other questions will be dealt with further in the next chapter, which will describe the debate on regional policy that has marked the recent period.

5. REGIONAL DEVELOPMENT UNDER DEBATE

Problems of regional planning and its priorities are discussed in the Soviet press, although certainly not in the form in which they would appear in the Western mass media. The discussants must keep within very well-defined limits which are ultimately set by the Communist Party. Even so, some extremely interesting information can be gleaned from the material presented. On a number of occasions the problems of regional development have been debated on quite open (for the Soviet Union) terms, and union agencies such as ministries and planning authorities have had to undergo some heavy criticism from republic representatives.

This chapter will present some of the contributions to the Soviet debate on regional development. The main focus will be on some of the current trends in the debate, as exemplified in the contributions made by pace-setting representatives from the republics, rather than on how in general regional development is dealt with in the Soviet press. The articles selected for review are analyzed with regard to the author's position on the problems of regional distribution and the degree of administrative autonomy enjoyed at the republic level.

The background of policy decisions on the regional situation will be explored, and a number of the goals of regional policy examined. The focal point of the discussions is the question of how future investments are to be distributed among the different regions.

There are two separate but recurrent themes in particular that run throughout the discussions, which we might call the east-west problem and the north-south problem. The east-west problem has to do with the allocations of investments within the RSFSR and, accordingly, how large a share Siberia is to receive. Another important issue is the structure to be given to the Siberian economy: limited or differentiated development. The north-south problem concerns the relationship between the industrialized regions in Europe and the much less developed republics in Central Asia, and whether measures should be taken to stimulate development in the latter and if so when. One of the undertones of this issue is the rapid population increase in Central Asia.

Other problems are also touched upon in the debate; for example, the union ministries and the Gosplan are often criticized (in many cases quite sharply) for a lack of interest in the problems of regional development, especially by representatives of the Baltic republics, but also by the Central Asian republics.

The Europeans and the Siberiaks

The debate between those who represent the interests of the European regions and those who represent the development of Siberia centers on two mutually related problems: The first is the role Siberia is to play in the Soviet Union's economy. The ambitious development of Siberia has brought representatives of the European republics to question its rationality. Other discussants claim that it is necessary to develop Siberia to guarantee the Soviet Union's future growth.

But *how* Siberia should be developed is also an issue, and on this question two basically different standpoints may be discerned. The one says that development of Siberia should be circumscribed, i.e., Siberia should be relied on mainly for energy and other raw materials. The other standpoint—represented by, *inter alia*, researchers at the Institute for Economics and Industrial Organization at the Novosibirsk branch of the Academy of Sciences—calls for a differentiated development. Industries should be established in the various regions and the economic development of Siberia as a whole should be stimulated. It is this latter issue, i.e., limited or differentiated development of Siberia, which set the main tone of the discussions in the 1970s and 1980s.

Even in the '60s, voices could be heard that opposed the huge development projects east of the Ural mountains. It was then that the extraordinarily difficult problems that had to be surmounted in Siberia became fully apparent. It was found that although huge investments had been made, the returns were low. Development in Siberia was also hindered by a severe and permanent shortage of labor, and to recruit new labor to Siberia was an especially difficult task.[1]

Scientists and planners from Belorussia and the Ukraine were the most critical of the rapid expansion in Siberia, claiming that there were unutilized energy resources in their republics and elsewhere in the western Soviet Union and if these were not soon developed an energy shortage might begin to be felt in the European Soviet Union. They argued that the transport of energy from Siberia would entail a number of problems, with electricity being a case in point, and would be extremely costly whatever the case.[2]

The Belorussian economist V. G. Udovenko pointed out that reserves of energy and raw materials in the European Soviet Union were ample enough to warrant greater investments in this region. According to Udovenko, the conditions in Belorussia for expanding oil extraction were especially good.[3]

Representatives of the western regions of the USSR have put forth various arguments to promote their own regions. Arguments similar to Udovenko's had been presented earlier by S. Malinin, the Chairman of the BSSR Gosplan, who pointed out that Belorussia not only had oil, it also had other valuable sources of energy such as peat, coal, and water power. Further, Belorussia had a good climate for industrial development.[4]

Of course at the time only a small portion of total energy resources were believed to be located in the westernmost parts of the Soviet Union, but they had the advantage of being in a region with a favorable climate. Hence the resources in Europe, it was argued, should be used up before the attempt was made to develop the relatively inaccessible resources in other parts of the union.[5]

It was not only the Belorussian economists who argued for intensifying economic development in the European USSR; some discontent was also voiced with regard to regional policy priorities in the Ukraine. That region has enjoyed a rapid economic growth for some time, made possible, among other things, by an effective utilization of labor resources. But some imbalances emerged in the '60s in the Ukrainian economy, and intraregional differences have since grown rapidly.[6]

The European economists do not openly criticize the rapid development of Siberia, which becomes evident from a reanalysis of the sources used by Leslie Dienes. Their argument is extremely cautious, with the participants limiting themselves essentially to emphasizing the favorable conditions existing in their own republics. It is interesting, however, that the time in which the Ukrainian economy began to run into difficulties, i.e., the 1960s, coincided with the stepped-up development of Siberia.[7]

It is clear from talks given by Ukrainian politicians at Party Congresses that a real discontent does exist with the current policy; the criticism against the Gosplan of the USSR is particularly cogent.[8]

The pro-Siberian argument in the 1960s and 1970s was first and foremost concerned with demonstrating that it was rational to process raw materials at the site of extraction and avoid more costly transportation. Siberian industry, so went the argument, should therefore be developed and the extracted raw materials should be processed in Siberia to a greater degree than heretofore.[9]

The proponents of a continued development of Siberia seem to have won the support of the central political leadership at this time. Siberia continued to receive 15–16% of capital investments. Several new and large projects were undertaken, e.g., the building of the water power station in Ust-Ilimsk, opening up the oilfields in the Tiumen' region and the construction of the Baikal-Amur railway north of the existing Trans-Siberian railway.

But even persons in central positions, e.g., the Chairman of the Department for Economic Geography of Moscow University's Geographic Institute, Aleksei Mints, have voiced doubts concerning the development of Siberia. Mints argues that the European parts of the Soviet Union should continue in its role as the country's economic hub well into the future, and in Siberia, only those industries should be built up that had to be located near raw materials or were in need of large amounts of energy. According to Mints, development of the production potential in Kazakhstan and Central Asia was also an important task.[10]

Mints premised his argument on the need for regional specialization. Since a well-functioning industry already existed in Europe, there was every reason to continue to maintain this industry intact; Siberia's contribution would then be to provide the rest of the Soviet Union with raw materials. This may be regarded as a typical example of an argument advocating a limited development of Siberia.

Another argument resembling that of Mints was put forth a few years later in 1977 by the geographer N. V. Alisov, who maintained that the development of the European parts of the country should be given priority, for three reasons: First, the Soviet Union had entered a period of intensive economic development, different from the earlier extensive development, and hence the European USSR, where the major share of industry is located, must be given priority. Secondly, modernization and renovation, which are also an aspect of intensive development, are more efficient in the European regions where a good portion of plant and equipment is old. Thirdly, it is essential to develop further the western regions in view of the ever-growing economic integration of the CMEA.[11]

These considerations, i.e., orientation toward intensive rather than extensive development, and cooperation with the CMEA, were also mentioned in the latest five-year plans. The obvious inference is that arguments such as Alisov's carry considerable weight, but there are also weighty arguments for the alternative option, namely, a differentiated development of Siberia.

A. G. Granberg from the Institute for Economics and Industrial Organizations in Novosibirsk is one of the most influential advocates of a differentiated development of Siberia. Granberg maintains that Siberia moved into an important position in the Soviet economy during the '70s. Siberia's national income, for example, is now larger than the Ukraine's, and economic development in Siberia has been more rapid than in any of the other republics.[12]

The development of Siberia is also marked by a number of problems. Difficulty in recruiting labor is a serious impediment, and labor costs are also higher than elsewhere in the Soviet Union. Due to climatic and other factors, the initial costs of new construction projects are very high.[12]

But these problems need not mean that economic growth must decline in Siberia; on the contrary, new investments are necessary, says Granberg, to resolve them. Continued development of Siberia is an absolute necessity if the Soviet Union is to have sufficient energy for its industrial output. Furthermore, the USSR can also earn hard currency from its Siberian exports, and if the Siberian economy is differentiated and the infrastructure is built up, it will also be easier to recruit a work force.[13]

Another argument for expanding Siberia's economy is that Siberia's industry is more effective than industry in other regions. An analysis of effectiveness will show, according to Granberg, that Siberia is at a disadvantage under the existing price system. For instance, if world market prices for energy were used, Siberia's contribution to the Soviet national economy would be much greater.[14]

Economists at the Novosibirsk section of the Soviet Academy of Sciences have simulated the future development of the Soviet economy, and Granberg maintains that according to their findings the continued development of the Siberian economy is vital to the future growth of the Soviet economy as a whole. Despite the decline in the growth of total Soviet investments, Siberia's share must be increased to over 15%.[16]

There are, in fact, many signs that Siberia will continue to receive priority. The data show that Siberia's share in total Soviet investments approached 20% in the late '70s, although it is very uncertain whether this should be understood to imply that Soviet policymakers have opted for a differentiated growth strategy for Siberia. A good portion of investment is clearly used for energy production.

But Western scholars have arrived at another evaluation of Siberia's development potential. The geographer Theodore Shabad, drawing on Mints and Alisov, has claimed that there has been a shift in Soviet regional policy and that the European parts of the country have been given priority over Siberia in consideration of the more intensive development of the economy of European Russia and cooperation within the SEV.[17]

But it seems much too early to draw such far-reaching conclusions as does Shabad. Energy production in Siberia is certain to continue to play a crucial role for the Soviet Union far into the future, although it is undeniable that some differentiation is also taking place in Siberia— within, for instance, the territorial production complexes.

Criticism of *Vedomstvennost'*

The debate between the Europeans and the Siberiaks in the first instance concerned the priorities in West and East, respectively. A second topic in the discussion of Soviet regional policy has been the status of the Central Asian republics. The early 1980s saw a number of publications on this problem, written by top-ranking persons within the Party and the state apparatus in the Central Asian and Caucasian republics, which are well worth scrutiny if only because of the sometimes very strong criticism levied at the ministries and the planning bodies.

N. Khudaiberdiev, Chairman of the Council of Ministers of the Uzbek SSR, has analyzed economic problems in Uzbekistan in the light of its rapid population growth. In the period from 1970 to 1980 Uzbekistan's population rose from 11.8 to 16.2 million, which is equivalent to a 3% annual growth, and the trend is, moreover, expected to continue. To employ the extra manpower that this will create, industrial growth must also occur at a more rapid pace than previously. But housing, occupational training schools, and preschool institutions must also be built. The Uzbeks expect aid from the union Gosplan and from the various union ministries for these projects.[18]

Thus Uzbekistan's head of government was demanding prompt action from the central administration to deal with his republic's economic problems. It is unusual for representatives of the republics to demand prompt action from all-union bodies in this way. Khudaiberdiev returned frequently to the question of population growth and cautioned that the situation could well give rise to serious problems.

Z. Pataridze, Chairman of Georgia's Council of Ministers, mounts an extremely harsh criticism of the all-union ministers in an article written in 1981. Georgia's economic growth, he observes, had not been wholly satisfactory. The republic lags behind the union average on a number of social and economic growth indicators, and in certain areas there has even been a decline. The blame, suggests Pataridze, lies almost exclusively with the errant policy of the union ministries, which have failed to allocate sufficient funds to capital investments in Georgian industry. The Ministry for the Chemical Industry is a case in point, although it may be fairly said that the union ministries in general are encumbered by a certain narrowness of vision, insofar as they are concerned exclusively with the interests of their own sector, and often take decisions of major significance for the republics without representatives of this administrative level being given the opportunity to present their views.[19]

Pataridze's criticism is directed toward what the Soviets call *vedomstvennost'*, i.e., excessive and unwarranted concern for the interests of one's own administrative area. The union ministries are singled out especially, since they have no special representation in the republics. According to Pataridze the republics have much too little influence. The implied remedy is a devolution of decisionmaking powers in certain matters to the republic level.

The Tadzhiks have also called on the union administrative bodies to act. K. Makhamov, Chairman of Tadzhikistan's Gosplan, says that economic development in Tadzhikistan has been profoundly affected by the creation of the southern Tadzhik TPC, with its concentration on the chemical industry. But more measures are necessary, in particular more housing, and more social and cultural facilities are needed; investments in those areas must be increased promptly.[20]

The target of Makhamov's criticism was the same as that of Khudaiberdiev and Pataridze: the central ministries and the Gosplan of the USSR; the same motif may be also found in articles written by representatives for Azerbaidzhan and Kazakhstan.

M. Allakhverdiev from Azerbaidzhan notes that equalization among the republics in economic growth has come a relatively long way, but that Azerbaidzhan was still lagging behind in this respect in

the '60s and early '70s. However, measures had been taken subsequent-
ly to stimulate industrial growth in Azerbaidzhan, and the plentiful
supply of labor has of course been a positive factor. But the expansion
of industry into medium-sized and small population areas and even into
the countryside is necessary if the plentiful labor reserves are to be put
to their fullest use. Azerbaidzhan's economic problems are concentrated to a quite significant degree in the construction sector. The Ministry
for the Building Materials Industry and Gosplan have failed to allocate
the necessary investment capital to this sector.[21]

Azerbaidzhan also shows a tendency toward the accumulation of a
surplus labor reserve, especially in the smaller population areas and in
the countryside. Allakhverdiev calls for the expansion of industry into
these locations, a proposal that recurs time and again in the debate.

The harsh criticism of *vedomstvennost'* is continued in an article by
S. Takezhanov who acknowledges in his analysis of development in
Kazakhstan that the republics have gained more influence on planning
in the recent period, although the ministries and the narrowminded
view they represent continue to dominate. The position of the regional
and local authorities in the planning process must therefore be strengthened considerably, he says, especially as regards the location of enterprises within the republics.[22]

A common feature of all these contributions from the Caucasus and
Central Asia is the urgency of their pleas for quick and concrete action
to hasten industrial development. Numerous references are made to the
rapid population growth. The labor supply is regarded as a positive
factor over the short term, but a distinct uneasiness about the future in
this respect is discernible between the lines. The harsh criticism of
the passivity of the central authorities is conspicuous, and judging from
the tone of the debate, the representatives of republic Councils of
Ministers and planning authorities do more than merely mechanically
carry out decisions made higher up in the hierarchy; they also articulate
the interests of their own republics and exercise some upward influence
within the hierarchy.

Vedomstvennost' has not been the exclusive target of representatives
from the republics: Moscow economists have also let themselves be
heard. Iu. V. Subotskii complains that too many tasks and functions
have been concentrated in the ministries, preventing them from focus-
ing their activities on those areas that are most vital to the economy as a
whole.[23]

It is clear from a report at a conference held at the Institute for State and Law of the Academy of Sciences in December 1981 that difficulties in combining sectoral policy and regional policy are common to all the socialist countries. The abundance of ministries with their far-ranging responsibilities has been an encumbrance in their planning systems and one of the major sources of *vedomstvennost'*. Experiences with other types of administrative structure, e.g., the system of economic councils, merit study.[24]

There have been recurrent references to the Sovnarkhoz system in the recent debate, with both the advantages and disadvantages of strengthening the influence of the regional administrative level through such a system being pointed out. One of the reasons the Sovnarkhoz system has been revived in the discussion is the general sentiment that the ministries have much too broad powers, a view that seems to be shared by experts at both central and regional levels.

One area in which regional interests are specially well articulated is the issue of the reversal of the Siberian rivers, the *perebroska*. The aim of the project is to divert waters from the Siberian rivers the Irtysh and Ob, and other northern rivers, southward to irrigate lands in Uzbekistan, Turkmenistan, and Kazakhstan. Those who support the project claim that it will be a boon to the cotton industry and agriculture in general in the southern republics, and moreover will create jobs. Its opponents have stressed ecological arguments: deterioration of the climate, salinization of the soil, etc.[25]

Khudaiberdiev, from Uzbekistan, cited earlier, argues that the project brooks no further delay,[26] and the same line of thinking is echoed in numerous articles in the local Uzbek press.[27] At the 26th Party Congress in 1981, Party leaders from the three southern republics standing to gain most from the reversal of the rivers, i.e., Uzbekistan, Kazakhstan, and Turkmenistan, suggested that the project should be initiated during the 11th Five-year Plan. But in the guidelines for the five-year plan it is merely stated that the scientific preconditions for the project must be further investigated.[28] Thus as far as this issue is concerned, regional opinion has had no influence on policymaking at the central level, at least not on this occasion. The project will be returned to later in the section discussing the 1981 Party Congress and the 11th Five-year Plan.

The Baltic republics also called for changes in regional policy in the early 1980s, but their criticism of the central authorities has been more cautious and has concentrated more on increasing the republics' independence in making economic policy. Karl Vaino, First Secretary of the

Estonian Communist Party, observed that one of the most pressing economic problems of that republic was its shortage of labor. Considerable efforts have therefore been expended with a view to improving efficiency and labor productivity. The introduction of new indicators in the context of the 1979 economic reform brought about a perceptible improvement in this area, although according to Vaino several ministries have been rather dilatory in implementing the reform and have opposed local initiative in this direction.[29]

In a similar vein, J. Ruben, the Chairman of the Council of Ministers in Latvia, criticized the passivity of the ministries and the planning bureaucracy. In Lithuania the prime problems seem to lie with material supplies and the transportation system.[30] V. Zaikauskas, from Lithuania, argues that the republic and local soviets should be given a broader influence on planning and on the use of labor resources, and that republic bodies should also be given a say with regard to capital investments; republic representatives ought always to be asked before changes are made in plans, and special departments should be set up in the ministries and Council of Ministers committees to oversee the territorial aspects of planning.[31]

The criticism of the union ministries' conduct in the Baltic republics continued during Andropov's time as Party General Secretary. Coordination between the union ministries and the republic ministries continued to be defective. The situation clearly required that the republic level be given a greater say in determining economic policy, maintained I. Manjušis, and an organizational reform was necessary. According to Manjušis, the existing organizational structure was too complex to function well.[32]

Manjušis's criticism has been reiterated by other commentators. The greatest obstacle to improving the efficiency of the Soviet economy lies in the existing organizational structure of the ministries, claims A. Zamakhin.[33]

A rather unambiguous picture of the conduct of the ministries and the ministerial council committees emerges from this debate. One case after another of inefficiency and inertia are pointed out, while in matters of planning the overriding tendency is for each ministry to give first consideration to the interests of its own sector. This leads to serious problems, and not only at the republic level. The conclusion, therefore, is that regional influence on planning and economic policy should be strengthened.

While only a few representative portions of the debate have been mentioned, even this limited material shows clearly enough that Soviet policy with regard to the republics is hampered considerably by the bureaucratic ways of the ministries and ministerial council committees. One subtle difference between the representatives of the Caucasian and Central Asian republics on the one hand and the Baltic republics on the other is that the former still expect forceful action from the central authorities, whereas the latter tend rather to advocate giving the republics greater independence in setting economic policy.

Three Development Strategies

The problems of regional development have hardly been an exclusive concern of republic representatives; representatives for the central planning authorities have also addressed the issue. The Vice-Chairman of the Gosplan of the USSR, A. Batiurin, explored the future prospects of regional development in terms of available manpower.

The situation, he acknowledges, is extremely serious and places distinct limitations on economic policy. In some areas, e.g., Europe and Siberia, there is a severe labor shortage, whereas in Central Asia and Azerbaidzhan the problem is to "guarantee full employment" for the growing labor force.[34]

Batyurin calls for greater labor discipline and more advanced training of the work force as a general measure to reduce the problems created by a shortage of manpower. The different regions have developed each in their several ways in this regard. For instance, the rapid economic development in Siberia has made it necessary for a large number of workers and officials to transfer there from other areas. But here too complications have arisen: the labor force in the European USSR has been experiencing a declining growth and signs of a serious labor shortage are beginning to appear in Siberia as well. According to Batiurin, a way to a solution to the problem is to refrain from expanding labor-intensive industries in Siberia.[35]

The obvious implication is that priority should be given to capital-intensive industry, which would mean that large capital investment projects would continue into the future. Interestingly, Batiurin skirts the question of transferring labor from Central Asia to Siberia, a measure that he apparently regards as unfeasible.

Batyurin recommends instead another development model for Central Asia, where favorable conditions exist for the development of small industries that could certainly take advantage of the plentiful and growing labor reserves in that region. Of course, small industry would have to be organized in a way that did not conflict with the traditions of the indigenous population. The areas most suited for new small industries are the Uzbek SSR, Tadzhik SSR, Turkmen SSR, Kirghiz SSR, and Azerbaidzhan SSR, as well as the southern parts of the Kazakh SSR.[36]

It is clear from Batiurin's article that something must be done quickly to avoid a serious underemployment in Central Asia, and his proposal to develop small industry is interesting in that respect. Nonetheless, the development of Siberia, along with continued industrial growth in the European parts of the USSR, still seems to enjoy a higher priority.

A number of different models for future regional development are distinguishable in the debate. Three approaches to the distribution of new investments, i.e., developmental strategies, were discussed, all feasible alternatives for regional policy in the future.

The first, strategy 1, places the European parts of the Soviet Union at the center of economic activity on into the future. Industry would be revamped and brought up to date, and reorganized to make it more efficient; cooperation within the CMEA would be stepped up; and energy and raw materials would be obtained from the European parts of the country and from the eastern regions. Quite a number of scientists have advocated this strategy, and the most recent five-year plans have also concentrated on the updating of industry.

In strategy 2, Siberia's industrialization would be accelerated considerably. Raw materials would be processed in Siberia using locally available energy resources; but Siberia would also continue to provide other parts of the Soviet Union with energy. It is too late to change this, but in strategy 2 the resources would be worked over to a much greater extent in Siberia itself. Strategy 2 is supported mainly by experts from Siberia, but also probably by certain groups among the planners.

In strategy 3, Central Asia would be further industrialized. Industrial output, energy production, and agriculture would be stimulated by taking advantage of the local labor force; development of small industries would be a key component; and the river reversal project could fit into strategy 3 as well. The main supporters of this strategy are a group of regional politicians and experts from Central Asia.

All these strategies represent feasible alternatives for the political leadership, but in view of the inability of the Soviet system to implement comprehensive changes, which Seweryn Bialer has pointed out, strategy 1 is perhaps the most probable since it entails few or no changes in the existing situation. But other factors that will also influence the choice, such as population growth and available labor resources, will certainly come to play a major role over the long term. It will also become more difficult to set priorities considering the narrowing margin for capital investments. Available resources must be utilized efficiently so as to yield maximum economic returns, yet at the same time maintain a reasonable regional balance. Of course, various combinations of these strategies are also possible.

In Chapter 2, I discussed the role played by experts and bureaucrats outside the central leadership, in particular at the regional level, in political decisionmaking. It seems to be clear from the foregoing analysis that various options are discussed in the press, in several leading periodicals, after which the political leadership makes its decision. Existing regional priorities are in fact challenged by the strategical options described above, which would seem to support hypotheses 3 and 4 in Chapter 2. However, it is rather difficult to assess whether the existence of policy options is actually of any importance in the central political decisionmaking process.

The Communist Party and the Soviet administrative bodies are of course also concerned with the aims of Soviet regional policy and the setting of priorities. The next chapter will analyze official political decisions in this area.

6. DECISIONS ON REGIONAL POLICY

Regional differences in level of development, the Soviet planning organization, and the debate on regional development have so far been discussed. The present chapter will attempt to analyze a number of important decisions that have been of significance for regional policy. For example, the 1979 economic reform gave republic and local administrative bodies a broader influence on policymaking, and two years later the reform was consolidated by a decree from the Central Committee.

Some of the most important decisions in the early 1980s of direct consequence for regional development were made at Party Congresses at the republic and union levels in 1981 and on the occasion of the adoption of the 11th Five-year Plan in the same year. The 26th union Party Congress was preceded, as is customary, by congresses in the fourteen republics that have their own Party organization (the RSFSR is an exception in this respect). Regional development problems were discussed at several of these, although there was hardly any open criticism of current policy. Regional development was discussed on a number of occasions at the union Party Congress, and Brezhnev indeed touched on the issue explicitly in his report. Tikhonov took up regional problems in his detailed discussion of the draft five-year plan, and the speeches given by the various republic leaders at the Congress illuminated the topic further. Altogether, the materials from the Party Congress are a valuable source of information on the views of the political leadership on regional development.

More specific information on economic development in the republics is to be found in the five-year plans adopted by the Supreme Soviets of the union and of the republics in the fall of 1981. The data they contain help to fill in the picture of the kind of development desired by the political leadership, and provide clues on whether the planned development will reduce regional differences. Plans for three of the most developed republics, the RSFSR, Estonia, and Latvia, and for two of the less developed republics, Uzbekistan and Turkmenistan, may be profitably compared in this regard.

An analysis of these political decisions should help to determine the direction of regional development and the pattern of distribution of state allocations among the different regions. First, however, it would be useful to examine some of the decisions that should, in principle at least, give broader decisionmaking powers to regional and local administrative bodies in matters of planning.

The 1979 Economic Reform

Decisions on economic reforms have been taken on several occasions in the period after Stalin's death. As mentioned above, the Sovnarkhoz system was introduced in 1957, and in 1965 the sectoral ministries were restored and new planning indicators (e.g., profits) were given greater importance. In the 1973 reform the decision was taken to permit enterprises to form *ob"edineniia*, i.e., industrial or production associations. The two latter reforms were implemented slowly and cautiously, and on the whole exemplify the inertia that in general seems to attend reform efforts (cf. Bialer[1]).

In July 1979 the Central Committee and the Council of Ministers adopted a resolution entitled "Improving planning and reinforcing the effects of the economic mechanism on raising effectiveness in production and improving the quality of work."[2] The reform provided for changes within the existing economic system, with the intention of making the existing economic mechanisms more effective. Detailed central planning was to continue, and according to the reform would even be reinforced. Enterprises were given no new rights of the kind introduced in Hungary, for instance.

The July reform had several aims: Resources would be concentrated to cope better with certain major national problems, and narrow sectoral interests would no longer be allowed to decisively influence planning; conditions were to be created to enable priorities to be correctly set among the various sectors and the various economic regions, especially with regard to the distribution of investment funds.[3]

Thus the resolution dealt with the very same problems that had also been discussed in the debate in the Soviet press at the time. As was brought out in Chapter 5, republic representatives often called attention to narrow sectoral attitudes and the difficulties in setting priorities correctly among the different regions. Interestingly, the same views are still to be heard today, several years after the decision ratifying the July reform, indicating that even this reform was slow in its implementation.

The July reform introduces certain modifications in the indicator system; e.g., "the weight indicators," which had long been particularly important in Soviet planning, will be eliminated. Secondly, planning will draw on the results of scientific research to a greater degree than heretofore. Special programs are to be developed in research and development, especially in technology, by Gosplan, the research institutes of the USSR Academy of Sciences, and other research centers.[5]

The July reform also calls for a strengthening of territorial planning, which indicates that the union ministries and the USSR Gosplan will give greater heed to territorial considerations in compiling their plans. The republic Councils of Ministers are to be drawn into planning activity, and they will also be kept informed on the details of the activities of all-union enterprises located in the territory of their respective republics. Further, republic Councils of Ministers will be given the opportunity to present their views on plans for union-managed enterprises, and the plan indicators for the latter will be integrated into republic plans for social and economic development.[6]

Material resources and labor reserves will be put to better advantage; Gosplan SSR and other central authorities will maintain territorial production balance sheets in collaboration with the republic Council of Ministers, which will then serve as a statistical basis for the territorial distribution of output. Special programs for the problems of regional development will be compiled for the TPCs.[7]

The growing economic importance of Siberia and the Far East requires special action, for which special development programs are to be worked out. The July resolution charges the Gosplan USSR and the Council of Ministers of the RSFSR with the task of planning the regional distribution of output and working out a development program for these areas, with special attention focused on the production complexes. In developing these programs, it will be a matter of indifference under which ministry a particular enterprise belongs.[8]

Territorial concerns will be given special consideration in calculating labor resources, and it is recommended that special labor balance sheets be compiled with the collaboration of republic and local administrative authorities to facilitate the territorial distribution of the work force.[9]

The 1979 economic reform represents a clear decision to give greater consideration to territorial aspects in managing the economy. Even though the main focus of the reform lies elsewhere, the new functions it gives to the republic and local authorities nonetheless represent a definite change.

The aim of the reform with regard to territorial planning seems to be to enhance the role of republic and local administrative authorities in it. Henceforth, as has been mentioned, republic Councils of Ministers will be kept better informed on the activity of all-union enterprises, and will also be able to present their views in planning that activity, although they have not formally been given any additional decisionmaking powers in this respect. Republic authorities will also have a say in working out the special regional development programs.

The same line of thinking on regional development that guided the July resolution is described in a decree issued jointly in 1981 by the Central Committee, the Presidium of the Supreme Soviet, and the Council of Ministers entitled ''A further strengthening of the importance of the Soviets of Peoples Deputies in building the economy.'' In it the focus is mainly on the local soviets, i.e., the oblast and krai soviets, the Supreme Soviets of the ASSRs, and levels below them. The gist of the decree is that the coordinating controlling functions of the Soviets should be strengthened.[10]

According to the decree, the centrally compiled plans will be submitted to the appropriate local soviets for their views on the utilization of land, environmental protection, utilization of labor, etc., and the union and republic administrative bodies to give due consideration to these views. The decree even moots the possibility of devolving authority over some enterprises from the union to lower administrative levels.[11]

Thus the 1981 decree clearly states that local administrative bodies are to have greater influence, if mainly in an advisory and consultant capacity, while formal decisions concerning enterprises under the authority of all-union ministries will still be taken at the union level. But the wording of the decree indicates that policymakers have realized the need for better coordination between union enterprises and those administered by local authorities. This issue—the relationship between union enterprises and enterprises under local Soviets—recurred in dis-

cussions during the Party Congresses of 1981 and in the adoption of the
11th Five-year Plan.

The 1981 Republic Party Congresses

The major decisions taken by the Party Congress and the Supreme
Soviet when the five-year plans are adopted normally follow a definite
formal pattern. The 26th Party Congress was preceded by several
preparatory actions, e.g., the Soviet republics held their Congresses
during which issues of social and economic development were discussed, to be later decided upon at the union Party Congress. The basic
guidelines for the economy in 1981–85 and for the period up to 1990
were laid down at the Party Congress, as had similarly been done at
earlier congresses. These guidelines were then further developed, after
which the Supreme Soviet ratified the five-year plan in its autumn
session. The decision ratifying the five-year plan is in the form of a law.
After the union Supreme Soviet took its decision, the Supreme Soviets
of the republics met and passed laws ratifying the five-year plans in
their respective republics.

Thus both Party and state authorities are involved in the ratification
of the five-year plan, although the Party's decision, formally speaking,
consists only of recommendations. Regional policy issues came up on
several occasions during the discussions of the five-year plans. It will
be useful to begin with a review of some of the republic Congresses:
The Estonian and Lithuanian Party Congresses will serve to elucidate
the situation in the more developed regions, while Uzbekistan and
Turkmenistan may be taken as representative of the less developed
republics.

By and large the republic congresses are organized similarly to the
Union Congress. The Party First Secretary reports on actions taken by
the Central Committee and the supreme Party bodies since the previous
Congress, after which the Chairman of the Council of Ministers (or in
the exceptional case the chairman of the republic's Gosplan) reports on
the guidelines for the five-year plan. After the discussions, resolutions
are passed approving the annual reports and the five-year plan. A new
Central Committee, as well as republic representatives to the CPSU's
Congress, are also elected.

At the Estonian Communist Party's 18th Congress in January 1981,
First Secretary Vaino gave the main report. It was full of laudatory
phrases for the union Party's support to Estonia and, in particular, for

General Secretary Brezhnev's efforts. A generally bright picture was painted of the economic situation in Estonia, where industry had purportedly overfulfilled the plans each year in the five-year period just passed. Total industrial output increased by 24%, which in fact was projected in the plan.[12]

But economic growth was attended by a number of problems. The rise in productivity was much too slow, and planned renovation of industry was unsatisfactory in many areas. According to Vaino, these problems could have serious consequences for development during the 11th five-year planning period. According to the draft guidelines for the planning period, set forth at the Central Committee's October Plenum in 1980, growth in industrial output in Estonia should be between 14 and 17%. But "the growth in labor productivity, given the severe labor shortage, will be of crucial importance both for the growth of industry and for the fulfillment of the plan." The implication is that the previous plan target for labor productivity was not fulfilled.[13]

Thus Vaino foresees problems in meeting targets in the upcoming five-year plan. A further increase in the productivity of labor is necessary, and the ministries and state committees are called upon to take suitable action to improve the situation.[14]

Vaino did not question any of the proposals set forth in the guidelines, but in carefully chosen words he did allude to the severe labor shortage and the problems it entails with regard to plan fulfillment. The situation was similar in the other republic congresses as well; planning problems having to do with the work force, while perhaps varying in their forms, were regularly addressed at all the Congresses.

V. Klauson, Chairman of the Estonian Council of Ministers, took up the same issue in his speech on the five-year plan. The importance of improving the management of the economy is also stressed, and with regard to the July 1979 reform Klauson reports that the new indicators are about to be introduced in Estonia. The purpose of the reform was to improve the economy's efficiency, and further efforts should therefore be made to bring together sectoral and territorial planning, according to Klauson.[15]

Capital investments will have a lower growth rate in Estonia in the following five-year planning period than earlier—as indeed is the case for the union as a whole—and the need to improve efficiency and labor productivity thus becomes even more patent.[16]

The speeches of the Party Secretary and the head of government indicate that there are two important restrictions on Estonia's future growth, namely the shortage of labor and the decline in the growth rate of capital investments. Since Estonia ranks among the most developed regions of the Soviet Union, a relatively slower growth will contribute to equalization among the republics, provided of course that the less developed republics have not suffered similar restrictions on their growth. Moreover, Estonia could if necessary compensate for its labor shortage and the declining growth of investments by improving efficiency in production.

Lithuania's Communist Party's 23rd Congress was held in Riga in late January-early February 1981. First Secretary A. Voss reported that the results of the 10th Five-year Plan were very good. The plan targets for industrial output had been achieved almost a month before the end of the planning period, and performance within the ministry for local industry and among the fishing kolkhozes was especially satisfactory. This successful development was also reflected in the growth of national income, which was 21%. Industrial growth increased by 21%, and capital investments by 17%.[17]

Like Vaino, Voss also took up the problems of the republic's development, which was unsatisfactory in several sectors, among them light industry and the construction materials industry.[18]

Industrial output was projected to increase by 15–18% during the 11th five-year planning period, a target that was difficult to achieve, said Voss. Just as in Estonia, to meet this goal, efficiency would have to be improved because of the serious labor shortage; greater labor discipline was also necessary. The 1979 economic reform improved the chances to fulfill the plan, and Voss called on the republic's Gosplan to hasten the introduction of the new indicators; coordination between sectoral and territorial planning was also needed.[19]

Iu. Ruben, chairman of Latvia's Council of Ministers, agreed with Voss's analysis of the economic problems in his survey of the draft guidelines for the upcoming five-year period, which projected a 15–18% growth in industrial output, while labor productivity was to increase by 19%.[20]

Economic development seems to follow similar patterns in Estonia and Latvia. Both republics have a highly developed industry and a high per capita national income, and indeed, according to available statistics, they have the highest growth rate in the whole Soviet Union. Growth will probably slow in the future, because the increment in the work force is so small. According to the Party's guidelines, the increase in capital investments will also be slower. In the guidelines for the five-year plan, the industrial growth rate of these two republics is projected to be the lowest in the entire Soviet Union. Nevertheless, this development was not challenged at the Party Congress, criticism being aimed exclusively at activities within certain ministries at the republic level.

The participants in the Uzbekistan Communist Party's 20th Congress heard Sh. Rashidov's report on the period just passed. Like his Estonian and Latvian colleagues, Rashidov, who was the Party First Secretary in Uzbekistan and also Candidate Member in the CPSU's Politburo, gave a retrospective picture of five years of intensive effort in the republic. The plan targets for industrial output were achieved before the end of the planning period, and industrial output had increased by almost 25%.[21]

However, Rashidov also criticized various ministries and committees, in doing so following the somewhat stereotyped patterns usually encountered at Party Congresses. Efficiency was much too low within the sectors covered by some republic ministries, and a number of plan targets remained unachieved.[22]

During the 11th five-year planning period industrial output was projected to increase very rapidly, by between 28% and 31%, with the most rapid growth projected for machinery construction, the chemical industry, and the consumer goods industry. Thus output was to grow more rapidly during the 11th five-year planning period than during the 10th. This would be impossible, said Rashidov, if labor discipline and labor productivity were not improved.[23]

Capital investments are to grow by 22–25% during the planning period, which is almost double that for the country as a whole.[24] Uzbekistan, a relatively poor republic, will thus be allocated a proportionately higher share of capital investment funds than the more developed regions. To what extent this in practice led to an economic equalization will be dealt with later on.

Uzbekistan is mainly an agricultural republic, with cotton being the key crop. A good share of Rashidov's speech dealt with problems in agriculture, perhaps the most important of which was the water supply. Agriculture will continue to grow in Uzbekistan only if great care is exercised in the use of its water resources.[25]

Rashidov took up the river reversal projects once again, and said that the diverting of water from the Siberian rivers to Central Asia was an absolute necessity if the enormous potential of Uzbek agriculture was to be fully used. "Uzbekistan's Communist Party Central Committee should like to pose straightforwardly the question of whether the practical work should not be hastened and begun during this present five-year period,''[26] he said, reflecting the strong feelings found in the Central Asian republics on this question.

Water supply is indeed an important issue in the Uzbek economy and in its politics, but employment is perhaps no less serious. Rashidov pointed out that the natural population growth in Uzbekistan is extremely rapid and the population is expected to grow from 16 million in 1980 to over 22 million by 1990. "This requires a considerable increase in the number of job opportunities," he said, and moreover they must be evenly distributed throughout the republic so that employment can be maintained even in smaller villages and towns. Rashidov foresaw an increase in the number of small enterprises and of branches of larger enterprises to be built in these smaller localities.[27]

Uzbekistan's great economic and political problems, the water supply and employment of the available labor, were also dealt with in N. Khudaiberdiev's presentation of the guidelines for the five-year plan. A high level of employment among the rapidly growing population is an absolute necessity, he stated.[28]

Khudaiberdiev also touched on the question of diverting water from the Siberian rivers, and said that both the Central Committee and the Party Congress felt that the work on the project should begin immediately. He supported that view with positive statements from the all-union ministry for agriculture and waterways and from the Gosstroi SSSR.[29]

In the main, Khudaiberdiev shared Rashidov's views on future employment in the republic, and called the population growth "a serious demographic problem"; new job opportunities were absolutely necessary.[30]

In Uzbekistan, regional development problems are, according to the political leadership, closely connected with the water supply and employment problems. It was evident enough from the speeches at the Uzbek Party Congress that these two issues are extremely important for the region. If the water supply is not expanded, no further growth can reasonably be expected of Uzbek agriculture.

But the gravest problem seems to be employment. Uzbekistan has a "serious demographic problem" and it will be difficult to find employment for the rapidly growing population, especially in the countryside, where so far there has been no industrial activity worth mentioning. The employment situation was already serious at the beginning of the

1980s; a relatively small proportion of the population, about one-third, is employed, so it is easy to understand the uneasiness of the political leadership over future development. The word unemployment was not uttered in the Congress speeches, but from the gist of them it may well be conjectured whether unemployment may not actually already exist in Uzbekistan.

Thus the labor problem has different countenances in the Baltic republics, where labor is in short supply, and in Uzbekistan, where a surplus exists. But the possibility of transferring labor from one region to another was not so much as mentioned in the Congress reports.

At the Turkmenistan Communist Party's 22nd Congress, First Secretary M. Gapurov noted that the growth in industrial output was 12% between 1956 and 1980, which was still short of the plan target. The reasons given were problems in the Turkmenistan oil industry, e.g., declining well output and a cutback in refining, which led the USSR's Council of Ministers to issue a special decree calling for improved efficiency.[31]

An increase of 26–28% in industrial output was forecast for the planning period 1981–85, reported Ch. Karriev, Chairman of the Council of Ministers, in his presentation of the five-year plan. He also predicted problems in the utilization of labor and natural resources; labor productivity had in fact shown no growth at all during the planning period 1976–80.[32]

Turkmenistan's economic situation is similar to that of Uzbekistan, with regard to, for instance, the water supply and employment, but there seem also to be problems in the oil industry.

At first glance the republic Party Congresses give the appearance of stereotyped well-orchestrated performances. Praise is heaped on ministries and enterprises that merit it, while others are criticized for inefficiency, and of course the General Secretary also receives his share of the encomiums for showing special concern for the republics.

Yet above and beyond the stereotypes some quite interesting material is still to be gleaned from the Party Congresses. No one doubts that the employment problem is considered to be extremely serious in Central Asia, and the same applies to the water supply problem, while in the Baltic republics, the labor shortage is a grave concern.

The republic representatives also made indirect allusion to their need for more resources to deal with their problems, although there was no discussion of how priorities should be set at the union level. The proportioning of new investment funds outlined in the five-year plan guidelines is accepted as given.

The scenario at the Estonian, Latvian, Uzbek, and Turkmen Party Congresses was reproduced at the congresses of the other republics. E. Shevarnadze, Georgia's First Party Secretary, reported a 41% industrial growth during the planning period just passed, and announced a projected growth of 30–33% for the 11th five-year planning period. Corruption and relations between nationalities were other problems touched upon.[33]

The Belorussian Communist Party's 29th Congress concentrated on ways to improve agricultural output. Party Secretary T. Kiselev called for greater emphasis on the production of consumer goods and food. During the 10th five-year planning period industrial growth was 42%, and according to the guidelines, it should be 20–29% during the 11th five-year planning period.[34]

First Secretary T. Usubaliev addressed the Kirghiz Communist Party's 17th Congress with a speech that was distinguished by his criticism of the activities of a number of union ministries, charging them with a reluctance to make capital investments in Kirghizia (especially in the light industry sector).[35]

At the Moldavian Communist Party's 15th Congress, First Secretary S. Grossu focused on economic problems in agriculture, saying that although results from the 10th five-year plan were satisfactory, a number of plan targets had not been achieved. There were "fundamental flaws in economic activity," most notably with regard to labor productivity, he said.[36]

Congresses were also held in the other republics (with the exception, of course, of the RSFSR) during January and February 1981, and the issues brought up in the republic Congresses were taken up again on several occasions at the union Party Congress, where the republic leaders spoke on regional development in their respective areas. But Brezhnev, General Secretary of the Party, and Tikhonov, Chairman of the Council of Ministers, also broached the question of regional development. The next section will examine the statements of the union top-level political leadership on regional issues.

To sum up, the republic Party Congresses dealt in the first instance with problems specific to their respective regions. Increased investments, and union assistance in dealing with the labor problem were called for. As mentioned above, republic representatives also made contributions to the regional policy debate in the periodical literature, where, however, they formulated their demands in sharper tones.

Thus it would appear that republic representatives do make certain demands on central policymakers, as for instance in connection with preparations for the upcoming five-year plan. This is certainly fully in line with the official position that proposals for improvements in the guidelines should be openly put forward. The call for increased resources to the republics was of course more carefully formulated, but there is no mistaking that republic representatives do watch over their own republics' interests in various ways, in any event as evidenced in their official statements. Moreover, there is no reason to doubt that these statements also reflect real problems.

The 26th Party Congress

The 26th Party Congress dealt with more general problems than the republic Congresses, discussing and assessing the economic performance and concrete achievements of the union as a whole during the 10th planning period, and a new and slightly amended version of the basic guidelines document was presented. The territorial aspects of economic development, with special focus on Siberia and Central Asia, came up quite often in the discussion.

Of course Leonid Brezhnev's reading of the report on the period following the 25th Congress was the main highlight of the Congress, but all the republic leaders also spoke, as is the custom, after the General Secretary's speech. Finally, as a third highlight, Nikolai Tikhonov reported on the upcoming five-year plan.

Brezhnev announced that the Soviet Union had undergone major changes during the 1970s, in particular with regard to the localization of industry. The decision had been taken at the 25th Party Congress to form TPCs in several areas within the European RSFSR, in the Urals, in Siberia, in Kazakhstan and Tadzhikistan, and during the 10th five-year planning period these complexes accounted for the whole of growth in output of oil, gas, and coal, with energy production in Western Siberia of course heading the list.[37]

The prime task for the 11th Five-year Plan, said Brezhnev, was to further improve the welfare of Soviet citizens. This would entail a transition to a more intensive phase of development for the economy, in which the national income was projected to increase by between 18 and 20% during the 11th five-year planning period.[38] The decisions taken in the 1979 economic reform would be especially important when the transition to more intensive economic growth takes place. The task for the future was to implement these decisions, he said, going on to point out that managing the economy had political as well as its economic aspects.[39] Brezhnev indicated that the implementation of the 1979 reform had been slow (a familiar tune, as mentioned from earlier reforms).

Brezhnev also dealt with relationships between the different regions of the Soviet Union and said that it was necessary to

> reduce social differences at the territorial level, so to speak. Cultural resources and living conditions vary from one part of our vast land to the other. Such differences not infrequently complicate the labor situation in a number of localities. The implementation of the development programs for Western Siberia, the Baikal-Amur area and other regions in the Asiatic parts of our country has stepped up the influx of population to these regions, but people still prefer to move from north to south or from east to west, even though a rational location of the productive forces would require movement in the opposite directions.[40]

Brezhnev's speech is a virtual distillation of several of the Soviet social problems of a territorial nature. There are clear differences in living conditions among the different regions, so that it is natural that the population should make their way to more flourishing areas, even though that it may not necessarily be more advantageous for the nation's economy as a whole.

"An effective demographic policy" must therefore be developed. The living conditions in Siberia must be radically improved, with more housing, more consumer goods, etc., while for Central Asia measures must be taken to employ the "surplus labor."[41]

Thus forceful action is necessary to deal with the problems in Siberia and Central Asia, which in the latter case includes a labor surplus, but according to Brezhnev, these actions are wholly in line with the policy that had been pursued for a long time already.

> Since the time Soviet power was first established our economic and social policy has been formulated with a view toward bringing the non-Russian parts of Russia up to the same level of development as the central parts as rapidly as possible. This task has been solved with outstanding success and the close cooperation between all the different nations of our country, and above all the Russian people's selfless assistance, have played a prime role in this.[42]

Thus in the official Soviet view there are no longer any notable differences in the level of socioeconomic development among the different regions, although there are some differences still remaining in living conditions on an individual basis. The Russian people are given a good deal of the credit for the progress that has been made.

Again, according to Brezhnev, several areas in the Soviet Union needed help from the central authorities, especially Siberia and Central Asia. Tikhonov's speech also singled out these areas, and mentioned that the growth of industrial output for the entire union was projected to be 26–28% during the upcoming plan period, compared with a growth of 24% during the 10th five-year period. Capital investment would grow by 12–15% compared with the preceding plan, whereas the corresponding figure for the 1976–80 period was 29%.[43] It should be stressed that the analysis and evaluation in this book refer to the 11th Five-year Plan. In 1986, decisions were taken by Party and state authorities concerning the 1986–90 Plan.

Judging from Tikhonov's statistics, the growth rate for capital investments should have declined sharply—indeed, by about 50%—for the period 1981–85. Tikhonov also voiced severe criticism of flaws in the economy: e.g., the rise in labor productivity targeted by the 10th Five-year Plan was not achieved. "Inertia, tradition, and habits" from the time when planning emphasized the quantitative aspects of production were the causes of the problems, according to Tikhonov.[44] For the upcoming planning period a growth of 23–25% was projected in labor productivity in industry, compared with 17% for the period 1976–80.[45]

Tikhonov also said that "the dispersion of the forces of production" would be further improved during the plan period, which means that the economies of all the Soviet republics will continue to grow and further approach an equal level of development. Again, the importance of development in Siberia was particularly stressed; the Baikal-Amur railway would open up new areas rich in raw materials; and the new TPCs in Siberia, Central Asia, and other regions will also grow rapidly during the upcoming plan period.[46]

Pursuant to Tikhonov's proposal the Congress adopted "The basic guidelines for the USSR's economic and social development in 1981–85 and the period up to 1990." These guidelines concentrate in particular on the location of industry and on the growth of the fifteen republics, with the following main points stressed:

1. Growth in the eastern regions will be accelerated, with particular stress on energy production in Siberia and Kazakhstan.

2. Better use will be made of the labor reserves of Central Asia; and the training of the labor force will be improved in this region.

3. Enterprises will be remodelled and technologically revamped in

the European parts of the country; existing resources will be put to better use.

4. The territorial production complexes will be further improved.

5. The role of local Soviets in planning will be strengthened pursuant to the 1979 reform.[47]

It was presumably no coincidence that the development of the eastern region heads the list of actions to be undertaken during the planning period. Far more resources are required in Siberia than for equivalent undertakings elsewhere. The use of available labor in Central Asia and the modernization of industries in Europe are of course also costly, but by no means as costly as the development of Siberia.

Herein seems to lie part of the explanation of the persistence of regional differences. A further factor adding to the costs of development in Siberia is that, as increasingly more difficult areas are penetrated for development, the sources of raw materials that had been relied on in the past are depleted.

The fifteen republics were also given special instructions on how they should organize their activities during the planning period; of special interest were the growth figures for industrial output and agricultural output (Table 6.1).

It should be borne in mind that, because the results of the 11th Five-year Plan have not yet been published, the following discussion refers to the projected figures rather than figures that have by now been tabulated. Table 6.1 shows that industrial production is expected to grow more rapidly in the less developed republics that in those that are relatively highly developed: e.g., 15% for Estonia and Latvia, but 20–30% growth rates for industry in Central Asia during the planning period. This might be interpreted as a deliberate attempt of the leadership to further equalize the respective levels of development. But the planned growth in Central Asia (with the exception of Uzbekistan) is still lower than the union average, and it is uncertain whether the absolute differences really diminished as projected in the plan figures. A 15% growth in a highly developed industry may mean more than 30% growth in absolute figures in a poorly developed industry. That question will be taken up later. It should be pointed out that these were only suggested plan targets; the actual result after five years could well be quite different.

A near-average industrial growth is projected for the RSFSR for 1981–85, with priority being given to machinery construction, and the gas and chemical industries. In Siberia, priority was given to fuel

Table 6.1

Industrial Output and Agricultural Output: Percent Growth during the 11th Five-year Planning Period According to the Decision Taken at the 26th Party Congress

Republic	Industry	Agriculture
RSFSR	24–27	12–14
Estonia	14–17	11–13
Latvia	15–18	12–14
Lithuania	21–24	8–10
Ukraine	20–23	12–14
Belorussia	26–29	10–12
Moldavia	30–33	20–22
Georgia	30–33	22–24
Armenia	29–32	10–12
Azerbaidzhan	29–32	15–17
Kazakhstan	22–25	11–13
Uzbekistan	28–31	17–19
Tadzikistan	21–24	8–10
Kirghizia	24–27	12–14
Turkmenistan	21–24	14–16
USSR	26–28	12–14

Source: *Materialy*, pp. 185ff, p. 103.

extraction, electrical energy, the chemical industry, and the paper pulp industry, i.e., the processing of available raw materials. The Western Siberian TPC was to be further expanded during the planning period, while the construction of the hydraulic power plant in Boguchany, of the Baikal-Amur railway and the Southern Iakut TPC, was to continue.[48]

Thus, while the major projects in Siberia were scheduled to continue during the 11th five-year planning period, no mention at all was made that the BAM should be completed during this period, nor for that matter is there any mention of the diversion of waters from the Siberian rivers. Although representatives from the Central Asian republics have again and again called for work to begin on this project, they were evidently unable to gain an audience.

In Estonia industrial output was to increase by only 15%, which corresponds to about half the union average. Priority was to be given to the oil shale industry, and the electronic and electrical engineering industries, while modernization was also planned in some sectors. Although growth was to be modest in Estonia, effort was concentrated on the technologically highly advanced industries.

The growth of industrial output in Latvia is expected to be low compared with the union as a whole, but even here a growth is projected in the advanced sectors such as the electronics industry and the manufacture of radios and TV sets.

Thus the pattern of growth in Estonia and Latvia resembles to a certain extent that in Western Europe: absolute growth has diminished considerably, although some technologically advanced sectors continue to grow.

Industrial growth is also below average in Lithuania, but not so low as in Estonia and Latvia. The food industry continues to be an important sector in Lithuania in the 11th five-year planning period, along with the electronic and radio engineering industries.

In the Ukraine, industrial output was planned to grow 20–23%, somewhat below average. A number of new atomic power plants were scheduled to begin operations before 1985, and coalmining and the mining of metal ores were to be expanded, all of which means a considerable growth in energy production. Priority continues to be given to heavy industry, and food production will continue to grow.

According to the draft plan, industrial output in Belorussia should grow at about the union average. Machinery construction and the radiotechnical and electronic industries are top-priority sectors.

Moldavia is projected to have the most rapid industrial growth of all the republics, several percentage points over the union average. Agriculture has traditionally been the mainstay of Moldavia's economy, and continues to be so during the 11th five-year planning period.

Industrial growth is planned to be very rapid in Georgia as well, although it is not among the most backward republics. The electronic and radio engineering industries are expanding sectors, and agriculture should also grow at a rapid pace.

Armenian industry is projected to grow at a rate of about 30%, i.e., above the union average, with considerable investments in the electronics industry and the iron and steel industry.

Azerbaidzhan's industry is to grow by 30%, with the electronics industry being favored. Petroleum production continues, although in somewhat lower volumes than previously.

Industrial growth in Kazakhstan is somewhat below the average. Metalworking, machinery construction, and the chemical industry are important sectors, while coalmining and the production of electrical energy are key to the republic's economy.

Industrial growth in Uzbekistan is planned to be about 30%, with investments concentrated in the production of electrical energy and the extraction of metals. Cotton growing continues to be the key industry.

Kirghizia's industrial growth is projected at 21–24%, which is several percentage points below the union average. Thus industry will grow slowly, despite the fact that Kirghizia has one of the lowest growth rates in the Soviet Union. Investments are concentrated on energy production and the textile industry.

Tadzhikistan's industrial growth should be 24–27%, i.e., just under the union average. Tadzhikistan, like Kirghizia, is one of the most backward republics in industrial development. The Southern Tadzhik TPC, which includes an electrochemical factory and an aluminum plant, will assume a positive place in the republic's economy.

Turkmenistan's industrial growth is also below the union average, with the chemical industry and the foods industry enjoying priority. Oil production and oil refining are other important sectors.

Thus the indications are that the political leadership intended to carry equalization further during the 1981–85 five-year period. The most developed republics, Estonia and Latvia, were planned to have a low industrial growth rate, while Uzbekistan, industrially relatively backward, was to have an industrial growth distinctly above the union average.

However, other signs indicate that regional differences will continue to exist. Three of the Central Asian republics with a low level of socioeconomic development, Kirghizia, Tadzhikistan, and Turkmenistan, were to grow at a rate below that for the union as a whole, according to the draft plan. Some republics occupying an intermediate level with regard to industrial development, namely Georgia, Armenia, and Azerbaidzhan, were to have a more rapid growth rate than the Central Asian republics. Moreover, the emphasis was not necessarily on agricultural output in the three Central Asian republics. For example, in Kirghizia, agricultural output was to increase by only 10%, which is below the union average.

Three of the Central Asian republics, Kirghizia, Tadzhikistan, and Turkmenistan, show signs of relative stagnation. If regional equality were a priority objective in Soviet politics, the economic growth indicators could be reasonably expected to be much higher than the average for these relatively backward republics. But quite probably, other factors, e.g., assessments of economic efficiency and strategic military considerations, have carried more weight than regional equalization. This issue will be explored further when the implementation and results of regional policy are examined.

But what did the republic leaders think of planned growth for the period 1981–85? The First Secretaries in the republic Communist Parties had the opportunity to comment once again upon the draft guidelines following Brezhnev's and Tikhonov's speeches to the Party Congress.

The issues discussed at the republic Party Congresses were taken up again in the republic Party Secretaries' speeches at the all-union Congress: e.g., labor resources, inefficiency in production, and the contradictions between sectoral and territorial planning.

Latvian Party Secretary August Voss called attention to the severe labor shortage in his republic, and said that to cope with this problem republic authorities were forced to set limits to the overall size of the work force in any given enterprise. But some all-union ministries had considerably exceeded these personnel limits, charged Voss, and this considerably undermined efforts to raise total labor productivity in Latvia. The ministries' conduct also jeopardized the complex target programs (*kompleksno-tselevye programmy*) which the republic authorities had worked out following the 1979 reform to come to terms with some of the key economic problems caused, for instance, by sectoral barriers. Voss called upon Gosplan USSR to take action preventing ministries from recruiting labor.[49]

Petras Griškevičius, First Secretary of the Lithuanian Communist Party, named the shortage of labor as the republic's principal problem. The only way to increase production was to raise labor productivity, and according to Griškevičius this should be done by modernizing existing enterprises and providing them with more advanced technical equipment. Greater attention to this problem from the ministries, including the all-union ministries, would be welcomed, intimated Griškevičius.[50]

Karl Vaino from Estonia's Communist Party had more specific things in mind than the other Baltic Party leaders in his demand for action from central authorities: namely improved technical equipment to gather and crush rocks and stones on arable land. According to Vaino, 10–12% of the labor force worked in the countryside doing heavy labor clearing fields by hand.[51]

The Latvian and Lithuanian Party leaders had been quite strong in their criticism of the all-union ministries, charging them with being directly responsible for the problems encountered in attempts to raise labor productivity. The ministries had recruited excessively large work forces for their enterprises and moreover were dragging their heels in the technological updating of them. But Vaino's speech was different, in that, aside from the demand for technical equipment for clearing fields, it consisted mainly of panegyrics for Leonid Brezhnev.

The four Central Asian Party Secretaries, from Kazakhstan, Uzbekistan, Kirghizia, and Turkmenistan, had one last opportunity to stress the importance of the Siberian river water diversion project before the Party Congress closed. As mentioned, the course adopted was not that advocated by the Central Asian Party leaders, and nothing was said in the directives that the work should begin during the 11th five-year planning period.

The arguments presented at the union Party Congress in favor of the project were the same as at the republic congresses. D. Kunaev, First Secretary of the Kazakhstan Communist Party, and member of the Politburo, argued that the diverting of waters was necessary for the future economic and social growth in Central Asia.[52] Interestingly, even Kunaev, a member of the Politburo, the Party's highest body, was unable to gain an audience for the proposal.

The Uzbek Party Secretary Rashidov made a direct reference to the five-year plan guidelines in his speech, and said that a positive decision on the Siberian river project would be of tremendous importance for agriculture in Central Asia. Dozens of millions of hectares would be brought under cultivation.[53] According to T. Usubaliev, Kirghizia's First Party Secretary, Kirghizia could draw advantages from the project as well.[54] M. Gapurov, Turkmenistan's First Secretary, stressed that he was expecting a proposal on the *perebroska* and called upon the Central Committee and the Council of Ministers to come forth with a positive decision.[55]

Republic representatives spelled out their demands for improvements in their own republics each in their different way. D. Rasulov, Tadzhikistan's Party Secretary, requested the Council of Ministers and the USSR Gosplan for help with economic growth, in particular in the extraction of metals.[56] Kunaev's speech had a totally different tone. He severely criticized Gosplan and Gossnab for not keeping pace with developments, e.g., with regard to the metal ore mining and the lumber industry.[57] The same sharp tone marked A. P. Liashko's speech (Liashko is the former chairman of the Ukrainian Council of Ministers). He said that a sharp increase in capital investments in the Ukraine was necessary,[58] and made no effort to hide his dissatisfaction with the insufficient investments in the Ukraine. As mentioned earlier in the chapter on the regional policy debate, comprehensive discussions had been carried out earlier on whether the western or the eastern parts of the country should be given priority in growth.

Several of the republic leaders called attention to earlier Party decisions concerning the development of specific republics. In 1979 the Central Committee passed a resolution on improving Party work in Kirghizia, and some action had already been taken in this respect.[59] Economic growth had been quite slow in Azerbaidzhan in the 1960s and on the encouragement of the Central Committee a number of changes were made in the economy with positive results, according to First Secretary G. Aliev.[60] The situation was the same in Georgia, where a number of decisions on the republic's economic growth had been taken at the central level during the 1970s. Edvard Shevardnadze said that the situation had now improved tangibly.[61]

In the 1970s several of the Soviet republics had undergone relatively comprehensive changes, alluded to by the republic leaders. Azerbaidzhan experienced a change of leadership, when Aliev, former head of the state security service, was installed as Party leader. In Georgia, Shevardnadze was appointed Party Leader, which was followed by extensive purges. Armenia experienced similar shakeups. Behind these changes in Party leadership lay the central leadership's dissatisfaction with the slow economic growth, corruption, and black marketeering, etc., which had reached unacceptable proportions in these republics.

Shevardnadze's speech contained a far-ranging proposal: the time was ripe, he said, for changes in planning and the Party organizational structure at the raion level, and pointed out the positive experiences gleaned from the integration of planning and political work in the Abasha region.[62]

S. Grossu from Moldavia and K. Demirtian from Armenia made pleas for economic assistance to their respective republics' economies, and both said that the Gosplan USSR would have to accelerate its industrial modernization program in these republics.[63]

T. Ia. Kiselev, Party Secretary in Belorussia, also demanded action in his republic to bring its industry up to date technologically.[64]

M. S. Solomentsev, chairman of the RSFSR Council of Ministers, discussed Siberia, and in particular, the development of the territorial production complexes. The underdeveloped infrastructure in Siberia stood in crucial need of improvement in the upcoming 11th five-year planning period. Siberia would play an extremely important role in the Soviet Union's future development, he observed.[65]

A number of other representatives of Siberian Party organizations also spoke at the Congress and, like Solomentsev, focused on the underdeveloped infrastructure: not only communications, but the *social infrastructure*—housing, day nurseries, cultural institutions, etc.—must be improved.

G. P. Bogomiakov, First Secretary in the Tiumen' oblast, stressed the crucial need for housing construction and social services to keep pace with the build-up of industry in Siberia. Dilatoriness in building up the social infrastructure was just one of several signs of problems in coordination in the Siberian economy, although the situation had improved somewhat since the Council of Ministers committee for the Western Siberian territorial production complex was established.[66]

The almost insurmountable sectoral barriers, and the problems attendant on them, that had long plagued Soviet industry even after it had reached a relative maturity were clearly discernible in the new Siberian industries as well, pointed out B. N. Eltsin, First Party Secretary in the Sverdlovsk oblast:

> I should like to suggest that economic planning and economic cooperation is marked by a sectorally oriented, not to say a narrowly parochial structure. The objective possibilities and necessity of making thorough use of the resources of territories, the economic regions and districts are not given sufficient consideration.[67]

The problems with the underdeveloped social infrastructure and the excessively sectoral orientation are probably interrelated. The sectoral ministries tend to concentrate their activities on their own areas and neglect other aspects that do not directly concern them. Quite a number of speeches at the Congress adduced these problems.

An increased differentiation of the Siberian economy was also called for, albeit in guarded words. P. S. Fedirko, Party Secretary of the Krasnoiarsk krai, underscored the need for an "intensive development of the productive forces in Siberia," although the representatives of the union ministries apparently did not particularly warm to the idea, according to Fedirko.[68]

But no more explicit arguments for an extensive differentiation of the Siberian economy were presented at the Congress. Party representatives were much more cautious on this issue than the Siberian scientists, who had presented their radical proposals in the press. There could be several reasons for this cautiousness. First, the 11th Five-year Plan projected vast investment sums for Siberia, and it would therefore be unreasonable to demand even more resources. Secondly, the Siberian speakers were representatives from the oblast level, i.e., a relatively low level in the Party organization, and therefore probably had no chance to put forth any proposals that diverged drastically from the plan, which had already acquired practical definition.

The issues treated at the 1981 Party Congresses—labor resources, investments, efficiency, productivity, etc.—were also an important ingredient in the guidelines for the 11th Five-year Plan. These guidelines, which in principle are only recommendations, were then modified into more specific five-year plans in 1981. The 11th Five-year Plan was adopted by the Supreme Soviet in its fall session, after which the Supreme Soviets of the republics adopted their plan resolutions at the republic level; these will be analyzed in the next section.

The 11th Five-year Plan

The targets for economic growth in 1981–85 set at the 26th Party Congress were rather low compared with those of earlier plans, but the final ratification of the five-year plan by the Supreme Soviet set the plan targets even lower. Indeed, the projected growth rate for industry was the lowest since the five-year planning system was introduced.[69]

Details on the final five-year plan were published following the Central Committee meeting in November 1981, at which Brezhnev announced that capital investments had to be reduced to about 30 billion rubles below even the original target. This meant that total investments were to increase by 10% and not 12–15% as recommended in the guidelines.[70] Thus the growth rate for investments would continue to decline during the 11th five-year planning period.

The five-year plan was presented to the Supreme Soviet delegates by Nikolai Baibakov, vice chairman of the Council of Ministers and chairman of the Gosplan USSR, at which time the definitive plan targets were presented: a rise of 18% in national income, a 26% growth in industrial output, and a 10% increase in total capital inqestments, as called for earlier by Brezhnev. State investments were projected to increase by only 5.4%.[71]

Thus Baibakov confirmed the final plan targets were set lower than stipulated in the guidelines from the Party Congresses. The most significant consideration here was the low growth rate in investments, which left little actual new capital to be distributed among the various regions with a view to equalization.

Baibakov also gave specific directives for economic growth in the fifteen Soviet republics: continued development of the eastern regions was of absolutely prime importance, he said. Production of energy and raw materials was to be further promoted, the territorial production complexes were to continue their activities, and new TPCs would be formed. Better utilization of available labor resources in Central Asia was called for, and in Europe the revamping and technological updating of industry would bring about a more intensive utilization of available resources; if all these measures were carried out, regional differences should, it was projected, continue to diminish.

> The rapid growth of industry and agriculture in Central Asia, the Caucasus, and Moldavia is a guarantee for a continuing equalization in economic development between these regions and the other Soviet republics.[72]

So, despite the doctrine that equalization had in the main already been achieved, according to Baibakov it would continue during the 11th five-year planning period. Although Baibakov referred explicitly to the Central Asian and Caucasian republics, as well as Moldavia, as relatively underdeveloped, the planned growth rate for three of the four Central Asian republics was lower than the union average, as may be seen from Table 6.1.

Plan targets for the republics' industrial growth were also presented at the Supreme Soviet session: in all cases they remained within the latitudes defined by the Party Congress, although in many cases (the union as a whole, the RSFSR, and a few other republics) the figures were nearer to the lower limit (Table 6.2).

The targets for industrial growth during the 11th five-year planning period were much lower for all republics than their counterparts in the 10th Five-year Plan, and in the Central Asian republics would seem to be too low to make up for the differences in level of development that according to most Western scholars still exist.

The planned slowdown in industrial growth in the highly developed republics of Estonia and Latvia, i.e., 15%, and the rapid growth planned for industry in the Caucasus, Moldavia, and Uzbekistan, i.e., about 30%, are conducive to equalization. But a different trend is discernible in the other Central Asian republics. The growth rates in

Table 6.2

Growth in Industrial Output in Percent during the Period 1981–85 According to the Decision of the 26th Party Congress and the Law on Five-year Plans Adopted by the Supreme Soviet

Republic	Decision of Party Congress	Decision of Supreme Soviet
RSFSR	24–27	25
Estonia	14–17	15
Latvia	15–18	16
Lithuania	21–24	23
Ukraine	20–23	23
Belorussia	26–29	28
Moldavia	30–33	32
Georgia	30–33	31
Armenia	29–32	31
Azerbaidzhan	29–32	30
Kazakhstan	22–25	25
Uzbekistan	28–31	30
Tadzikistan	21–24	22
Kirghizia	24–27	27
Turkmenistan	21–24	21
USSR	26–28	26

Sources: *Materialy*, pp. 185ff., *Pravda*, 20 November 1981.

Kirghizia and Turkmenistan are even lower than the union average, while the RSFSR is expected to have a relatively rapid growth despite the fact that it is already industrially well developed. On the whole this means that the plan targets for industrial growth are such that regional differences will diminish negligibly or not at all.

Further, it must be borne in mind that the plan targets are adjusted during the plan period and that the republics do not always achieve their plan targets; this can reinforce the tendency for regional inequalities to persist (see the chapter on implementation and results).

As mentioned, the 11th Five-year Plan targets were at such a level that no appreciable evening out of regional differences was likely. If the plan targets are broken down to show annual growth, the suspicion is reinforced that regional equalization will not be

Table 6.3

Growth in Industrial Output in Percent of 1980 Level during the 11th Five-year Planning Period by Year (1981–85)

Republic	Year				
	1981	1982	1983	1984	1985
RSFSR	4	8	13	19	25
Estonia	2	4	7	11	15
Latvia	2	5	8	11	16
Uzbekistan	5	11	15	21	30
Turkmenistan	1	4	7	12	21

Sources: *Sovetskaia Rossiia*, 3 December 1981, *Sovetskaia Estoniia*, 3 December 1981, *Sovetskaia Latvia*, 6 December 1981, *Pravda Vostoka*, 28 November 1981, *Turkmenskaia iskra*, 29 November 1981.

furthered by the plan (Table 6.3).

The figures in Table 6.3, which covers the most highly developed republics, the RSFSR, Estonia, and Latvia, and the two relatively less developed republics, Uzbekistan and Turkmenistan, show that the growth rate for the three former republics will be approximately the same for all five years. For Uzbekistan and Turkmenistan, a rather rapid increase was projected for 1985, i.e., the last year of the five-year Plan. In the light of what was said earlier on the degree of plan fulfillment, such a rapid growth rate in the very last year of the plan period would seem questionable.

For national income as well, the most rapid growth in the two Central Asian republics was projected for 1985 (Table 6.4), with a considerable risk that the plan would not be fulfilled.

The considerable covariance between the two indicators "industrial output" and "national income" is important to bear in mind. Western observers regard national income to be the best measure of socioeconomic development, and it does in fact give a good picture of development in a number of sectors.[73] The main reason industrial output is used as an indicator is that more data are available on it.

Labor productivity is also an important measure of economic growth, and the five-year plans clearly show that the industrially developed republics were to have the fastest growth in this respect as well, as indeed was explicitly stated in the Party Secretaries' speeches. But labor productivity was projected to increase more slowly in Turkmeni-

Table 6.4

Growth in National Income in Percent of 1980 Level during 11th Five-year Planning Period by Year (1981–85)

Republic	Year				
	1981	1982	1983	1984	1985
RSFSR	4	8	12	17	22
Estonia	2	5	8	11	15
Latvia	3	6	9	11	15
Uzbekistan	5	9	14	19	26
Turkmenistan	3	7	10	15	23

Sources: Same as for Table 6.3.

Table 6.5

Growth in Labor Productivity in Industry in Percent of 1980 Level during 11th Five-year Planning Period by Year (1981–85)

Republic	Year				
	1981	1982	1983	1984	1985
RSFSR	3	5	9	13	18
Estonia	2	5	8	11	16
Latvia	2	5	8	11	16
Uzbekistan	—	—	—	—	—
Turkmenistan	0	1	2	3	5

Sources: Same as for Table 6.3.
Note: Data on labor productivity were not published for Uzbekistan. The data for Turkmenistan cover only union-republic and republic industries (e.g., only 60% of all the industries in Turkmenistan).

stan (Table 6.5), where economic growth will be contingent on putting more people to work.

Table 6.6 shows that capital investments were to decline in the most developed republics during the 11th planning period, although they would increase in Turkmenistan, showing a trend which at least over the long term will lead to greater equalization. But these figures refer only to republic and local investments; no data on union investments are available, but there is nothing to indicate that the pattern in these

Table 6.6

Growth in Capital Investments in Percent of 1980 Level during 11th Five-year Planning Period by Year (1981–85)

Republic	1981	1982	Year 1983	1984	1985
RSFSR	−2	−4	−4	−3	−3
Estonia	—	—	—	—	—
Latvia	1	−4	−5	−5	−5
Uzbekistan	3	3	4	6	7
Turkmenistan	17	24	25	28	27

Sources: Same as for Table 6.3.
Note: Data on capital investments were not published for Estonia. The figures are probably near to those for Lithuania. The data cover only investments in union-republic and republic industries.

cases would diverge notably from the others.

The conclusion from this analysis of the plan figures is that a certain measure of equalization among the republics is aimed for in planning. For instance, industrial output and national income would increase relatively rapidly in some of the less developed republics, which would also receive new capital investment allocations, but the pace of equalization seems to be quite slow. For some republics, e.g., Turkmenistan, it is doubtful whether the distance from the national union average will be appreciably narrowed at all.

In addition, some of the plan targets for the least developed republics seem to be rather unrealistically high, so that the result will be that these republics will probably register the lowest degree of plan fulfillment. This will of course enhance regional differences.

Development after the 26th Party Congress

In 1982, regional economic issues were given special attention in official policy on two occasions. The first was in the Central Committee's resolution on "The Soviet Union's food program for the period up to 1990" in May. Sizeable transfers to agriculture and a more decentralized management were the measures announced to deal with growing problems in food production.[74]

The investment in agriculture, about 30 billion rubles, is of roughly the same magnitude as the reduction in plan targets for capital investments in 1981. The greater regional influence allowed is also interesting, although the program contains no specifications of how regional decisionmaking powers were to be broadened.

The republics were also the focus of attention in December 1982 at the celebration of the 60th anniversary of the formation of the Soviet Union. Iurii Andropov, at that time the General Secretary of the CPSU, stated at a ceremonial meeting with the Central Committee and the Supreme Soviets of the USSR and the RSFSR, that every Soviet republic was doing more than its share for developing the Soviet Union's economy, but this was particularly true of the Russian republic. Integration of the Soviet society must continue, said Andropov, until the final goal, a merging of nations, was reached, in accordance with Lenin's nationality doctrine.[75]

Thus Andropov laid strong emphasis on the continued assimilation of the republics and nations, although that goal was still a long way off, he said. The ultimate goal of integration will therefore probably have no direct consequences for the Soviet republics.

The problems with regional planning and distribution continued into Andropov's brief period at the helm, and there was no evidence that any fundamental changes were contemplated in the economic policy mapped out at the 26th Party Congress. In 1983, however, a number of minor changes were made in the system of economic planning and management regarding the position of the enterprise work force, enterprise power to influence planning, and improving labor discipline.

At its June 1982 session the Supreme Soviet passed the law on enterprise personnel, giving workers a greater say in enterprise management, and sharpening labor discipline.[76]

The law focused especially on worker brigades, and their heightened role. Not only would workers henceforth be permitted a say in decisions bearing on the day-to-day management of enterprises; they would also be responsible in certain measure for improving productivity and reinforcing labor discipline. The law also specifies that decisions taken by worker brigades on matters concerning their own work would be binding for enterprise management.[77]

It is unlikely that the law will bring about any decisive changes in enterprise operations; it is interesting, however, insofar as it indicates that policymakers have realized that increased employee participation can be conducive to greater productivity.

The *economic experiments* ratified in July 1983 were of major importance for the Soviet economy insofar as they represent the attempt to give concerns and enterprises greater influence on planning and transfer greater responsibility for the results of production to the plant level.[78]

The intention was to strengthen the status of enterprises in the Soviet economy. This change was preceded by experiments limited to a few sectors in some republics. The experiments cover the sectors administered by the Ministry for Heavy and Transport Machine Building and the Ministry for the Electrical Equipment Industry; the Ministry for the Food Industry in the Ukraine, the Ministry for Light Industry in Belorussia, and the Ministry for Local Industry in Lithuania are also involved.[79]

The economic experiments give enterprises broader powers to influence their plan targets, with stress placed more on quality than quantity. Further, enterprise managers also have been given broader latitude in deciding on bonus payments to employees. Enterprises will also be offered incentives to introduce new technology; they will participate in all stages of planning and have greater independence from the central authorities.[80]

In formal terms, the economic experiments entail a decentralization of decisionmaking to the concern or enterprise level. But the changes are relatively limited, and not at all similar to the far-reaching changes introduced in Hungary. The experiments were begun in early 1984, but it will probably be some time before they are completed. When exactly a change affecting the entire Soviet economy will come about, i.e., not merely changes within five ministries, it is impossible to say, and it is wholly within the realm of possibility that such a reform will never take place at all. As discussed in the introduction, partial reforms in the Soviet economy tend to be less successful.[81]

When the economic experiments were ratified, measures were also approved by the Central Committee and the Council of Ministers to facilitate cooperation between the agricultural sector and other sectors of the economy[82] inasmuch as the experiments also concerned some aspects of the food sector.

Andropov's campaign for greater labor discipline culminated in August 1983 in a joint decree from the Central Committee, the Council of Ministers, and the Central Council for Trade Unions, entitled "More intensive methods to improve socialist labor discipline."[83]

The measures adopted provided for a package of rewards and punishments in all sectors, leading to wage differences between those who are hard working and those who work deficiently. The decree supplements the law on labor discipline passed in June.

The changes introduced under Andropov were on a small scale. To the extent that enterprises actually do acquire broader powers, the lower administrative levels will of course also acquire more influence. In terms of regional policy, it is interesting to note that it was republic ministries in the Ukraine, Belorussia, and Lithuania that were chosen for the experiments. The Lithuanians especially had been openly discontent with the central interference down to the most minute detail in the management of the republic's economy.

The decisionmaking surrounding approval of the 11th Five-year Plan, together with developments thereafter, help to provide a more concrete idea of how official regional policy is shaped in the Soviet Union. A number of general conclusions may be drawn from studies of regional policy decisions made in 1979–83:

1. Regional policy is a part of general economic policy in the Soviet Union and is not always distinguished from other aspects of economic development; however, regional economic factors often receive attention, e.g., when decisions are taken on republic plan targets. The location of industries is also often taken up for consideration.

2. Priorities are also influenced by the fact that new funds for capital investments declined during the 11th five-year planning period. However, a certain amount of other resources became available through the reduction of investments in some of the western republics.

3. Equalization among the republics is an explicitly stated aim of regional policy and resources are being transferred to the Central Asian republics, although in insufficient volume to eliminate regional differences, which may hence be expected to remain during the 11th five-year planning period.

4. The eastern regions are at present the Soviet Union's leading recipients of new investments. Although precise data are difficult to obtain, it is clear that extremely large sums are being allocated to the production of energy and raw materials. There is no doubt that securing energy resources is a more important goal of economic policy than regional equalization.

5. Economic growth is somewhat slower in the European Soviet Union, and this contributes somewhat to economic equalization; but this is offset by the fact that industry in the European parts is to be modernized and stimulated. Technologically advanced sectors such as

the electronics industry are growing rapidly in several of the European republics.

6. There were clear differences between representatives of the union level and those of the republic level in the public debate. Republic representatives often demanded increased resources, and not infrequently ventured some rather harsh criticism of the activities of union bodies. Conflicts of interests, however, were held within definite limits, but it would not appear that the political function of the republic level is confined to the mere passive implementation of centrally made decisions, but rather that republic authorities do actually propose specific policy alternatives. The evidence therefore seems to support the third and fourth hypotheses formulated in Chapter 2.

7. During Andropov's time in power, a number of minor changes were ratified; for example, the position of the enterprise work force was strengthened, and enterprises were given broader powers. Implicit in these changes was a certain recognition of the need to decentralize the economy, although it is uncertain whether these experiments in fact resulted in any real change.

The 11th Five-year Plan set extremely important tasks for both Europe and Siberia. In Europe, there was to be a transition to more intensive development, and in Siberia, considerable resources were invested in energy production. Thus, the growth strategies 1 and 2 seem currently to be the most pertinent. However, development of Siberia will probably require more capital than the revamping of industry in the European USSR, and the differentiation of Siberia's economy will probably be a slow process.

There is a correlation between investment strategies and the articulation of republic interests with regional interests. The three investment strategies are personified in three loose groups, blocs, or lobbies, consisting of scientists, politicians, etc., all demanding more resources for their own region.

The *Central Asian bloc* consists of politicians and scientists who wish to promote the social and economic development of Central Asia and have accordingly given voice to their interests at Party Congresses and in the debate in the press. Representatives for the Central Asian bloc have been relatively outspoken about their views, but there is reason to believe that this bloc does not have a particularly strong influence on Soviet policy. Central Asia has been allocated relatively fewer resources in the five-year plans than the other republics. Moreover, the river reversal project was not incorporated in the 11th Five-year Plan, despite intensive campaigning for it by the Central Asian lobby.

The advocates of continued rapid development of Siberia, the *Siberian bloc*, have tended to present their views mainly in the press, especially in scientific periodicals. Most of those who call for a differentiated development of the Siberian economy are scientists from the Novosibirsk branch of the Soviet Academy of Sciences; they are probably also supported by politicians, although the arguments presented by Siberian politicians at the 26th Party Congress were quite guarded. This bloc may also be assumed to have the support of influential politicians in Moscow, inasmuch as the development of Siberia is one of the cornerstones of present Soviet economic policy.

A third bloc is also distinguishable. On several different occasions, politicians and scientists from the western parts of the Soviet Union have insisted that the European USSR should not be neglected, pointing out that there are valuable raw materials in this region of the country as well. Proximity to trading partners in the CMEA is also important.

The *European bloc* is more heterogeneous than the other blocs, and contains an important subgroup of Ukrainian and Belorussian politicians and scientists that seems to be well represented among central decisionmakers in Moscow. Another group is of Baltic origin: politicians and scientists from the three Baltic republics have on several occasions pointed out flaws in the planning system and called for increased autonomy for the Soviet republics.

Ethnic Russians are of course also included in the European bloc. Many scientists, especially economists, have stressed the importance of continued rapid development of the European region. Caucasian politicians and scientists may also be considered part of the European bloc although they have been much less active in the discussions on regional development than representatives of the other regions.

But it may be questioned whether the blocs can influence central decisionmaking in Moscow, given their varied composition and lack of formal organization; still, the representatives of the different regions are very active in discussions and sometimes present clear alternatives to the current policy. Since their arguments are permitted in the Soviet press and at the Party Congresses, they must enjoy some measure of approval and recognition from the central decisionmakers in Moscow.

The third hypothesis concerning distribution of power in the Soviet Union (presented in the chapter on theoretical premises) postulates that outside participants are able to influence decisionmaking, although influence seems to be limited to the formulation of policy alternatives for political leaders who then take the final decisions.

Quite clear alternative policies may be discerned in the Central Asian and Baltic arguments, namely increased investments to bolster the local economy in the one case, and more autonomy for concerns and enterprises in the other, and other policy alternatives may be distinguished as well. All in all, therefore, if the present analysis is correct, the third hypothesis seems to give a good description of how Soviet society functions.

The different blocs can in a certain sense be compared with competing organizations that present the case for their regional interests to the decisionmaking bodies. The speeches of the regional Party Secretaries at the all-union Party Congress summed up the demands of the regional organizations, backed up by reasoned arguments why resources should be allocated to their respective regions. In another sense, the routine might be compared with how certain bureaucracies function when they are beset by internal budget conflicts.

But analogies with organizations or bureaucracies in the West yield only a smattering of the real picture. All activity takes place within a firmly centrally regulated system. The various bloc representatives must work within narrow limits that are ultimately defined by the Communist Party. It is interesting to ascertain that these blocs do exist, however, and that their activity has increased in the recent period, in particular, the last part of Brezhnev's time in power. The regional interest groups seem to have been especially active in the drafting of the 11th Five-year Plan.

To obtain a wholly correct picture of regional policy, however, how that policy is implemented must also be studied, and the outcomes of the plans will therefore be examined in the next chapter, along with the policies implemented in the three major regions, Europe, Siberia, and Central Asia. Finally, the principles governing the location of industry will be reexamined.

7. IMPLEMENTATION AND RESULTS

In an earlier section the goals of regional policy and various decisions bearing on it were examined. The present chapter will discuss the implementation of regional policy and attempt to evaluate its results.

Unfortunately, as is often the case in Soviet research, there are problems gaining access to the relevant data. Attention will therefore be concentrated on certain key features that may reasonably be expected to shed light on regional policy, namely investments, regional wage differentials, and transferrals via the Soviet state budget. Quantitative indicators such as per capita national income and national per capita income of the working age population will be drawn on to determine the effects of regional policy, although some qualitative indicators, as for example the national or ethnic factor, will also be taken into account in the evaluation.

Definition of Terms

In American research on the implementation of policy and its assessment three important concepts are distinguished: input, output, and outcome. The *input* to a political program is the various types of resources, personnel as well as material. *Output* refers to the decisions taken on actions to be implemented, e.g., an organizational reshuffling. *Outcome* describes the actual changes that have occurred as a result of output.[1]

The distinction between output and outcome is extremely important. In many cases, and not the least in the Soviet context, the content of decisions and the actual result may differ appreciably. The novelty in the latest techniques such as implementation analysis and evaluation research is that this distinction is heeded more carefully.

Investigation of the implementation of political decisions is sometimes referred to as the study of postdecisional politics, i.e., a political analysis of that part of the political process that is set into motion after a formal decision has been made.[2]

In the implementation stage the original decisions may be modified in that the social bodies that are charged with implementing them may make their own interpretations that will diverge from the original intentions. This is especially true of decisions containing unclear or contradictory elements; moreover, it sometimes occurs that the implementing bodies may even actively resist a decision.[3]

A policy may also be evaluated in different policy areas, either by the authorities charged with implementing it, or by others, e.g., researchers. Evaluation is "any systematic study of the fulfillment of actually ratified goals by administrative bodies and their effects upon goals."[4] Evaluation is a stage in the political and administrative decisionmaking process which itself contains the following stages: (1) preparation of a decision, (2) formal ratification of the decision, (3) implementation, (4) evaluation, (5) information feedback to the original decisionmaker. After this feedback, the next round of decisionmaking takes place with the same sequence of stages.[5]

Of course this is merely a model, not an exact description, of the decisionmaking process; in reality, the stages are hardly so clearly delimited.

Evaluation can be further defined in terms of a number of questions:

1. Have the goals formulated for the system of control been achieved?

2. Has the system of control contributed to the achievement of the goals?

3. What other effects has the system of control had?[6]

For an evaluation to be meaningful, changes in the actual situation (or the failure of such changes to take place) must be related to the aim of the undertaking. Thus evaluation measures the effects achieved against the intended aim. There are also different ways to locate policy aims. According to some observers, evaluation analysts should proceed from the aims as officially formulated in policy declarations.[7]

The emphasis in the present study has been on official goal formulations, and Soviet regional policy will accordingly be evaluated in relation to these goals, although it is also warranted to ask what the real goals of Soviet regional policy are. Moreover, the three main types of goals, economic, social, and political, may also vary with regard to their actual importance for the policy being pursued.

Evidence was presented earlier indicating that some degree of regional equalization is still aspired to by Soviet policymakers. The 11th Five-year Plan contains plan targets which, if the plans were implemented fully, should help to reduce regional differences. Of course it could validly be claimed that the posed goals were inadequate to achieve total equalization; still, they do entail some reduction in regional differences at the end of the planning period as compared with the beginning.

A possible explanation for the persistence of regional differences despite plan decisions designed to eliminate them may lie in a discrepancy between goal and result. The inference would then be that the implementation of political decisions is quite difficult in the Soviet system.

The Problem of Implementation

Western research on Soviet regional development reviewed in the chapter on regional differences was based mainly on 1960 and 1970 data. However, it is quite probable that the pattern has remained largely unchanged into the 1980s, and current Soviet data, presented in the following, indicate that this is indeed the case.

According to Western studies several clusters with varying levels of development may be distinguished among the republics. These clusters were strikingly often congruent with self-contained geographic areas. Thus the Baltic republics, especially Estonia and Latvia, and the RSFSR feature a relatively high level of socioeconomic development, with the other European republics following suit. The Caucasian republics and Kazakhstan come next, with the Central Asian republics, Uzbekistan, Tadzhikistan, Kirghizia, and Turkmenistan at the bottom of the scale with the lowest indicators of socioeconomic development.[8]

Thus there is evidence for rejecting the official Soviet claim that regional differences have basically disappeared. To be sure, some equalization has certainly taken place over the years, yet major differences still remain. The division of the republics into groups in terms of their level of development is also supported by the findings of Soviet researchers (cf. the chapter on regional differences).

In Chapter 1 the difficulties in implementing far-ranging reforms in Soviet society were pointed out. Bialer, for instance, shows that reforms are absorbed into the existing planning system. Reform intentions may be good enough, but according to Bialer they are often implemented on a much too limited scale.[9] The same difficulties in implementing economic reforms have been observed in Eastern Europe.[10]

This is in general a fitting description of how Soviet regional policy has fared as well. It may be presumed that the intention of the leadership has been to bring about improvements in the least developed regions of the Soviet Union, so as to achieve some regional equalization. But efforts have been too slack; changes are nullified by the inertia at lower levels in the planning and management system.

Similar assessments of the problems encountered in implementing economic decisions may also be found in Soviet reports, which show in effect that economic changes often remain on paper. The responsibility for this lies mainly with the ministries, which do not always carry out their functions as they should. The former chairman of Gosplan USSR, N. Baibakov, described this in the following way:

> Not infrequently, measures planned by the ministries to improve management and to raise the efficiency of production and improve the quality of work remain on paper, since there is no ongoing monitoring of their practical implementation, and as a result the targeted goals are not achieved.[11]

Thus the good intentions of the leadership are not matched by a commensurate ability to carry out the planned measures in practice. There is, for instance, poor control over whether changes have actually been implemented.

It is in this context that the discipline campaign initiated by Andropov—and continued by Gorbachev—should be seen. One of the reasons for the difficulties in implementing decisions is the poor work discipline at both administrative and production levels.

Often, the watchdog function of ensuring that decisions are implemented is alleged to be the task of the Communist Party. Accordingly the criticism of faulty implementation may be seen as an indirect criticism of how the Party is doing its job, in particular at the lower organizational levels.

An article from *Kommunist* in 1983 written by B. Shcherbitskii, member of the Politburo and First Secretary in Ukraine, exemplifies this view of the Party as key to the implementation of decisions once they have been ratified. The title of the article is ''The supervision and monitoring of decision implementation is the most important function in the Party's leadership of the society.'' In the article, lower-level Party organizations are instructed in the art of monitoring the implementation of decisions taken at higher levels.[12]

At a Politburo meeting in early December 1983 an open criticism was mounted of the way lower-level Party organizations carried out the economic reforms, and the contents of the meeting were reported in most of the major Soviet daily newspapers, including a number of newspapers published in the republic capitals.[13]

It seems that the economic experiment decided upon in summer 1983, and begun in January 1984, had already encountered difficulties in its preparatory stages. A number of guideline documents were drawn up and approved, but after these concrete preliminary steps, serious hitches emerged in the practical implementation of the reform. The ministries concerned, i.e., the Ministry for Heavy and Transport Machine Building, were dilatory in taking the necessary measures. For example, the firms involved in the experiment did not receive workable instructions, and some Party organizations did not understand the significance or scope of the reform.[14]

The 1983 reform, or the economic experiments, as it is usually referred to in the press, bore a number of similarities with its predecessors. The difficulties in implementing the political decisions have been considerable, and in the report from the Politburo meeting two ministries are even named and criticized. This fits well with Bialer's description of difficulties in implementing changes in the Soviet Union. Strikingly often, it is at the ministerial level, i.e., the level just below the highest decisionmaking bodies, where tendencies to alter the course of the reform emerge.

The five-year planning system is one area where it is possible to follow the implementation of decisions directly, and accordingly in the next section the goals and the results of planning will be compared.

Plan Targets and Plan Fulfillment

In the chapter on regional policy decisions it was pointed out that most of the plan targets in the 11th Five-year Plan had been set lower than in the earlier five-year plans: the projected growth in industrial output and the rate of growth in capital investments are typical examples. Yet an analysis of plan fulfillment during the five-year plan shows that the Soviet economy has in fact found it difficult to achieve even these relatively low plan targets. It became evident in the first year or so that some plan targets were beyond reach and that a revision was necessary.

It is of interest to determine which republics will achieve their plan

Table 7.1

Growth in Industrial Output in Percent during 9th and 10th Five-year Plans

Republic	1971–75 outcome	1976–80 plan	1976–80 outcome	1981–85 plan
RSFSR	42	36	22	25
Estonia	41	26	24	15
Latvia	36	27	20	16
Lithuania	49	32	26	23
Ukraine	41	33	21	23
Belorussia	64	43	42	28
Moldavia	55	47	32	32
Georgia	39	41	40	31
Armenia	45	46	46	31
Azerbaidzhan	50	39	47	30
Kazakhstan	42	40	18	25
Uzbekistan	39	39	30	22
Tadzhikistan	39	39	30	22
Kirghizia	52	37	27	27
Turkmenistan	54	30	12	21
USSR	43	36	24	26

Sources: *Nar. khoz. 1980*, pp. 130ff; *Pravda*, 30 October 1976, 20 November 1981.

targets and which will not, how the plan is revised during the plan period, which republics are given revised targets, and finally whether there are differences in this respect between the more industrially developed republics in the western Soviet Union and the more agriculturally oriented republics in the south.

Table 7.1 shows that there can sometimes be major differences between plan targets and plan fulfillment. Only two republics, Georgia and Armenia, achieved their plan targets for the 10th Five-year Plan. In some republics, e.g., Turkmenistan and Kazakhstan, growth was much lower than planned, while in several other republics growth may fairly be regarded as relatively low compared with the planned figures.

Real growth in industrial output declined compared with the 9th and 10th Five-year Plans for all republics except Georgia and Armenia, and in some cases, e.g., in Turkmenistan and Kazakhstan, quite drastically.

Table 7.2

Growth in National Income, Industrial Output, and Labor Productivity in Industrial Output, and Labor Productivity in Industry Plan Target and Plan Outcome for the Entire Soviet Union (Percent of Preceding Year)

	Plan 1981	Outcome 1981	Plan 1982	Outcome 1982	Plan 1983	Outcome 1983
National income	3.4	3.2	3.0	2.6	3.3	3.1
Industrial output	4.1	3.4	4.7	2.8	3.2	4.0
Labor productivity	3.6	2.7	4.1	2.1	2.9	3.5

Sources: *Pravda*, 20 November 1981; "SSSR i soiuznye respubliki v 1981 godu, SSSR i soiuznye respubliki v 1982 godu," *Pravda*, 25 November 1982; 23 January 1984.

During the first years of the 11th five-year planning period overall, growth continued at a relatively slow pace. According to plans, industrial output was to have increased by 4.1% in 1981 and 4.7% in 1982 for the union as a whole, but the actual figures were 3.4% and 2.8%, quite low for the Soviet Union. National income also grew more slowly than the planned figures for 1981 and 1982. There was some improvement in 1983, although the higher growth figures for this year should be seen against the background of the relatively poor showing in 1982 (Table 7.2).

The rate of growth of capital investments was targeted lower, the planners relying instead on labor productivity as the major source of economic growth. Table 7.2 shows, however, that even the rise in that factor will be lower than projected. Data thus far therefore indicate that the actual result of the 11th Five-year Plan, like many earlier plans, was poorer than targeted.

The growth rate of capital investments declined on target to 2–3% per year during the first two plan years; but in 1983 investments grew by 5% over 1982.[15]

Although the outcome is lower than planned, there is no zero growth. National income in the Soviet Union is rising by about 3% per year, which is probably more rapidly than in many Western countries. Although particular figures may of course be questioned, it would seem that most observers now accept that the growth rate is 3% or slightly lower.[16]

The important question, however, is how the growth rate varies among the republics. Have the more developed republics found it easier or more difficult to achieve their plan targets? Have the Central Asian republics, with their low level of industrial development, fared better or worse? All of these questions are crucial in assessing implemented policy.

The following analysis is based on a select sample of the relatively advanced (the RSFSR, Estonia, and Latvia), and the relatively backward Soviet republics (Uzbekistan and Turkmenistan). The selection is more or less the same as that used earlier in discussing the republic Party Congresses.

For the RSFSR, the plan outcome roughly parallels the results for the union as a whole. The rise in national income was lower than the planned figure for the entire period for 1981 to 1983. Growth of industrial output and in labor productivity was closer to the plan figures (Table 7.3).

But in one area the plan was overfulfilled: capital investments increased by several percentage points more than planned throughout the entire period from 1981 to 1983, continuing a pattern generally observed in the past for investments in the RSFSR. Although the published statistical data in this area are not unambiguous, the growth of investments suggests a growing concentration on Siberia. One presumable explanation for this is that a greater need for capital investments has arisen in Siberia since the plan period began, e.g., because plant installations were more expensive than calculated. This applies equally to capital-intensive sectors (energy production, iron and steel, chemical industry, and forestry industry) and to the planned expansion of the production apparatus and of the infrastructure.[17]

Plan fulfillment for Estonia and Latvia seems to be near or above 100% for most indicators. The 1983 results were good in both republics. Estonia's national income rose by 5% this year compared with the planned 3.4% (Tables 7.4 and 7.5). Growth has continued in these republics despite the decline in capital investments. In 1983, investments declined in Estonia by 11%,[18] but in the future economic growth will probably decline if the downward trend in the rate of capital investments continues.

Whereas Estonia and Latvia have, with the exception of only a few indicators, fulfilled or overfulfilled the plan targets, the picture for Uzbekistan and Turkmenistan is spottier. For 1981 the plan result was relatively good, but the results for 1982 were somewhat poorer; in 1983 the plan target for industrial output was overfulfilled in Uzbekistan while in Turkmenistan the planned targets for none of the important

Table 7.3

Growth in National Income, Industrial Output, and Labor Productivity in Industry—Plan Target and Plan Outcome for RSFSR (Percent of Preceding Year)

	Plan 1981	Outcome 1981	Plan 1982	Outcome 1982	Plan 1983	Outcome 1983
National income	3.6	3.0	3.3	2.8	3.7	3.3
Industrial output	4.0	3.0	3.8	2.5	3.0	3.6
Labor productivity	3.3	2.9	1.4	2.2	3.2	3.6

Sources: Same as for Table 7.2, *Sovetskaia Rossiia*, 3 December 1981, 2 December 1981, 1 February 1984.

Table 7.4

Growth in National Income, Industrial Output, and Labor Productivity in Industry—Plan Target and Plan Outcome for Estonian SSR (Percent of Preceding Year)

	Plan 1981	Outcome 1981	Plan 1982	Outcome 1982	Plan 1983	Outcome 1983
National income	2.0	1.4	3.5	3.7	3.4	5.0
Industrial output	2.0	2.1	2.0	1.6	2.7	3.6
Labor productivity	2.0	2.1	2.1	1.6	2.5	3.8

Sources: Same as for Table 7.2; *Sovetskaia Estoniia*, 3 December 1981, 5 December 1982, 31 January 1984.

Table 7.5

Growth in National Income, Industrial Output, and Labor Productivity in Industry—Plan Target and Plan Outcome for Latvian SSR (Percent of Preceding Year)

	Plan 1981	Outcome 1981	Plan 1982	Outcome 1982	Plan 1983	Outcome 1983
National income	3.0	3.0	2.5	2.0	3.0	3.0
Industrial output	2.1	3.1	2.5	2.7	2.0	2.6
Labor productivity	2.1	3.0	2.5	2.5	2.0	2.6

Sources: Same as for Table 7.2; *Sovetskaia Latviia*, 3 December 1981, 5 December 1982, 1 February 1984.

Table 7.6

Growth in National Income, Industrial Output, and Labor Productivity in Industry—Plan Target and Plan Outcome for Uzbek SSR (Percent of Preceding Year)

	Plan 1981	Outcome 1981	Plan 1982	Outcome 1982	Plan 1983	Outcome 1983
National income	4.5	7.1	3.5	3.2	4.2	3.8
Industrial output	5.0	6.1	4.2	3.8	4.0	5.1
Labor productivity	—	3.2	—	1.0	—	2.4

Sources: Same as for Table 7.2; *Pravda Vostoka*, 28 November 1981, 2 December 1982, 1 February 1984.

Table 7.7

Growth in National Income, Industrial Output, and Labor Productivity in Industry—Plan Target and Plan Outcome for Turkmen SSR (Percent of Preceding Year)

	Plan 1981	Outcome 1981	Plan 1982	Outcome 1982	Plan 1983	Outcome 1983
National income	3.0	3.1	3.6	3.1	3.8	3.6
Industrial output	1.3	2.5	1.5	1.1	3.8	3.0
Labor productivity	0.0	0.9	0.7	0.0	1.6	1.3

Sources: As in Table 7.2; *Turkmenskaia iskra*, 2 February 1981, 5 December 1982, 2 February 1984.
Note: Data for labor productivity cover union-republic and republic industries.

indicators—national income, industrial output and labor productivity—were achieved (Tables 7.6 and 7.7).

Plan targets for the Central Asian republics were, as mentioned earlier, set with a view toward equalization. But since plan fulfillment lagged in Uzbekistan and Turkmenistan, the equalizing effect that had been built into the plan was nullified.

Unfortunately, because data are lacking on a number of important points, analysis suffers. The data that do exist, however, show that economic development in Turkmenistan is beset by serious problems. Labor productivity is rising insignificantly at a rate between 0.0% and 1.3%, and growth in investments was only about a fourth of the planned figure for 1981–82. For Uzbekistan the investment picture was somewhat better.

As pointed out earlier, the plan targets for a number of important indicators have not been achieved, and a part of the reason has been the poor showing of the RSFSR in this respect. The most developed republics, Estonia and Latvia, in general achieved their targets, but for two of the Central Asian republics the picture was more uneven, although available data indicate that on the whole plan fulfillment left something to be desired.

Similar differences in plan fulfillment marked the 10th Five-year Plan as well. Table 7.1 shows that the degree of plan fulfillment was higher in the European parts of the Soviet Union and in the Caucasus than in Kazakhstan and Central Asia. All the Central Asian republics fell far short of their original plan targets. Turkmenistan's industrial output increased by only 12% compared with a planned figure of 30%, which moreover was lower than the target of 36% for the Union as a whole. Thus regional differences in plan fulfillment have not been conducive to regional equalization.

The plan targets for the one-year plans were also readjusted downward from the original five-year plan targets from 1981. Thus, union growth in national income for 1983 was to be 3.5% over 1982, but the annual plan for 1983 projected 3.3%. The original plan target for industrial output was 4.3%, but the revised figure was 3.2%. The figures for labor productivity were 4.1% and 2.9% respectively.

The figures are not completely comparable since they refer to different actual 1982 values, but the general picture is clearly one of a downward adjustment, and there were no differences between the developed and relatively underdeveloped republics in this respect.

Even the relatively slight shift toward more regional equalization that might have come about as a result of economic growth during the 11th Five-year Plan was therefore probably not achieved. Regional differences, which have persisted through the years, will remain untouched, merely duplicating the pattern observed during the 10th five-year planning period. The reasons are in part that some plan targets were not fulfilled, and in part that a larger portion of capital investments presumably have been allocated to capital-intensive production in Siberia. Thus regional differences persist, neither increasing nor decreasing to any notable degree.

The Instruments of Regional Policy

The centralized Soviet planning system creates means to distribute resources among the regions in a way that the political leadership deems fitting. The five-year plans contain several instruments that may be used to influence regional balance. As should be evident from the foregoing, regional variations do exist in the degree of plan fulfillment. Incomplete plan fulfillment is one of the reasons why regional differences have been so little affected despite the fact that plan targets were set so as to allow at least some regional equalization. Plan targets are normally expressed in growth figures, i.e., relative figures. Now, however, let us examine some of the changes that have taken place in absolute terms in capital investments in particular, but also in other instruments of regional policy.

Investment policy is one of the most important instruments of regional policy. Political leadership can influence regional balance by modifying the distribution of investments over certain regions. Elisabeth Lauschmann, quoted in the introduction as an example of the dominant tradition in Western research on regional policy, has emphasized especially the role of such instruments of regional policy as investment,[19] and similar discussions on means and ends, or instruments, occur from time to time in the Soviet literature as well.[20]

Capital investments are of course an extremely important factor in economic growth in a particular area. An analysis of the absolute figures for investments and changes in their regional distribution will give some idea of how regional policy is implemented. Soviet regional economists, like many of their Western counterparts, insist that there is a close correlation between capital investments, the structure of the work force, and economic growth.[21]

Capital investments are a reflection of the extent to which leadership in a planned economy wishes to stimulate growth within a particular region. Table 7.8 shows the regional distribution of capital investments, which include the construction of new enterprises, remodelling, and expansion and improvement of existing enterprises in industry, agriculture, the transport sector, commerce, etc. The construction sector is also included.[22]

Capital investment in the Soviet Union is a major problem, ranging

Table 7.8

Capital Investments in the Soviet Union in 1970, 1980, and 1982 by Region (Percent of Total Investments)

Region	1970	1980	1982
RSFSR	59.5	62.4	62.9
Baltic	3.2	2.8	2.8
Rest of Europe	20.6	18.6	17.9
Caucasus	3.9	3.6	3.9
Kazakhstan	6.6	6.1	5.9
Central Asia	6.4	6.4	6.6
Total	100.2	99.9	100.0

Sources: Nar. khoz. SSSR 1970, p. 488; *Nar. khoz. SSSR 1980*, p. 344; *Nar. khoz. SSSR 1982*, p. 345.

from those of a general nature, to those concerning the sectoral distribution of investments, and investment efficiency, i.e., return on investment. The present study will be concerned solely with their regional distribution.

Clearly, investment funds are utilized in different ways in different regions. Costs will vary; but the magnitude of capital investments is still a relatively accurate indication of the relative importance attached by the political leadership to the various regions (Table 7.8).

The figures reveal a relatively high degree of stability. The distribution among the regions is basically unchanged. The most important difference between 1970 and 1982 is a growth of over 3% for the RSFSR, which in 1982 received more than 60% of investments; indeed, over 80% of all investment is allocated to the RSFSR and the European republics. Kazakhstan receives 6–7%, the Caucasus 3.4%, and Central Asia about 6.5% of total investments. Despite the great population growth in Central Asia, which now has about 10% of the Union's population, no noteworthy change took place there between 1970 and 1982.

In this area too, there is quite broad agreement with the findings of earlier Western studies. Only the increase for the RSFSR is somewhat out of line with the general pattern, so that it would be worthwhile to study this republic further and attempt to gather statistical data for Siberia. No official data for Siberia is available after 1975, although one Soviet scientist, Minas Chentemirov, reported that 20% of total

Table 7.9

Capital Investments in the Soviet Union in 1970, 1975, and 1980, by Macroregions (Percent of Total Investments), at Comparable Prices

Region	1970	1975	1980
Europe	67.9	67.6	63.8
Siberia	15.4	16.8	20.0
Caucasus and Central Asia	16.9	15.7	16.1
Total	100.2	100.1	99.9

Sources: *Nar. khoz. SSSR 1970*, p. 488; *Nar. khoz. RSFSR 1975*, p. 330; *Nar. khoz. 1980*, p. 344; *Problems of Communism*, September-October 1982.

investment in 1978 was allocated to Siberia, and assuming that this figure holds for 1980 as well, the following regional distribution picture emerges (Table 7.9).

But the figure of 20% for Siberia may be much too high. In an article written in 1980, the Siberian economist Granberg called for an increase in Siberia's share of investment funds to 15%,[23] which would mean that the pattern established in 1970–75 would have undergone no notable changes. But it is possible that Granberg was referring to the western and eastern Siberian economic regions. If another 4.5% (the proportion allocated to the Far East) is added to the figure given by Granberg, the sum is 20%.

A report in the Soviet press in 1982 confirms that Siberia's share in investments really was about 20% in the early 1980s. The chairman of the Gosplan RSFSR, N. I. Maslennikov, stated in his speech to the December 1982 session of the RSFSR Supreme Soviet that more than 27 billion rubles, or close to 21% of the total investment sum, would be allocated to Siberia in the form of investments in 1983.[24] The available data, i.e., both official statistics and isolated data provided by scholars, indicate that investments in Siberia increased during the 1970s. After all, according to Soviet scientists and politicians, investment in Siberia is the Party's *general line* with regard to the territorial distribution of the forces of production.[25] Similarly, the share of the other areas shows a declining tendency. These changes should be seen in the light of the fact that the growth rate of total investments in the Soviet Union has declined. Investments can also be adjudged in terms of the size of the population in a particular region. This will give a per capita value

Table 7.10

Investments in Rubles per Capita, 1970, 1980, and 1982

Region	1970	1980	1982
RSFSR	375	600	644
Estonia	428	556	547
Latvia	377	506	561
Lithuania	365	471	530
Ukraine	280	382	387
Belorussia	299	436	472
Moldavia	266	375	400
Georgia	237	352	410
Armenia	332	368	387
Azerbaidzhan	233	327	372
Kazakhstan	414	543	552
Uzbekistan	265	339	365
Tadzhikistan	219	249	243
Kirghizia	246	276	278
Turkmenistan	366	433	476
USSR	340	505	535

Sources: *Nar. khoz. 1970*, p.10; *Nar. khoz. 1980*, p. 11; *Nar. khoz. 1922–82*, p. 12; *Nar. khoz. 1982*, p.345.

reflecting the relationship between growth and economic activity, on the one hand, and the size of the population, on the other (Table 7.10).

The distribution of investments shows a perfect match with the clusters demonstrated to exist in *Soviet Regional Policy*. Turkmenistan is an exception inasmuch as major investments were made during the period between 1970 and 1980, in particular in the petroleum industry. It should be noted that the calculations are made on a per capita basis, which means that republics with a large proportion of non-working age population show lower figures than if the figures were expressed in terms of the employable population, as will be done later on in this study.

Expressed per capita, investments per capita investments show the familiar pattern of "rich" and "poor" republics described in other studies. The RSFSR and the Baltic, as well as Kazakhstan, are high up the scale with regard to per capita investments, with the Ukraine and

Belorussia following closely on their heels; in the Caucasian republics about 400 rubles per capita is invested. In Central Asia the pattern is more varied. Tadzhikistan and Kirghizia rank very low, while Uzbekistan and Turkmenistan fare somewhat better.

For Siberia, the figures would be: 498 rubles per capita in 1970 and 941 rubles per capita in 1980. This means that in terms of per capita investments, Siberia is favored over the other areas, although clearly many investments do not benefit the Siberian population directly. Energy and raw materials are transported to Europe, and in addition Siberia covers a vast area yet is only sparsely populated (about 28 million in 1980).[26]

Interestingly, the RSFSR, which has the highest per capita investment rate, also has the highest growth rate for investments, on a par, in fact, with that of Lithuania and Latvia. Growth is moderate in the other republics, and some show none at all. In Tadzhikistan, the population is growing more rapidly than investments; hence, per capita investment even decreased in 1980–82.

The rapid population growth in Central Asia can make per capita calculations misleading. It is advisable, therefore, to subtract the non-working age population when calculating regional differences in capital investments (Table 7.11).

Expressing investments in terms of the employable population alters the picture of regional distribution of investments very little. The western republics and Kazakhstan still lead the list, Turkmenistan is on a par with the western republics, while the rest of the republics show the same pattern as with per capita calculations.

Up to now no distinction has been drawn among the different types of investments. But the *investment structure* is illuminating in evaluating the regional distribution of capital investments. Data on allocations to the various sectors in each republic are sparse, but some information is accessible, in the five-year plans, for example.

The basic guidelines for the 11th Five-year Plan call for high growth rates for the electronic and appliance industries in Estonia, Latvia, and Lithuania. In many of the Central Asian republics, light industry and the chemical industry were to be favored, while in the other republics, emphasis was to be on machinery construction and light industry.[27]

Thus the high-tech sectors are being promoted in the Baltic republics, while more traditional sectors are given preference in Central Asia. There can be no doubt, then, that the structure of investments tends to reinforce regional economic inequality.

Table 7.11

Capital Investments in Rubles per Working Age Population (15–54 or 59 Years), 1980

Republic	Investments
RSFSR	996
Estonia	994
Latvia	886
Lithuania	801
Ukraine	646
Belorussia	751
Moldavia	645
Georgia	616
Armenia	642
Azerbaidzhan	605
Kazakhstan	923
Uzbekistan	724
Tadzhikistan	527
Kirghizia	537
Turkmenistan	882
USSR	964

Sources: Baldwin, p. 128; *Nar. khoz. 1982*, p. 345.
Note: For the concept working age see the section on employment below.

Investment decisions in the Soviet Union are in the main made centrally, although since 1979, when a minor economic reform was put through, the regional and local levels have enjoyed more influence. The importance of the fact that the territorial aspects of the economy are also included in the plans is being underscored with increasing frequency.[28]

Resources are also allocated to the republics in other ways than through investments, e.g. through the budgets, which basically reflect the five-year plans, and in fact are drawn up at the same time as the latter (and the one-year plans as well), representing a kind of translation of the plans into budgetary language. Budgets are also drawn up at the republic and lower administrative levels.[29]

In the recent period, only two republics have received extra allocations via the union budget. In the 10th Five-year Plan, transfers from the union budget to Kazakhstan's budget were increased from 197 to

Table 7.12

Transfers from Union to Republic Budgets during the 10th Five-year Plan (Millions of Rubles)

Republic	1976	1977	1978	1979	1980
Kazakhstan	197	149	389	449	587
Turkmenistan	65	—	14	3	—

Source: *Gosudarstvennyi biudzet SSSR i biudzety soiuznykh respublik 1976–1980*, pp. 105 and 108.

587 million rubles, or from 2.8% to 6.3% of Kazakhstan's total budget.[30]

Turkmenistan is the only other republic that received direct transfers from the union budget, although the sums were smaller than those received by Kazakhstan: 65 million rubles in 1976, or 7.1% of revenues, and 3 million in 1979, or 0.3%. In 1980 there were no direct budget transfers to Turkmenistan (Table 7.12).

Thus transfers are being channeled into two regions targeted for major industrial investments. A number of new TPCs have been formed in Kazakhstan, and in Turkmenistan huge investments are being made in the oil industry. The transferred funds will most likely be invested in projects of union importance in these regions, although the transfer data at hand are not sufficient to permit definitive conclusions to be drawn in this regard.[31]

Thus only one of the poor republics of Central Asia, Turkmenistan, receives extra funds from the state budget, a finding that accords with observations made in earlier chapters. The Central Asian republics are relatively disadvantaged compared with the other regions of the Soviet Union; the gap between the wealthier and the poorer republics has remained. On the other hand, the differences are not permitted to get out of hand, and transfers from the union budget is one way to prevent this from happening. Other means are surely used as well, e.g., hidden transfers,[32] but the lack of data makes analysis difficult.

The republic budgets for 1984 were compiled early in the year. Their size and per capita distribution by and large parallel the regional distribution of investments (Table 7.13), although it should be observed that the republic budgets cover only 58% of the cost of economic development.[33] The remainder is financed from the union budgets. The most important budget expenditures are in economic growth,

Table 7.13

Republic Budgets 1984, Absolute Figures (Millions of Rubles) and Rubles per Capita (Population Jan. 1, 1983)

Republic	Millions of rubles	Rubles per capita
RSFSR	88,790	630
Estonia	1,446	960
Latvia	2,153	830
Lithuania	3,236	923
Ukraine	27,766	550
Belorussia	6,692	682
Moldavia	2,262	558
Georgia	2,778	541
Armenia	1,772	550
Azerbaidzhan	2,547	398
Kazakhstan	10,475	678
Uzbekistan	7,244	425
Tadzhikistan	1,509	356
Kirghizia	1,786	470
Turkmenistan	1,344	442
USSR	161,800	597

Source: *Ekonomicheskaia gazeta 1984/2; Nar. khoz. 1982*, p. 8.
Note: The data cover the sum of revenues and expenditures in the budget.

education, health, social security, and defense.[34]

Another method that has been used to influence regional balance is the system of *wage coefficients*. A supplement is added to the basic wages of persons employed in certain areas where it has been difficult to recruit labor, in particular, in Siberia and the Far East. The wage coefficients are calculated at the raion level and, usually, separately for each sector. Table 7.14 shows the coefficients in industry, aggregated at the economic region level. The figures are for 1970 and may be somewhat different today. However, data for more recent years are lacking in the official Soviet statistics.

These wage supplements, which in certain areas are as high as 100% of the basic wage, are intended as an incentive to workers to migrate to areas with a labor shortage, e.g., eastern Siberia and the Far East. Persons who have worked for a relatively long period in the northern

Table 7.14

Wage Coefficients for Industry in Economic Regions, about 1970

Region	Coefficient
Central	1.00
Baltic	1.07
Urals	1.10
Western Siberia	1.15
Eastern Siberia	1.33
Far East	1.66
Caucasus	1.00
Central Asia	1.00

Source: Murray Feshbach, "Regional and Branch Wage Differentials in the Soviet Union," *The Association for Comparative Economic Studies* 2–3 (1975), pp. 57–59.

regions receive an extra wage supplement in addition to the wage coefficients. Other benefits, e.g., longer holidays, are also given. But it is not certain whether the extra benefits are sufficient to cover the higher cost of living in Siberia and the Far East. Problems with the social infrastructure in Siberia are so serious that higher wages alone are hardly a sufficient incentive for workers to move there.[35]

Wage coefficients have been in use since 1968. Initially they were established for Siberia and the Far East, but have since then been used in some economic sectors in the Urals, Kazakhstan, and Central Asia. In general, their role in the Soviet wage structure has been growing.[36]

At the 26th Party Congress Tikhonov said that the regional wage supplement system would be expanded to include workers in the Urals, Kazakhstan, and certain regions in Siberia and the Far East.[37] It remains, however, a less important instrument of regional policy than capital investments.

The Effects of Regional Policy

As stated in the chapter on problems of regional development, it is difficult to distinguish between the results of regional policy and the regional effects of general economic policy, and in fact it is sometimes all but impossible to draw such a clear distinction in either a market economy or a centrally planned economy. Nevertheless, upon closer scrutiny a number of regional effects of general policy may be discerned. Action will be taken regionally if the regional balance is tipped in an undesired direction. Regional policy, therefore, may be fairly considered to be subordinate to general policy.

Although a general assessment of the effects of regional policy must remain incomplete in the present context, some are, indeed, quite clear, and their evaluation, together with an analysis of goals, decisions, and implementation, will give a good picture of Soviet regional policy.

The most important question is whether regional balance has been affected by regional policy discussions and its answer is already implicit in the foregoing discussion. The original decisions on regional policy tended toward regional equalization, although the pace of equalization projected in the 11th Five-year Plan was slow. But even the slight change that was to have been achieved has in the main been cancelled out by the lower level of plan fulfillment in the most backward republics.

This conclusion is borne out by the figures on plan fulfillment in 1983. Most republics achieved their 1983 annual plan targets, with the most advanced republics showing a somewhat higher performance in this respect. The differences are greater with regard to labor productivity, with Tadzhikistan showing 100.2% and Estonia 103.8% plan fulfillment.[38]

An examination of national income, one of the most important parameters available for measuring economic growth in the Soviet Union[39] shows persisting regional differences among the fifteen republics. Table 7.15, showing the 1982 national income figures for the different republics, reveals the same general pattern as other indicators. The Baltic republics and RSFSR top the list, with the Central Asian republics bringing up the rear. There were a number of minor shifts in the general pattern between 1970 and 1982, and it should be also noted that the per capita national income decreased in Kazakhstan, Tadzhikistan, and Turkmenistan between 1980 and 1982.

Like capital investments, national income can also be correlated with the working age population to eliminate the influence of the large segment of the under-15-year-old population on the statistics. But the same basic pattern remains (Table 7.16).

The data in Table 7.16, presented in index form, match Zakumbaev's index for industrial development (see Chapter 3). The years 1970 to 1980 can now be compared on the basis of the two calculations of national income per capita working age population (Table 7.17). Several changes took place during this period, with Kazakhstan losing ground, but otherwise the basic pattern remains: the western European

Table 7.15

National Income in Rubles per Capita (Comparable Prices), 1970, 1980, and 1982

Republic	1970	1980	1982
RSFSR	1,335	2,059	2,171
Estonia	1,622	2,374	2,473
Latvia	1,565	2,293	2,469
Lithuania	1,343	1,813	1,957
Ukraine	1,161	1,622	1,708
Belorussia	1,100	1,966	2,155
Moldavia	981	1,411	1,540
Georgia	875	1,527	1,686
Armenia	923	1,561	1,704
Azerbaidzhan	743	1,276	1,380
Kazakhstan	984	1,299	1,233
Uzbekistan	737	1,009	1,103
Tadzhikistan	690	872	850
Kirghizia	818	1,031	1,047
Turkmenistan	880	955	943
USSR	1,199	1,786	1,887

Sources: Dellenbrant, ''Soviet Social and Political Indicators,'' p. 37; *Nar. khoz. 1979*, p. 10; *Nar. khoz. 1922–82*, p. 11; *Nar. khoz. 1982*, p. 379. See also *SSSR i soiuznye respubliki v. 1982 g.*
Note: National income is calculated on the basis of figures published in *Narodnoe khoziaistvo Latviiskoi SSSR v 1971 godu* and growth figures published in *Narodnoe khoziaistvo SSSR*. See Dellenbrant, ''Soviet Social and Political Indicators,'' for more detailed information on the method of calculation.

republics rank the highest, while the four southern Central Asian republics still ranked lowest in 1980.

The effects of regional policy have thus been relatively minor, at least if it is assumed that the national income per capita working age population is to any degree an accurate measure of Soviet realities. Earlier on in the discussion some of the factors explaining such minor changes as do occur were pointed out. The equalizing potential of plan targets is very low, and because of general inertia and ever-present bottlenecks in the administration and planning system, it is difficult to implement policy once it has been decided upon.

In the following, several other factors (e.g., employment, and various cultural and national problems) influencing the implementation of

Table 7.16

National Income, Rubles per Individual of Working Age (15–54 or 59), 1980

Republic	National income	Index (USSR = 100)
RSFSR	3,400	111
Estonia	4,197	138
Latvia	3,997	131
Lithuania	3,155	103
Ukraine	2,766	91
Belorussia	3,300	108
Moldavia	2,411	79
Georgia	2,569	84
Armenia	2,703	89
Azerbaidzhan	2,360	77
Kazakhstan	2,228	73
Uzbekistan	2,100	69
Tadzhikistan	1,846	60
Kirghizia	1,972	65
Turkmenistan	1,936	63
USSR	3,052	100

Sources: Baldwin, p. 128; *Nar. khoz. 1982*, p. 379; Dellenbrant, "Soviet Social and Political Indicators," p. 37.

regional policy will be discussed, and finally, a reanalysis of location criteria will be made in this light.

Employment

As indicated earlier, the shortage of labor is considerable in some regions, while in others labor is plentiful. A study of the level of employment in the various republics should accordingly shed further light on the problems attendant on implementation of Soviet regional policy. The 1979 census shows that about a third of the population in Central Asia is employed, while for Europe the figure is one-half (Table 7.18).

These differences in the level of employment correlate with the other data on regional differences; they also partially explain existing in-

Table 7.17

National Income per Individual of Working Age 1972 and 1980 (USSR = 100)

Republic	1972	1980	Rank 1972	Rank 1980
RSFSR	108	111	4	3
Estonia	146	138	1	1
Latvia	131	131	2	2
Lithuania	127	103	3	5
Ukraine	96	91	6	6
Belorussia	94	108	7	4
Moldavia	69	79	11	9
Georgia	75	84	9	8
Armenia	78	89	8	7
Azerbaidzhan	72	77	10	10
Kazakhstan	98	73	5	11
Uzbekistan	65	69	14	13
Tadzhikistan	55	60	15	15
Kirghizia	68	65	12	12
Turkmenistan	68	63	13	14
USSR	100	100	—	—

Sources: Zakumbaev, p. 10 and same sources as for Table 7.16.

equalities. If a republic with a low level of employment is to provide the same standard of living and the same level of services as a republic with a higher level of employment, either productivity must be higher, which is most probably not the case in Central Asia, or transfers must take place from other republics.

At the republic Party Congresses in 1981, complaints were raised about the labor shortage in the Baltic republics, although from another vantage point such a shortage may be regarded as a consequence of the maximum utilization of labor reserves at a given level of labor productivity. The Central Asian republics, on the other hand, expressed concern over their prospects of being able to utilize available labor reserves to the fullest. It is evident that underemployment exists in these republics.

Table 7.19 shows a high level of variation among the republics in level of employment. In Central Asia about 40% of the population is

Table 7.18

Employed Population in Percent of Total Population

Region	1970	1979
RSFSR	49.9	54.0
Estonia	53.3	54.5
Latvia	53.5	54.8
Lithuania	49.1	51.6
Ukraine	49.5	52.1
Belorussia	47.8	52.2
Moldavia	50.1	52.1
Georgia	44.9	50.4
Armenia	39.3	47.4
Azerbaidzhan	34.2	43.2
Kazakhstan	42.2	46.9
Uzbekistan	36.0	40.8
Tadzhikistan	34.7	39.2
Kirghizia	38.3	42.4
Turkmenistan	37.2	41.2
USSR	47.2	51.5

Source: *Vestnik statistiki* 1 (1981), pp. 64ff. No data on Siberia were available.

working, while in the RSFSR, Estonia, and Latvia the figure is 54–55%. The relatively greater breadwinning burden on the shoulders of the employed undoubtedly shackles economic growth somewhat in Central Asia.

Further, the female and rural populations in the Central Asian republics have an especially low level of employment, much lower than the average for the Soviet population as a whole (Table 7.19). A good one-third of the rural population in Central Asia is employed, while over 50% of the population are supported in various ways by others. State pensioners or subsidy recipients constitute another group. The group of support recipients (*izhdiventsy*) is, however, astonishingly large. This segment of the population includes those who are employed only in private agriculture, so that hidden unemployment is a possibility here.

Soviet scholars have estimated the group of persons employed only in private agriculture to be about 17% of the population in Turkmenistan.[40] Special job-creating measures will presumably be undertaken for this group.

Table 7.19

Employment Rate for the Entire Population, the Female Population, and the Rural Population in 1979 (Percent of Total Population)

	Entire population	Female population	Rural population
RSFSR	54.0	49.8	47.9
Estonia	54.5	50.2	46.3
Latvia	54.8	51.3	47.2
Lithuania	51.6	48.4	44.8
Ukraine	52.1	48.3	47.9
Belorussia	52.2	48.7	46.2
Moldavia	52.1	49.7	49.6
Georgia	50.4	47.4	49.0
Armenia	47.4	44.8	45.1
Azerbaidzhan	43.2	41.1	40.9
Kazakhstan	46.9	43.4	41.8
Uzbekistan	40.8	38.4	37.7
Tadzhikistan	39.2	37.0	36.9
Kirghizia	42.4	39.5	38.5
Turkmenistan	41.2	38.4	38.6
USSR	51.5	47.8	45.6

Source: *Vestnik statistiki* 1 (1981), pp. 64–65.

Differences in the level of employment among women account for a good deal of regional differences. For cultural reasons, or because of large families, etc., the number of new recruits to the labor force in Central Asia from among the female population cannot be expected to be very large.

As mentioned earlier, calculations of the number of employed in relation to the total population can give a somewhat misleading picture. Republics with a rapid population growth and hence a large number of persons under the age of 18 will for that reason automatically show a lower level of employment. An alternative approach is to calculate the number of employed in relation to the working age population. This index will give a more accurate picture of the level of employment, although a disadvantage is that this index includes people who are employed but who are not within the working age range (16 to 59 years for men, 16 to 54 years for women), e.g., working pensioners.

Table 7.20

Employed Population (Percent of Working Age Population 1970 and 1979)

Region	1970	1979
RSFSR	88.8	88.6
Estonia	94.8	95.7
Latvia	94.6	94.5
Lithuania	91.2	89.0
Ukraine	88.8	88.2
Belorussia	90.2	86.6
Moldavia	94.2	88.7
Georgia	85.2	84.1
Armenia	81.5	81.1
Azerbaidzhan	84.7	79.6
Kazakhstan	84.7	79.6
Uzbekistan	85.1	81.9
Tadzhikistan	82.1	81.1
Kirghizia	84.8	79.6
Turkmenistan	84.5	81.7
USSR	88.3	87.1

Sources: *Itogi 1970*, vol. 2, table 3, and vol. 5, tables 4 and 10. *Vestnik statistiki* 1 (1981), p. 63. Baldwin, p. 128.

But as is evident from Table 7.20, the regional pattern is not notably changed even if the calculations are made in terms of the working age population. The Central Asian republics and Azerbaidzhan and Armenia still show the lowest employment. About 20% of the population of working age in Azerbaidzhan have no work, although this group includes the ill and the handicapped, students (receiving subsidies), women working in the home, and persons employed in private agriculture as well.

Thus regional variations in level of employment remain regardless of what method of calculation is used (in relation to the total population or to the working age population). Table 7.20 also shows a decline in the level of employment from 1970 to 1979 in all republics (except Estonia). This is perhaps accurate, at least for Central Asia. One possible source of error, however, is that the data on the working age population had to be taken from secondary analyses of the Soviet statistics since such data are not published in the official statistics. However, the figures used in the table come from Godfrey Baldwin's secondary source analyses,[41] which are of very high quality and have been used by quite a number of Western scholars.

Nevertheless, the political leadership is clearly concerned about the surplus labor problem and the growth of the population in Central Asia. At the 26th Party Congress Brezhnev spoke of the need for a demographic policy at the territorial level, and Soviet scientists have warned about possible problems in this area in the future.[42]

As mentioned, capital investments during the 11th five-year planning period cannot be expected to have a tangible equalizing effect among the republics. The low level of employment in Central Asia will remain unchanged, so that a rapid economic growth is not very likely to come from the existing labor force. Regional differences will thus remain.

In addition to the factors already mentioned—plan fulfillment in general, capital investment and employment—cultural factors are also operative. The Central Asian republics in the main lack industrial traditions. The traditional Moslem culture can hardly be said to facilitate industrial development of the European type, a view shared by Soviet experts as well.[43]

Cultural and National Factors

The problems of implementation in Soviet society have already been mentioned. Often, the sectoral all-union ministries in Moscow will act autonomously and moreover in a way that obstructs the implementation of economic policy. Changes at the territorial level are often hindered by sectoral barriers.

But there are also local and regional factors that obstruct the implementation of political decisions, in particular those associated with cultural and national traditions, and work at cross purposes to the course of development projected in the five-year plans.

Iulian Bromlei, the Soviet anthropologist and academician, has on several occasions made the point that the relative economic backwardness in some of the Soviet republics, especially Central Asia, had to do with the insufficient industrial tradition in these areas. Economic efficiency, claims Bromlei, can be improved by greater knowledge of national traditions and peculiarities, especially on the part of planners.[44]

Bromlei and Shkaratan point out that the structure of the Central Asian economy is ill-suited to the traditions of the population; for example it was hardly rational to build huge plants in areas where the population had traditionally been employed in crafts and small industry, and the economic results reflect this circumstance as well. Although capital investments in the 1960s were above the union average, growth in output and productivity was below that level.[45]

The result of this lack of congruence between the structure of the economy and national traditions has been that the indigenous nationalities of Central Asia are now underrepresented in industry. In Tadzhikistan, in 1979, 59% of the total population but only 48% of industrial workers were Tadzhiks (1977). In the technologically more advanced sectors, machinery construction and the metal industries, only 28% of the workers are Tadzhiks.[46]

Instead, Russians are the largest single ethnic group among industrial workers. Soviet leadership has criticized this situation, and Iurii Andropov stated in his speech on the 60th anniversary of the founding of the Soviet state that the position of the indigenous nationalities within the working class must be strengthened. Women are particularly underrepresented among the employed population[47] (cf. the section on employment).

But should the Russian segment of the population truly be so totally dominant among industrial workers that other nationalities play but a secondary and subordinate role? That would certainly give a new perspective on regional policy. But presumably other groups, e.g., the Balts, Belorussians, and Ukrainians, have also had much valuable experience with advanced industrial work. The most interesting question, however, is whether industrial development of backward areas relies mainly on migrated Russians, passing by the indigenous nationalities. The planning system would then be such that Russians and perhaps other nationalities from the western Soviet Union would be given the key role in industrial expansion.[48]

The issue therefore is the *relationship between nationality policy and regional development*. The evidence is that not only do Russians dominate among industrial workers, they also make up the majority of the population in the highly developed regions of the Soviet Union. The connection between national policy and regional policy may then be described as follows:

1. The regions with a majority Russian population have been favored by regional policy.

But there is a second possibility: according to the official Soviet view, policy has aimed at bringing the relatively backward regions up to the same level of development as the most advanced regions, which of course has meant that areas populated by non-Russian nationalities have received more support. An egalitarian policy such as this would mean that:

2. The regions populated by non-Russians have been favored by regional policy.

Finally, a third possibility would be that no national group is especially favored by development:

3. There is no special pattern discernible in the relationship between nationalities and regional policy as implemented.

What actually is the relationship between nationality policy and regional development? To assess this problem, aggregation at various levels may be employed. First the situation should be assessed on the basis of data for the entire union and the various regions within it. The data can then be disaggregated at lower levels to determine whether any particular nationalities or regions are favored by social and economic development. The size of investments allocated to a particular region is an important measure of the extent to which the leadership in a planned economy wishes to stimulate growth within a region, as was pointed out in the section on the instruments of regional policy. Investments will then reflect the disposition of political and economic policymakers to influence future growth rather than the actual absolute level of development.

Of course investment funds are used in different ways in different regions. Costs may also vary. But the total sum of capital investments does give some measure of the extent to which the leadership is disposed to invest in various regions over the long term. If equalization is genuinely sought, it is certainly sensible to allocate more investment capital to areas with a relatively low level of development.

The regional breakdown used in this study—the RSFSR, the Baltic republics, the rest of Europe (e.g., the Ukraine, Belorussia, and Moldavia), the Caucasus, and Central Asia—has the advantage that it corresponds to the pattern shown by regional differences in level of socioeconomic development. It should therefore be possible to ascertain whether capital investments continue to be allocated to the highly developed regions such as the RSFSR and the Baltic, or whether more investments are being channeled to Central Asia. Table 7.8 presents data on the distribution of investments, with the latter seen mainly as an

Table 7.21

Capital Investments in the Soviet Union 1960 and 1980, by Regions (Percent of Total Investments) at Comparable Prices

Region	1960	1980
RSFSR	63.5	62.4
Baltic	2.3	2.8
Rest of Europe	18.5	18.6
Caucasus	4.7	3.6
Kazakhstan	6.8	6.1
Central Asia	4.2	6.4
USSR	100.0	99.9

Sources: *Nar. khoz. SSSR 1960*, pp. 589–99, *Nar. khoz. SSSR 1980*, pp. 10 and 344.

instrument of regional policy. Table 7.21 provides a longer-term perspective in an endeavor to shed light on the relationship between regional policy and nationality policy.

This table and the others in this section compare the years 1960 and 1980. This time span allows long-term changes to be discerned. The period also includes the census years 1959 and 1979, which means that data were more readily accessible for lower aggregation levels, and were perhaps more reliable as well. Some of the tables, however, have had to use other years because no data for 1960 and 1980 were available.

Table 7.21 shows that over 80% of investments were allocated to the RSFSR and the European regions in both 1960 and 1980. The Central Asian share in total investments increased somewhat, but changes were minor for the other regions. All in all, the figures reveal a rather stable regional investment pattern, so that it is hardly surprising that regional differences in level of socioeconomic development should also have changed negligibly over time.

But in addition to distribution, investments can also be compared relative to the size of the population in a particular area; Table 7.22 shows that changes in capital investments have not kept pace with population growth.

The population of Central Asia has increased quite rapidly, almost doubling in twenty years. Growth was rapid in the Caucasus and Kazakhstan as well, but somewhat slower in the rest of the Soviet Union. The Central Asian republics today account for almost 10% of the total

Table 7.22

Population of the Soviet Union 1959 and 1979 (in Thousands and Percent of Total Population)

Region	Population		Percent	
	1959	1979	1959	1979
RSFSR	117,534	137,551	56.3	52.4
Baltic	6,001	7,385	2.9	2.8
Rest of Europe	52,810	63,262	25.3	24.1
Caucasus	9,505	14,074	4.6	5.4
Kazakhstan	9,295	14,684	4.5	5.6
Central Asia	13,682	25,480	6.6	9.7
USSR	208,827	262,436	100.2	100.0

Source: Nar. khoz. 1980, p. 10.

population. Every fifth Soviet citizen is now from the Caucasus, Kazakhstan, or Central Asia.

If the regional distribution of capital investment is compared with the regional distribution of the population, it will be found that the RSFSR and Kazakhstan have received a more than commensurate share of total investments. The RSFSR's share in total investments is 11% greater than its share of the total population, which would seem to indicate that relatively speaking the RSFSR has been favored by investment policy. Investments and population can also be compared on a per capita basis, as in Table 7.23.

In terms of these data the RSFSR and Kazakhstan were the most favored republics in both 1959–60 and 1979–80. The Central Asian republics show consistently lower figures. It may also be argued that the RSFSR is favored in another way in the Soviet Union, e.g., within the Communist Party.[49] In any event, the figures certainly give no evidence that there is any "closing of the gap" between the republics, as is often claimed in the Soviet press.[50]

If it can be shown that the RSFSR receives a higher proportion of investments than its proportion of the population would merit, then the question whether areas inhabited by Russians are favored by effective policy can in part be answered. The population of the RSFSR is over 80% Russian. But the picture is more complicated. There are Russians in other republics as well, as Table 7.24 shows.

The proportion of Russians is also high in Kazakhstan, Estonia, and

Table 7.23

Capital Investments per Capita 1959–60 and 1979–80 (Rubles per Capita)

Region	1959–60	1979–80
RSFSR	169	558
Baltic	121	422
Rest of Europe	109	334
Caucasus	153	327
Kazakhstan	229	532
Central Asia	95	305
USSR	149	462

Sources: Same as for Tables 7.15 and 7.16.
Note: "Rest of Europe" refers to the Ukraine, Belorussia, and Moldavia.

Table 7.24

Native (Indigenous) Population and Russians in the Fifteen Republics

Republic	Native population		Russian population	
	1959	1979	1959	1979
RSFSR	83.3	82.6	83.3	82.6
Estonia	74.6	64.7	20.1	27.9
Latvia	62.0	53.7	26.6	32.8
Lithuania	79.3	80.0	8.5	8.9
Ukraine	76.8	73.6	16.9	21.1
Belorussia	81.1	79.4	8.2	11.9
Moldavia	65.4	63.9	10.2	12.8
Georgia	64.3	68.8	10.1	7.4
Armenia	88.0	89.7	3.2	2.3
Azerbaidzhan	67.5	78.1	13.6	7.9
Kazakhstan	30.0	36.0	42.7	40.8
Uzbekistan	62.2	68.7	13.5	10.8
Kirghizia	40.5	47.9	30.2	25.9
Tadzhikistan	53.1	58.8	13.3	10.4
Turkmenistan	60.9	68.4	17.3	12.6

Sources: *Nar. khoz. SSSR 1960*, pp. 17ff., *Vestnik statistiki* 2 (1980), pp. 24ff.

Table 7.25

Capital Investments and Distribution of Population among Russian Regions and ASSRs within the RSFSR (Percent of Total Investments in 1975 and Total Population in 1975)

Regions	Investments	Population
Russian region	84.9	85.5
ASSRs	15.1	14.5
Total	100.0	100.0

Source: Nar. khoz. RSFSR 1975, pp. 6f. and 328f.

Latvia. As was just seen, the RSFSR and Kazakhstan have a privileged status with regard to capital investments. Estonia and Latvia are privileged in another way: they have the highest living standards in the USSR.[51]

A tentative conclusion would then be that areas with a large Russian population are favored by economic policy, certainly an important aspect of the russification of Soviet society.[52]

But these findings are based on data at a high aggregation level, and the situation may be different at lower levels. The fact that the RSFSR comprises vast sparsely populated areas such as Siberia, which, however, absorb large investment sums, should also be taken into consideration. It might therefore be useful to continue the investigation at a level below the union level, with special focus on the RSFSR.

The Russian republic is of major interest in view of the large sums that have been invested there both in absolute terms and relative to other areas. Furthermore, the RSFSR contains some areas where the Russian population is totally dominant and others where national minorities live.

The main question then will be to determine whether Russian-dominated areas are favored by economic policy. The RSFSR may be divided up into Russian oblasts (or equivalents) and ASSRs and the distribution of investments compared to the size of the population. National areas at the autonomous oblast level and below will be disregarded since the Russian population is usually totally dominant in them. Table 7.25 shows the comparative figures for Russian areas and ASSRs.

The pattern within the RSFSR differs from that observed at the union level. There is no notable difference between the distribution of

Table 7.26

Capital Investments in the RSFSR (Percent of Total Investments during 8th Five-year Plan 1966–70 and during 1975)

Regions	Investments 8th Five-year Plan	Investments 1975
European Russia	74.2	72.7
Siberia and the Far East	25.8	27.3
Total	100.0	100.0

Source: Nar. khoz. RSFSR 1975, pp. 6f. and 328f.

investments among Russian and national areas and the distribution of the population. The Russian population can therefore not be said to be privileged in this respect.

This finding differs from those of other scholars. Clem has demonstrated a significant difference between Russian and non-Russian areas in the RSFSR with regard to economic growth. The reason for the discrepancy is not clear, but a part of the explanation is doubtless to be sought in the fact that Clem used other indicators than investments, i.e., indicators based mainly on data concerning the degree of urbanization.[53]

Moreover, a comparison among Soviet republics based on per capita data may also be influenced by the circumstance that within the RSFSR considerable investments are made in areas where the population density is extremely low. It might be interesting, therefore, to determine whether investments in Siberia and the Far East are higher. Thus if figures for western Siberia, eastern Siberia, and the Far East economic regions are added together and compared with figures for the rest of the RSFSR, the results obtained are those in Table 7.26.

The share of investments in Siberia and the Far East may indeed be seen to have increased. However, the reference years that had to be chosen because of the lack of comparable data are too close together to permit any definitive conclusions.

Another circumstance, of especial importance with regard to investments in Siberia, is that it is by no means always certain whether investments within a region are of any direct benefit to the population in that region. Thus there are huge investments made in produce energy, oil, gas, and water power in Siberia, but a good deal of what is produced is consumed in European Russia. This must also be taken into account in evaluating the situation of nationalities.

The analysis of the capital investment pattern yielded no unambiguous results in respect to the nationality aspects of the RSFSR. But the pattern might be clearer at a lower regional level, in the Asian parts of the RSFSR, where considerable industrial expansion is taking place.

The Asian RSFSR consists of three economic regions: western Siberia, eastern Siberia, and the Far East, and considerable economic investments are being made in all, e.g., oil and gas production in western Siberia, the Bratsk-Ilimsk territorial production complex, and the Baikal-Amur railway. Development of Siberia and the Far East often takes the form of territorial production complexes (TPCs) in which energy is produced and raw materials extracted side by side, and the latter are to some extent processed as well. These TPCs are dispersed throughout the eastern regions, with the territories between them totally untouched.

The per capita distribution of capital investments by oblast or equivalent in Siberia and the Far East is shown in Table 7.27. The differences are considerable. The high figures for the Tiumen' region (in both absolute and relative terms) are due to the vast investments being made in oil and gas production. Other regions have also been the scene of major industrial expansion.

It is difficult to interpret the national component even at this level. There are three autonomous republics, Buriatia, Tuva, and Iakutia, in the Asian RSFSR, and two of these, Buriatia and Tuva, show relatively low indices, much lower than for the other regions in Siberia and the Far East, and lower than for the entire RSFSR. The third autonomous republic, Iakutia, shows a very high figure for per capita investment.

At the union level a correlation was found between the geographic location of the Russian population and the allocation of capital investments, while there was no such correlation discernible at the republic and regional levels. Does this mean that it simply does not exist at lower levels and that the correlation found at the union level is the result of a statistical misinterpretation, such as the ecological fallacy?

One possibility is that the correlation at the union level is totally coincidental and a product of the fact that the data were aggregated at a too high level; however, this is not likely considering that other investigators have also found a correlation between the nationality situation and economic development in the RSFSR.[54] It is most likely the case

Table 7.27

Capital Investments in Asian RSFSR (Rubles per Capita 1975)

Region	Investments per capita
Western Siberia	
Altai krai	416
Kemerovska oblast	446
Novosibirsk oblast	1,825
Omsk oblast	497
Tomsk oblast	647
Tiumen' oblast	1,994
Eastern Siberia	
Krasnoiarsk krai	494
Irkutsk oblast	794
Chita oblast	398
Buriat ASSR	508
Tuvin ASSR	466
Far East	
Primorsk krai	672
Khabarovsk krai	647
Amur oblast	905
Kamchatka oblast	838
Magadan oblast	1,346
Sakhalin oblast	896
Iakut ASSR	1,126
Total, Asian RSFSR	719

Source: *Nar. khoz. RSFSR 1975*, pp. 6f. and 328f.

that the correlation is too complex to be discerned with the relatively crude methods used. It might be useful, therefore, to attempt an analysis of the data at an even lower level.

Of the three autonomous republics in the Asian RSFSR economic development is most advanced in Iakutia. This republic shows high figures for capital investments in both the 1960s and 1970s (Table 7.28)

Development in Iakutia has been very rapid. In some respects the figures appear even too high considering Iakutia's large area and low population density (0.3 per square kilometer). The bulk of investments in Iakutsk has gone to the Southern Iakutsk TPC, which is the only TPC in the Far East, and is based on high-grade anthracite and mineral deposits, especially iron ore. Some of the capital investments in this

Table 7.28

Capital Investments in Autonomous Republics in the Asian RSFSR (Rubles per Capita 1965 and 1975)

Region	1965	1975
Buriatia	163	508
Tuva	206	466
Iakutia	757	1,126

Source: Same as for Table 7.27.

Table 7.29

Population Composition in the Autonomous Republics in the Asian RSFSR (Percent of Total Population 1959 and 1979)

Region	Native population		Russian population	
	1959	1979	1959	1979
Buriatia	20.2	23.0	74.6	72.0
Tuva	57.0	60.4	40.1	36.2
Iakutia	46.4	36.9	44.2	50.4

Sources: *Itogi vsesoiuznoi perepsisi naseleniia 1970 g.*, vol. IV, pp. 16ff., *Vestnik statistiki* 7 (1980), pp. 45ff.

TPC, especially machinery and equipment, came from Japanese firms. The construction of the Baikal-Amur railway, which passes just south of Iakutia, is of course of a major potential source of economic development for Iakutia. Urbanization, another indicator of growth in Iakutia, rose from 55% to 63% in 1979.[55]

Changes in the composition of the population of the three autonomous republics are shown in Table 7.29.

This indicator underwent a considerable change in Iakutia in the twenty-year period from 1959 to 1979: in effect, the Iakuts no longer comprise the largest single population group in the republic, having been surpassed by Russians, whose number had swelled to 50% of the population as of 1979. Changes in the other two republics have been less spectacular.

The Iakuts, who like most of the Central Asian peoples speak a Turkic language, have traditionally been herdsmen. Despite a relatively high level of formal education, they do not have a tradition of industrial work worthy of note.

Thus the rapid economic expansion in Iakutia has not been based on the Iakut population but has depended on a large influx of Russians and, to a lesser extent, other peoples of European origin. The increase in the Russian population in Iakutia, about 100% in twenty years compared with a 20% increase in the total Russian population of the Soviet Union during the same period, is not the result of natural population growth but of immigration, which has been considerable—mostly to cities and other industrial centers.

The correlation between *nationality policy* and *regional policy* is doubtless to be found at this level. Rapid economic development in a region is shouldered by Russians (who usually have better training and experience of industrial work) moving to that region.

If the practice illustrated here in a case study on Iakutia is generally valid for the entire Soviet Union, Russians will over the long term tend to concentrate in regions where a rapid industrial growth has taken place. In most cases this will also lead to a high living standard in those areas.

Thus the study of the relationship between nationality policy and regional policy, and more specifically the relation of the Russian population to non-Russian population groups, has yielded three possible hypotheses:

1. The Russian population is favored by the allocation of new investments to regions where they live;

2. Regions populated by non-Russians are allocated a proportionately higher share of new investments in accordance with the official doctrine of *sblizhenie*;

3. There is no significant difference between the Russian and non-Russian populations in this respect.

This case-study was conducted on four levels: union, republic, regional, and local. At the union level a correlation was found between the status of nationalities and capital investments, the key variable for measuring economic inputs, such that regions in which the Russian population was dominant, especially the RSFSR, received a proportionally larger share of investments.

A similar correlation could not be found at either the republic (RSFSR) or the regional level (Siberia and the Far East): there were no clearly discernible differences between Russian and non-Russian areas.

At the local level, i.e., ASSRs in Siberia and the Far East, some interesting nuances were found. Iakutia has undergone a rapid economic growth through the establishment of the Southern Iakutsk TPC, as a consequence of which a large number of Russians moved into the republic, and were hence responsible for a good share of the expansion and drew the corresponding benefits therefrom.

Thus it seems that a clear picture first emerges when analysis is undertaken *within* non-Russian regions. The next logical question is whether the same pattern is discernible in other regions and periods. In the Baltic republics, industry was rapidly restored during the 1940s and 1950s, at the same time as a massive influx of Russians occurred, particularly to Estonia and Latvia. Kazakhstan was the target of major economic inputs during the 1950s and 1960s, and in this republic Russians now are the largest single population group. The same process seems to have begun in Siberia in the 1970s and is now continuing into the 1980s.

Thus the evidence is not that Russian areas are especially favored by economic development but that Russians migrate to economically favored regions, where they gradually become the dominant population. (Of course such large movements of people cannot take place against the will of the ruling Communist Party.) There seems therefore to be a correlation between capital investments and Russian immigration, and perhaps also between these two phenomena and a growing Communist Party membership.

This result concurs with the findings made by other scholars, on the basis of other material, in similar areas. In the major study *Nationality and Population Change in Russia and the USSR* it is stated that "Available data indicate that in most cases the native nationalities have not received their proportional share of the benefits of industrialization."[56]

The results do not accord well with the claim, put forth in connection with the proclamation of the 60th anniversary of the Soviet Union's formation, that differences between nationalities and regions have in the main disappeared. It would seem more warranted to say that the Russian population plays an especially important role in Soviet society.

This, indeed, also comes out in Soviet views. In *Istoriia SSR* M. N. Rosenko says on the occasion of the 60th anniversary that the Russian national population has played a special role in developing and strengthening the unity of the Soviet people. The Russian federation plays a "leading role" in the economy of the Soviet Union, and the

Russian language has in reality become a national language because it is now the exclusive language of communication among the different nationalities. Rosenko goes on to say that the Russian people have had a hand in building the material and technological foundations for continued economic growth within the different regions of the Soviet Union.[57]

Indeed, if one looks beyond the official phraseology, Rosenko's assertions, which are not at all unique in the Soviet Union, are quite in line with the findings presented in the preceding section. The Russian people definitely play a major role in present-day Soviet society, especially with regard to economic development. The sheer size of the Russian population, its relatively good education, and its high degree of geographical mobility have been put to use in areas where a labor shortage has arisen as a consequence of rapid economic expansion, and this has of course had consequences for the national population within these areas.

The national factors examined in the foregoing, namely the lack of an industrial tradition in Central Asia and Russian dominance in areas undergoing rapid industrial growth, are certainly interrelated. As long as occupational training is inadequate in Central Asia and the population is relatively immobile and migration to the cities low-key, the same pattern may be said to continue. It is therefore uncertain what the outcome of experiments with small industries in Central Asia will be.

A Reanalysis of Location Criteria

The location criteria for Soviet industry reflect important aspects of the goals of Soviet regional policy. In Chapter 3 three principal sets of location criteria were distinguished; namely, economic, which were focused on economic growth and effectiveness; social, focused on equalization; and political, which gave priority to the exigencies of military strategy in locating Soviet industry.

The present study has been concerned mainly with the social criteria, i.e., the goal of equality, for several reasons. Regional equalization has been an oft-stated intention of Soviet leadership since the 1920s, and more lately still it has been applied not only to the Soviet Union, but to the entire CMEA where, according to doctrine, regional equality will some day be a fact.[58]

Moreover the ideal of regional equality is in harmony with socialism's ideology of equality in general. Accordingly it would be interesting to examine how this principle is applied in a country that is said to be socialist. If regional equality can be achieved in the Soviet Union, this certainly represents a significant difference from Western countries.

But the findings indicate the opposite, namely, that the social location criterion has in fact had a limited influence. The differences amongst Siberia, Central Asia, and the European USSR discussed in the introduction of this book seem to have persisted over time for various reasons, which we have tried to explain.

The results of Soviet regional policy will be more easily discernible from a closer examination of the Central Asian and Siberian macroregions. If it is clear that the Central Asian republics have a long way to go to catch up with the other republics in socioeconomic development, then it is relevant to ask what kind of relations exist between the center in Moscow and the Central Asian republics at the periphery. Can Central Asia be considered a colony, an *internal colony* of the Soviet Union?

One ground for such an assertion is the circumstance that raw materials, e.g., oil and cotton, are transported from these regions, which have relatively fewer industries, to the European USSR for processing.[59]

Another ground for regarding Central Asia as a Soviet colony is that the most important economic decisions concerning it are made elsewhere, in Moscow. Because of the centralized planning system, extremely few important decisions are made at lower levels. In addition, as the examination of the regional policy debate and the discussions at the Party Congress in 1981 shows, it is by no means always the case that local authorities are able to gain audience for their opinions and suggestions for change within their regions.

But regional differences in living standard are less than differences in industrial output, and some Soviet experts even say that wages are very high in some parts of the countryside in Central Asia and that the population is unwilling to migrate for that reason.[60]

But subsidies from the central level probably lie behind the relatively high standard of living in Central Asia; some figures on these subsidies have even been published in the official statistics (see the section on regional policy instruments). Finally, the underground economy in Central Asia probably helps to boost the living standard of some groups of people.

A relationship of this sort clearly differs from those that existed between the former empires and their colonies. The subsidies provide the Central Asian republics with a minimally acceptable standard in social services, health care, and housing, and in this respect these regions certainly compare well with the neighboring nations to the south.[61]

The present findings therefore agree with the conclusions of Martin Spechler, who studied development up to 1978 and found that some transfers to Central Asia have the purpose of guaranteeing these republics a somewhat higher standard than their level of industrial and economic development would actually warrant. The relation between the center and periphery in Central Asia might therefore be called a welfare colonialism.[62]

Spechler's conclusions also find agreement among Soviet experts. The geographer Khorev, quoted earlier, investigated the relationship between economic development measured in terms of per capita national income and in terms of living standard, defined with quantitative indicators, and found much greater differences among the republics in the former respect than in the latter. Thus the national income per capita in Kirghizia in 1979 was 60% of the union average, while the living standard was at almost the same level as for the union as a whole.[63]

The relation between the European USSR and Siberia coincides in several respects with the relationship existing between Europe and Central Asia. Considerable energy is produced in Siberia that is then used to cover needs at the union level. But a large portion of the energy sources is processed in Siberia, providing permanent employment. The Soviet Union's leaders have also invested much more capital in Siberia than in Central Asia.

Nevertheless it is valid to ask whether the population in Siberia has benefited from economic growth. The finding was that industrial expansion has been borne primarily by the Russian population. The huge investments in Siberia are almost exclusively for industrial plants, and investments in the social infrastructure are largely deficient. Complaints of problems with housing, day nurseries, etc., in Siberia are frequent.[64]

An article by Tatiana Zaslavskaia on the problems of social development in Siberia may serve as an example of such complaints from persons in high positions living in Siberia. Zaslavskaia discusses shortages and deficiencies in housing, services, cultural institutions etc. Incomes, especially in the countryside, are very low. According to

Zaslavskaia Siberia should have a much higher living standard than other regions to compensate for its inhospitable climate, and proposes a special program for social development in Siberia up to the year 2000 as part of the existing long-term economic program "Sibir."[65]

Thus, despite the vast investments made in Siberia, the standard of living is conspicuously low, and although major effort is being made to improve the situation, it will probably take some time for them to have a discernible effect.

Military considerations always are of major importance in Soviet planning. Enterprises and industrial centers are located with an eye to maximal defensibility. The construction of the Baikal-Amur railway north of the earlier trans-Siberian railroad may have been militarily motivated: the protective zone separating it from China will be much wider and easier to defend. On the whole, however, it is difficult to demonstrate directly the role of the military factor in regional planning, although it is surely not insignificant.[66]

It thus seems that the social location criterion, i.e., that of promoting regional equality, is only a long-term goal for the Soviet leadership and in competition with other important objectives even then. To be sure, the plan targets of the 11th Five-year Plan do make some concessions to regional equalization, but over the short term, other criteria, i.e., economic efficiency and military security, seem to be wholly dominant. One reason for this may be the bottlenecks and other problems that are constantly cropping up in the Soviet economy. The ad hoc investments that then must be made certainly lack the regional equalizing dimension.

The picture in general, however, seems to be that the less developed republics are assured a minimal level of industrial growth and a minimal living standard that must be maintained, and that is guaranteed by budget transfers and other mechanisms. If regional differences become too great, grave internal problems may arise in the poorer republics that could even go so far as to complicate the Soviet Union's foreign relations, especially in Asia, as well.

The conclusion is that the extent of regional differences is influenced but slightly by regional policy measures, which on the contrary tend to entrench regional differences more deeply, i.e., to maintain the existing balance, or perhaps rather imbalance, among the different regions.

8. REVIEW AND SUMMARY

This book has been an attempt to explore the following four topics of Soviet regional policy:

1. *The occurrence of regional differences in the Soviet Union.* Both Western and Soviet experts concur in their findings that considerable differences in level of socioeconomic development continue to exist among the republics during the 1970s and into the 1980s, and moreover are further borne out in official Soviet data. Differences in living standard seem to be somewhat less than differences in other spheres, e.g., production, investments, and employment.

2. *The content of political decisions on the distribution of resources.* The official Soviet view is that one of the major aims of regional policy has been to eliminate the remaining regional differences. This objective is said to have in the main been achieved during the 1970s, so that policy henceforth will be directed to maintaining regional balance. But analysis has shown that inequalities still exist. To be sure, considerable resources are allocated to areas lagging in economic development, but not in sufficient magnitude to enable the poorer regions to move abreast of the developed regions within the foreseeable future.

3. *The political decisionmaking process in regional policy.* The different regions are engaged in a continuous tug of war for funds for investments, etc. On certain occasions regional blocs are formed by politicians, scientists, etc., to promote development within a particular region. The regional blocs studied in this book were concerned with Siberia, Central Asia, and the European USSR.

4. *Implementation of decisions in regional policy.* It was found that regional policy decisions are implemented in a way that is detrimental to the poorer regions. Like other areas of policy, differences between

the announced objectives and the results of regional policy are considerable, so that in practice regional differences may even grow.

Thus there are regional differences in the level of socioeconomic development in the Soviet Union. These differences have persisted over time, and moreover showed no tendency to diminish when the Soviet economy entered a more advanced stage of development in the '70s and '80s. This would seem then to support Williamson's theory of regional development as being also applicable to the Soviet situation, at least judging from the available material.

One partial explanation of why the regional differential does not change over time rests with the complex administrative structures. This cumbersome and in some cases ill-defined organization generates a kind of inertia such that the effects of various reforms are not always those that had been desired. In addition, there are also contradictions between territorial and sectoral planning, and problems with sectoral barriers are regularly reported in the Soviet press.

A good portion of available resources for new investments is allocated to Siberia, the development of which is essential for its energy reserves, production, and probably for military reasons as well. Economic and political criteria for locating industry have priority over social criteria. The way investments are distributed in the Soviet Union supports Myrdal's thesis that economic activity spreads from the growth centers (Europe) to other priority areas (Siberia) which then has a backwash effect on other regions (Central Asia).

The growth in the labor force tends to reinforce the tendencies set into motion by investment policy. The employment rate in the Central Asian republics is much lower than in the other republics, especially among women and segments of the rural population. There is good evidence that underemployment exists in large parts of Central Asia; it is obviously difficult for a republic with a low level of employment to maintain an economic growth rate on a par with the growth in a republic with a high proportion of its population employed.

But the negative tendencies in Central Asia seem to a large degree to be offset by budgetary transfers to these republics. Differences in living standard among the republics are somewhat smaller than differences in other indicators, suggesting that Spechler's notion of welfare colonialism is a fair description of the relationship between the center and the periphery in the Soviet Union.

The social location criteria, i.e., measures aimed at regional equalization, are mainly of long-term importance in the Soviet Union, although, if the original targets of the five-year plans were fully achieved, a certain equalizing effect would be obtained. The other location criteria, i.e., economic and political, also have a long-term importance, but in the short term economic criteria probably dominate, since a large number of concrete economic problems must be dealt with promptly within the Soviet planning system and the regional dimension necessarily suffers some neglect.

The role of administrative levels lower down the hierarchy in the policymaking process was also examined, and two ways, in particular, were found where these levels are important:

1. In some issues policy takes shape as a result of an interplay between the central and regional levels, in which regional spokesmen articulate their interests at Party Congresses, in the press, etc.; however, since the factors determining central decisionmaking are not fully known, the most that can be demonstrated is a *correlation* between the articulation of interests and decisionmaking, but no *causal* relationship.

2. The lower administrative levels have a considerable influence on the implementation of political decisions: if implementation is delayed, the effects originally intended do not occur.

A test of the hypotheses presented in the second chapter clearly showed that it is important to take into account the lower administrative levels in the political decisionmaking process. Clear regional *policy alternatives* have indeed been formulated by the Siberian and Central Asian blocs, presenting diverse strategies for development for the Soviet regions.

The *Siberians* call for a greater differentiation of the Siberian economy. Siberia is already a highly favored region in the 11th Five-year Plan, but the alternative of the Siberians calls for even further expansion of the Siberian economy, development of several sectors, and more processing of raw materials in Siberia itself. In the situation as reflected in the 11th Five-year Plan, Siberia is effectively a major supplier of energy and raw materials to other parts of the USSR.

The *Central Asian* policy alternative calls for a rapid development of industry and agriculture in the southern republics. A major factor rendering such action necessary is the rapid population growth. Greater focus on smaller labor-intensive production units is proposed for industry.

The agricultural problem would also be solved by diverting waters from the Siberian rivers, but this proposal had little resonance in the Five-year Plan. On the other hand, the central planning authorities seem to have a somewhat more sympathetic ear for the need to renovate industry in Central Asia.

A *European* policy alternative, also discernible, calls for updating and expanding existing industry in the European USSR, with greater utilization made of raw materials from the western republics. The representatives of this view also feel that fewer resources should be allocated to the eastern regions.

It would appear, then, that Soviet regional policy is shaped in the first instance by central decisions made in the highest Party and state bodies, but before these decisions are made, policy alternatives are presented by various groups within the Soviet society. It is in this way, then, that outsiders come to have a say in central decisionmaking.

Four hypotheses on the relations between the central decisionmaking bodies and the periphery were formulated in the chapter on theoretical premises. The third and fourth hypotheses were found to best describe the current situation. Before definitive decisions are made on regional issues of major importance, various policy alternatives are formulated by representatives of various blocs. The fourth hypothesis contains a number of general statements on political phenomena, which it was impossible to investigate here. The *third hypothesis*, therefore, seems to best describe the situation in the Soviet Union, at least on the basis of the available data. Further, it is worth specifying that policy alternatives are not in the first instance formulated centrally, and in fact those that were studied specifically came from the regional level.

However, the influence of regional spokesmen may assume different forms in other policy areas. Regional policy is certainly an area of prime importance for the various republics and it is a reasonable presumption that republic leaders should show active concern in its regard. Studies of other areas of policy will presumably shed further light on the relationship between the union and the regional administrative levels.

But the importance of policy alternatives for later decisions should not be exaggerated; the Central Asian bloc failed to get an audience for its proposals on Soviet regional policy for the 1980s. Nevertheless, it is quite probable that specialists and bureaucrats have, with certain limitations, the possibility of influencing decisionmaking.

On the basis of regional policy data, policymaking in the Soviet Union can be described with a simple flow model, as follows (Figure 8.1).

Figure 8.1 Policymaking Stages in the Soviet Union

The inputs of the political process are goals (e.g., location criteria in regional policy) and priorities. The various demands for policy changes put forth by regional blocs may be included among inputs. Decisionmaking takes place in the political bodies at Party Congresses and Central Committee meetings. Outputs, e.g., the plan targets for the five-year plans, may be compared with outcomes, e.g., the actual results. As indicated earlier, the implementation phase, between output and outcome, is an important stage in the Soviet political process.

The explanatory value of the model in Figure 8.1 can of course be debated, but it is important at least to distinguish these different stages in the Soviet context. The implementation of political decisions in the Soviet Union is subject to various influences, which together often distort the content of the original decision.

The two factors complicating implementation upon which greatest emphasis was laid in the present study are the resistance of the large ministries to change and inadequate response at the local and regional levels. In the latter case, national and cultural factors play a by no means unimportant role.

Perhaps the most important factor of these two is the inertia that seems to inherently plague the Soviet bureaucracy. During the Brezhnev period an attempt was made to alter the relations between sector A and sector B in industry to the latter's advantage, but an analysis of plan fulfillment during all the various five-year plans shows that the actual outcome was a much smaller relative reduction of sector A than had been planned.[1]

The evolution of relations between sector A and sector B can be compared with regional policy. The discrepancy between political decisions and actual results is great in regional policy, and the unwillingness or inability to bring about changes on the part of officials in the large industrial ministries is probably the most important factor responsible for this discrepancy.

There is a general awareness of these problems, even in the Soviet

Union. The Soviet expert on constitutional law, B. P. Kurashvili, in an article entitled "The Objective Laws of State Control" written in October 1983, said that a thorough administrative reform was necessary in the Soviet Union and called attention to the inertia and resistance to change built into the state administrative structures.

> A democratization of the state administration reduces the number of tasks the administrative apparatus must handle but complicates the resolution of those tasks that remain. These require more sophisticated and refined administrative methods which administrative officials, trained under other circumstances, do not have. Nor are we speaking merely of the purely bureaucratic elements of administration for which a democratic reform would be like a sharp sword. . . . The struggle against inertia and bureaucratism must continue unremittingly within the state administration.[2]

But the "democratic" reform of the Soviet administration which Kurashvili is calling for seems to be a long way off. The bureaucracy's position is still unshaken, nor is there a lack of defenders of the existing administrative system. At about the same time as Kurashvili's article appeared, the Party's theoretical periodical *Kommunist* published an article by the editor-in-chief of *Planovoe Khoziaistvo*, P. Ignatovskii, with the revealing title "A Political View of the Economy."

In Ignatovskii's view, the central political bodies should continue to have the dominant influence on the economy. "Deviations" in economic life such as *vedomstvennost'* and *mestnichestvo* are seen by Ignatovskii as signs of deficient political control. The supremacy of this policy of course allows small possibilities for the regional and local administrative levels to influence central decisions. The margin for economic reforms is also extremely limited, according to Ignatovskii.[3]

Both Kurashvili and Ignatovskii deal with the central bureaucracy in their articles, but from different perspectives. Both point out the need for an analysis of the role of the bureaucracy in reforming Soviet society. As on earlier occasions, there seem to exist diverse views on the need for an economic reform.

An economic reform is of course of utmost importance for future regional policy. A much more thorough change in the existing planning and management system is necessary if regional policy is to change more substantially. Only after such a reform will the Siberian and Central Asian blocs be able to gain an audience for their demands for further development of their own regions.

EPILOGUE

The first half of the 1980s was marked by rapid shifts in the Soviet central leadership. Andropov's short reign was followed by Chernenko's equally brief period in power. The regional policy that had developed under Brezhnev was, in the main, continued during the Andropov and Chernenko periods.

Among the regionally based development projects the completion of the Baikal-Amur railway (BAM) is especially noteworthy. In October 1984, construction was finished after twelve years of work. However, it will take several years for the railroad to become fully operational and for new TPCs to be built in the BAM area.

Another giant development project remained in the planning stage. After several years of discussing the possible diversion of the Siberian rivers, the "project of the century" was raised at the Central Committee meeting in October 1984. The Chairman of the USSR Council of Ministers at that time, Nikolai Tikhonov, stated that in "the near future the preparatory work for the diversion of a part of the water from the Siberian rivers to Central Asia and Kazakhstan will be finished." This new so-called Sib-Aral Canal was, however, not mentioned in the 12th Five-year Plan. It seems, therefore, that this project has been postponed for an indefinite time.

According to the plan results 1984 was a relatively successful year in the Soviet economy. The national income showed a modest growth, although problems were reported in the energy sector, especially in oil and hard coal production.

The "large-scale economic experiment in industry," which was decided upon under Andropov and begun in January 1984, was continued in 1985. The main principle of the experiment is said to be "greater independence—greater responsibility" for the enterprises. The overall results appear to have been satisfactory. However, ministries and state committees have continued to act as before, which has had an adverse effect on the initiative of the enterprises.

The scope of the experiment was widened in January 1985, as 21 industrial ministries were transferred to the new system. In 1985, some 12% of industrial production originated from enterprises in the experiment. As of 1986, it appears that Soviet industry has been transferred to a modified experimental system, as have other sectors, such as the service sector in some of the republics.

During Gorbachev's period as Soviet leader further changes in the system of planning and management can be expected. These changes will, however, probably have a small impact on the regional policy. It seems clear that Gorbachev will continue to emphasize the development of Siberia and the Far East as well as the modernization of the western parts of the USSR. There are no indications that extra resources will be channeled to Soviet Central Asia to solve the severe problems in this region. This means that the regional imbalances will not decrease as a result of the new policy. Hence, the Soviet regional dilemma will continue to exist in the foreseeable future.

NOTES

1. The Problem of Regional Development

1. Seweryn Bialer, *Stalin's Successors*, p. 291.
2. Ibid., p. 304.
3. J. G. Williamson, "Regional Inequality and the Process of National Development," pp. 3ff.
4. Gunnar Myrdal, *Economic Theory and Underdeveloped Regions*, p. 26.
5. Ibid., pp. 27 and 31.
6. Albert O. Hirschman, *The Strategy of Economic Development*, p. 183.
7. Hugh Clout, ed., *Regional Development in Western Europe*, p. 10. Dudley Seers, ed., *Underdeveloped Europe: Studies in Core-Periphery Relations*, p. xix.
8. The term macroregion is used by N. N. Nekrasov in *Regional'naia ekonomika*, p. 22. The Caucasus could be considered a fourth macroregion. However, Georgia and Armenia feature a development in many respects similar to that in the western European parts of the Soviet Union. Azerbaidzhan shows similarities with Central Asia in a number of indicators. These problems are dealt with later on in the chapter on regional differences.
9. V. P. Mozhin, "Ratsional'noe razmeshchenie proizvoditel'nykh sil i sovershenstvovanie territorial'nykh proportsii," p. 4.
10. Cf. Hélène Carrère d'Encausse, "Determinants and Parameters of Soviet Nationality Policy."
11. Stephan M. Horek, ed., *Guide to the Study of the Soviet Nationalities*, p. 15.
12. Bengt Lorendahl, *Nordisk regionalekonomi*, pp. 14f.
13. Ibid., p. 17.
14. Ibid., p. 201.
15. Ibid.
16. Pär-Erik Back, "Regionalpolitik och beslutsnivå," p. 1.
17. Sven Godlund, *Regional politik i plan och verklighet*, p. 183.
18. Elisabeth Lauschmann, *Grundlagen einer Theorie der Regionalpolitik*, p. 1.
19. Ibid.
20. Ibid.
21. V. S. Khorev, *Territorial'naia organizatsiia obshchestva*, pp. 11ff.
22. Ibid., p. 12.
23. Ibid., p. 11.
24. Niles Hansen, ed., *Public Policy and Regional Economic Development*, pp. 1 and 17. See also Godlund, p. 180.
25. Lauschmann, p. 257.
26. Ibid., p. 259. The terms originate from M. Byé.

27. Nekrasov, pp. 24f.
28. Lauschmann, p. 288.
29. Hansen, pp. 24ff.
30. Lauschmann, pp. 330ff.
31. See Chapter 7, ''Implementation and Results.''
32. See Karl Deutsch, ''Social Mobilization and Political Development.''
33. John Blunden et al., *Regional Analysis and Development*.
34. Walter Isard, *Introduction to Regional Science*, p. 373.
35. Ibid., p. 432.
36. A. I. Vedishchev, ''Soizmerenie urovnei khoziaistvennogo rasvitiia ekonomicheskikh raionov SSSR,'' pp. 54f.
37. V. F. Maier, *Uroven' zhizni naseleniia SSSR*, p. 5.
38. *Obshchaia metodika razrabotki general'noi skhemy razmeshcheniia proizvoditel'nykh sil na 1971–80 gg*. This problem, i.e., the regional level of economic development, is discussed further in an interesting study by Mats-Olov Olsson, ''De sovjetiska unionsrepublikernas nationalinkomst.''
39. Nekrasov, pp. 34ff.

2. Theoretical Premises

1. The concepts concerning decisionmaking have been formulated following John Löwenhardt, *Decision Making in Soviet Politics*, pp. 9ff.
2. C. Wright Mills, *The Power Elite*, pp. 11ff. See also Floyd Hunter, *Community Power Structure*.
3. Robert A. Dahl, *Who Governs?*
4. Peter Bachrach and Morton Baratz, ''Two Faces of Power.''
5. Gudmund Hernes, *Makt og Avmakt*.
6. See above the beginning of Chapter 1, paragraph 3.
7. Alfred G. Meyer, ''USSR, Incorporated.''
8. Meyer, *The Soviet Political System: An Interpretation*, p. 468.
9. Cf. Astrid von Borcke and Gerhard Simon, *Neue Wege der Sowjetunion-Forschung*, pp. 129ff.
10. Graham T. Allison, *Essence of Decision: Explaining the Cuban Missile Crisis*, p. 144.
11. Ibid.
12. Hannah Arendt, *The Origins of Totalitarianism*.
13. Carl Friedrich and Zbigniew K. Brzezinski, *Totalitarian Dictatorship and Autocracy*, pp. 9ff.
14. Ibid., pp. 239ff.
15. Peter H. Solomon, Jr., *Soviet Criminologists and Criminal Policy*, p. 1.
16. Ibid.
17. Ibid.
18. Ibid., p. 2.
19. Ibid.
20. Thus the first hypothesis is similar to the totalitarian model while the third and fourth hypotheses fit the bureaucratic model. The second hypothesis is an intermediate form.
21. See Ruth Levitt, *Implementing Public Policy*.
22. Cf. Evert Vedung, *Energipolitiska utvärderingar 1973–81*.
23. Jan Åke Dellenbrant, *Soviet Regional Policy*.
24. Cf. I. S. Koropeckyj, ''Industrial Location Policy in the USSR during the Postwar Period.''

25. P. A. Minakir, *Ekonomicheskoe razvitie regiona: programnyi podkhod*, p. 32.
26. Cf. Martin C. Spechler, "Regional Developments in the USSR, 1958–78."

3. Regional Differences

1. *Pravda*, 2 February 1982.
2. Cf. F. C. Barghoorn, *Soviet Russian Nationalism*.
3. *Programmy i ustavy KPSS*, p. 41.
4. Ibid., p. 143.
5. *Pravda*, 22 December 1972, 21 February 1982.
6. *Metodicheskie ukazaniia k sostavleniiu plana razvitiia narodnogo khoziaistva SSSR*, p. 672.
7. *Metodicheskie ukazaniia k razrabotke gosudarstvennykh planov razvitiia narodnogo khoziaistva SSSR*, p. 559.
8. M. Chistiakov, "Metodicheskie ukazaniia k sostavleniiu odinnadtsatogo piatiletnogo plana."
9. Leonid I. Brezhnev, *Leninskim kursom. Rechi i statii*, p. 626.
10. *KPSS v rezoliutsiiakh i resheniiakh s"ezdov, konferentsii, i plenumov TsK.*
11. E. V. Taderoshan, "Sovetskii narod—sotsial'naia osnova sovetskogo mnogonatsional'nogo-obshchenarodnogo gosudarstva," p. 15 footnote.
12. Ibid., p. 15.
13. Ibid., p. 16.
14. Ibid., p. 17.
15. Hélène Carrère d'Encausse, p. 57.
16. "Shestdesiat let SSSR. Doklad Iu. V. Andropova."
17. "My gordy otechestvom svoim," p. 5.
18. R. I. Kosolapov, "Klassovye i natsional'nye otnosheniia na etape razvitogo sotsializma," 10.
19. "My gordy otechestvom svoim," p. 6.
20. V. Medvedev, "Narodnokhoziaistvennyi kompleks i mezhnational'nye otnosheniia," p. 46.
21. Iu. G. Saushkin, *Ekonomicheskaia geografiia*, p. 390.
23. Ibid.
24. Friedrich Engels, *Herr Eugen Dührings Umwälzung der Wissenschaft (Anti-Dühring)*, pp. 409ff.
25. I. S. Koropeckyj, "The Development of Soviet Location Theory before the Second World War—I," pp. 17f.
26. Koropeckyj, pp. 19f.
27. Ibid.
28. Ibid., p. 21f.
29. Alfred Weber, *Über den Standort der Industrien*.
30. Koropeckyj, "The Development of Soviet Location Theory before the Second World War—I," p. 52.
31. Ibid.
32. Cf. Saushkin, pp. 390ff and A. T. Khrushchev, *Geografiia promyshlennosti SSSR*, pp. 82ff.
33. Theodore Shabad and Victor L. Mote, *Gateway to Siberian Resources*, p. 13.
34. Koropeckyj, "Location Problems in Soviet Industry before the Second World War—I," pp. 55ff.
35. Ibid., p. 61.
36. Ibid.

37. Ia. G. Feigin, in Saushkin, *Ekonomicheskaiia geografiia*, pp. 392ff. See also Judith Pallot and Denis Shaw, *Planning in the Soviet Union*.
38. Cf. George A. Huzinec, "A Reexamination of Soviet Industrial Location Theory."
39. Gertrude E. Schroeder, "Regional Differences in Income in the 1970s," p. 25.
40. Ibid., p. 38.
41. Schroeder, "Regional Differences in Incomes and Levels of Living in the USSR," p. 187.
42. Schroeder, "Regional Living Standards," p. 129.
43. Koropeckyj, "Equalization of Regional Development in Socialist Countries: An Empirical Study," p. 73.
44. Ibid., p. 80.
45. Ibid., pp. 681 and 80.
46. Roland J. Fuchs and George J. Demko, "Geographic Inequality under Socialism," p. 305.
47. Ibid., p. 307.
48. Ibid., p. 308.
49. Ibid., p. 314.
50. Ibid., p. 315.
51. Ibid., p. 316.
52. Ibid., p. 318.
53. Ann Littman Rappoport, "Soviet Policies toward the Union Republics: A Compositional Analysis of 'National Integration,'" p. 214.
54. Ibid., p. 46.
55. Ibid., pp. 64ff. and 80ff.
56. Ibid., pp. 152ff.
57. Ibid., p. 167.
58. Martin C. Spechler, "Regional Developments in the USSR, 1958–78," p. 161.
59. Ibid., p. 145.
60. James W. Gillula, "The Economic Interdependence of Soviet Republics," p. 652.
61. Donna Lynn Bahry, "Republic Politics and Federal Budget Policy in the USSR," p. 132.
62. Jack Bielasiak, "Policy Choices and Regional Equality among the Soviet Republics."
63. Cf. Donna Bahry and Carol Nechemias, "Half-full or Half-empty?: The Debate over Soviet Regional Equality."
64. Ibid., p. 370.
65. Jan Åke Dellenbrant, *Soviet Regional Policy*.
66. Ibid., pp. 59ff.
67. Ibid., pp. 136ff.
68. Ibid., p. 102.
69. Ibid., p. 137.
70. J. G. Williamson, "Regional Inequality and the Process of National Development."
71. Cf. Richard E. Londsdale, "Regional Inequity and Soviet Concern for Rural and Small-town Industrialization," p. 593.
72. L. N. Telepko, *Urovni ekonomicheskogo razvitiia raionov SSSR*.
73. "My gordy otechestvom svoim," p. 6.
74. Ibid.
75. Medvedev, p. 53.
76. Telepko, p. 149.

77. Ibid., pp. 185ff.
78. I. Notkin, ed., *Proportsii vozproizvodstva v period razvitogo sotsializma.*
79. A. I. Vedishchev, "Soizmereniie urovnei khoziaistvennogo razvitiia ekonomicheskikh raionov SSSR."
80. Ibid., p. 10.
81. Ibid., p. 15.
82. N. M. Rutkevich, "Sblizheniie natsional'nykh respublik i natsii SSSR po sotsial'no-klassovoi strukture."
83. E. B. Alaiev and S. I. Khvatov, "Istoricheskii protsess vyravnivaniia urovnei ekonomicheskogo i sotsial'nogo razvitiia soiuznykh respublik," p. 25.
84. Ibid., p. 22.
85. Ibid., p. 24.

4. The Administrative Organization

1. Ronald Hill and Peter Frank, *The Soviet Communist Party*, p. 61. In principle, planning authorities at different levels would constitute a third administrative hierarchy; however, they are subordinate to the regular state hierarchy.
2. *Materialy XXVI s"ezda KPSS*, p. 130. The overview on this and following pages is primarily intended to serve as a background for those readers who are interested in regional policy without being Soviet experts.
3. Cf. Jerry Hough and Merle Fainsod, *How the Soviet Union Is Governed*, p. 458.
4. Ibid., pp. 412ff.
5. Ibid.
6. John Löwenhardt, *The Soviet Politbureau.*
7. *Who's Who in the Soviet Union*, p. 379.
8. Ibid., pp. 379-80.
9. Ibid.
10. E. A. Kepbanov, "Rol' Gosplana soiuznoi respubliki v obespechenii ego kompleksnogo razvitiia."
11. N. V. Tsapkin and P. S. Petrov, *Planirovanie narodnogo khoziaistva SSSR*, pp. 76ff.
12. Cf. H. Knop and A. Straszak, *The Bratsk-Ilimsk Territorial Production Complex*, p. 21, Tsapkin and Petrov, p. 78.
13. V. L. Kvint, "Politologicheskie i pravovye aspekty regional'noi nauchnotechnicheskoi politiki."
14. Ibid., p. 23.
15. Tsapkin and Petrov, p. 71.
16. Cf. Hough, pp. 480ff.
17. Andreas Ådahl, *Sovjetförvaltning*, p. 52.
18. Tsapkin and Petrov, p. 80.
19. Kepbanov, pp. 36ff.
20. Kvint, p. 32.
21. A detailed description of the Soviet republics may be found in Katz et al., *Handbook of Major Soviet Nationalities.*
22. Cf. Tsapkin and Petrov, p. 73.
23. Lars Ohlsson, *Lokal förvaltning i Sovjetunionen.*
24. J. C. Dewdney, "Patterns and Problems of Regionalization in the USSR," pp. 23ff.
25. Tsapkin and Petrov, p. 371.
26. Kopylov, p. 14.

27. For a more detailed description of the raions see Pallot and Shaw, pp. 62ff. See also N. Kopylov, "Novyi ekonomicheskii raion," p. 14.

28. Cf. Alec Nove, *The Soviet Economic System*, p. 65.

29. Rolf Eidem, *Planekonomi eller ramhushållning?*, pp. 149 ff.

30. The reform proposal was printed in *Pravda*, 3 April 1973.

31. Eidem, p. 153.

32. Compare the section below on administration problems and reforms.

33. Compare Chapter 5, below.

34. For a description of concern see Nove, pp. 80ff., Eidem, p. 164, and Alice Gorlin, "The Soviet Economic Associations," pp. 3ff.

35. See the law on work collectives and the enhanced role of the work collective in the management of enterprises and organizations, *Pravda*, 19 June 1983.

36. A. Kochetkov et al., "Upravlenie krupnymi proizvodstvennokhoziaistvennymi kompleksami," p. 64.

37. Cf. Peter de Souza, "The Structure of Territorial Production Complexes," pp. 6ff.

38. I. S. Barabasheva, "Upravlenie territorial'no-proizvodstvennym kompleksam (TPK)," p. 42.

39. E. Azarov, "Kogda sozdaiotsia territorial'no-proizvodstvennyi kompleks," p. 25.

40. M. K. Bandman, *Territorial'no-proizvodstvennye kompleksy*, pp. 4ff.

41. Kochetkov, p. 65.

42. Barabasheva, p. 46.

43. Ibid., p. 42.

44. Azarov, p. 26.

45. *Materialy XXVI s"ezda KPSS*, p. 50.

46. Ibid.

47. K. N. Iusupov, "Regional'nye mezhotraslevye kompleksy i ikh spetsializatsiia."

48. Nove, pp. 70ff.

49. S. A. Billon, "Centralization of authority and regional management," p. 220.

51. Ibid., pp. 291ff.

52. Ibid., p. 227.

53. V. M. Manokhin, " . . . S uchetom otraslevogo i territorial'nogo printsipov," p. 24.

54. T. M. Dzafarli et al., "Nekotorye aspekty uskoreniia nauchno-technikheskogo protsessa.

55. E. Afanasevskii, "Territorial'naia organizatsiia proizvodstva."

56. *Pravda*, 23 November 1982.

57. Ibid. The reference is surely in the first instance to Hungary.

58. Ibid., 14 March 1983.

5. Regional Development under Debate

1. Leslie Dienes, "Investment Priorities in Soviet Regions," p. 447.

2. Ibid., p. 448.

3. V. G. Udovenko, "Razvitiiu mineral'no-syrevoi bazy Belorussii—bol'she vnimaniia!"

4. S. Malinin, "Nuzhno respublike, vygodno strane," pp. 15 and 24.

5. V. G. Vasilev, "Razvitie poisko-razvedochnykh rabot na gaz v SSSR," pp. 4-6.

6. P. Voloboi and V. Poporkin, "O pokazateliakh khoziaistvennogo urovnia

raionov i oblastei," p. 59.
7. Dienes.
8. *Zasedaniia verkhovnogo soveta SSSR*, p. 78.
9. Ibid., p. 451.
10. A. A. Mints, *Resursy, sreda, rasselenie*, pp. 20ff.
11. N. V. Alisov, "Spatial Aspects of the New Soviet Strategy of Intensification of Industrial Production."
12. A. G. Granberg, "Sibir v narodnokhoziaistvennom komplekse," pp. 84ff.
13. Granberg, "Narodnokhoziaistvennaia effektivnost' uskorennogo razvitiia proizvoditel'nykh sil Sibiri," p. 75.
14. Granberg, "Sibir v narodnokhoziaistvennom komplekse."
15. Granberg, "Narodnokhoziaistvennaia effektivnost'," p. 75.
16. Granberg, "Sibir v narodnokhoziaistvennom komplekse," pp. 100ff.
17. Theodore Shabad, "Soviet Regional Policy and CMEA Integration."
18. N. Khudaiberdiev, "Perspektivy ekonomiki Uzbekistana," p. 12.
19. Z. Pataridze, "Ekonomika Sovetskoi Gruzii: dostizheniia i perspektivy," p. 7.
20. K. Makhkamov, "Formirovaniie i razvitiie Iuzhno-Tadzhikskogo TPK," p. 21.
21. M. Allakhverdiev, "Sovershenstvovanie struktury promyshlennogo proizvodstva Azerbaidzhana," pp. 135ff.
22. S. Takezhanov, "Nekotorye voprosy otraslevogo planirovaniia v usloviiakh respublika," p. 71.
23. Iu. V. Subotskii, "Otraslevaia sistema i ego tsentr upravleniia."
24. "Otraslevoe i territorial'noe upravlenie v SSSR i GDR," p. 135.
25. O. S. Kolbasov and A. I. Kazannik, "Okhrana prirody pri perebroske stoka severnykh i sibirskikh rek v iuzhnye raiony strany."
26. Khudaiberdiev, p. 10.
27. Cf. *Pravda Vostoka*, 20 December 1980, 8 January and 11 February 1981.
28. *Pravda*, 18 November 1981.
29. Karl Vaino, "Problemy i perspektivy povysheniia effektivnosti proizvodstva v respublike."
30. J. Ruben, "Plan i initsiativa."
31. B. Zaikauskas, "Razvitie khoziaistvennogo mekhanizma v respublike."
32. I. Manjušis, "Sochetanie otraslevogo i territorial'nogo upravleniia."
33. A. Zamakhin, "Na reslakh effektivnogo truda."
34. A. Bachurin, "Problemy uluchsheniia ispol'zovaniia trudovykh resursov," p. 25.
35. Ibid., p. 29.
36. Ibid., pp. 30ff.

6. Decisions and Regional Policy

1. Jan Åke Dellenbrant, *Reformists and Traditionalists*; Bialer, p. 304.
2. "Ob uluchshenii planirovaniia i usilenii vozdeistviia khoziaistvennogo mekhanizma na povyshenie effektivnosti proizvodstva i kachestva raboty."
3. Ibid. See also Dellenbrant and Perlowski, *Teknologisk utveckling i Sovietunionen*, pp. 100ff.
4. This indicator means that the output of the enterprise is planned in physical terms such as total weight of the products.
5. Ibid., pp. 13ff.
6. Ibid., p. 17.
7. Ibid., p. 18.

8. Ibid.
9. Ibid., p. 16.
10. "O dal'neishem povyshenii roli Sovetov narodnykh deputatov v khoziaistvennom stroitel'stve," *Pravda*, 29 March 1981.
11. Ibid.
12. "Otchet TsK Kompartii Estonii," *Sovetskaia Estoniia*, 29 January 1981.
13. Ibid.
14. Ibid.
15. "O proekte 'Osnovnye napravleniia razvitiia SSSR na 1981–85 gody,'" *Sovetskaia Estoniia*, 30 January 1981.
16. Ibid.
17. "Otchet TsK Kompartii Latvii," *Sovetskaia Latviia*, 30 January 1981.
18. Ibid.
19. Ibid.
20. "O proekta 'Osnovnye napravleniia razvitiia SSSR na 1981–85 gody,'" *Sovetskaia Latviia*, 31 January 1981.
21. "Otchet TsK Kompartii Uzbekistana," *Pravda Vostoka*, 4 February 1983.
22. Ibid.
23. Ibid.
24. Ibid.
25. Ibid.
26. Ibid., p. 4.
27. Ibid.
28. "O proekte TsK KPSS 'Osnovnye napravleniia razvitiia SSSR na 1981–85 gody,'" *Pravda Vostoka*, 5 February 1981.
29. Ibid.
30. Ibid.
31. "Otchet TsK Kompartii Turkmenistana," *Turkmenskaia iskra*, 17 January 1981.
32. "O proekte TsK KPSS 'Osnovnye napravleniia razvitiia SSSR na 1981–85 gody,'" *Turkmenskaia iskra*, 18 January 1981.
33. "Otchet TsK Kompartii Gruzii," *Zaria Vostoka*, 23 January 1981.
34. "Otchet TsK Kompartii Belorussii," *Sovetskaia Belorussiia*, 28 January 1981.
35. "Otchet TsK Kompartii Kirgizii," *Sovetskaia Kirgiziia*, 21 January 1981.
36. "Otchet TsK Kompartii Moldavii," *Sovetskaia Moldaviia*, 23 January 1981.
37. *Materialy XXVI s"ezda KPSS*, p. 33.
38. Ibid., p. 38.
39. Ibid., p. 51.
40. Ibid., p. 54.
41. Ibid.
42. Ibid., p. 55.
43. Ibid., p. 103.
44. Ibid., pp. 101ff.
45. Ibid., p. 108.
46. Ibid., pp. 120ff.
47. Ibid., p. 185.
48. For the guideline data on the republics see *Materialy*, pp. 186ff.
49. *Pravda*, 27 February 1981.
50. Ibid., 26 February 1981.
51. Ibid., 27 February 1981.
52. Ibid., 25 January 1981.
53. Ibid., 25 February 1981.

54. Ibid., 27 February 1981.
55. Ibid.
56. Ibid., 27 February 1981.
57. Ibid., 25 February 1981.
58. Ibid., 28 February 1981. Similar views, although in somewhat milder terms, were expressed in the speeches of the Ukrainian First Secretary and Politburo member V. V. Shcherbitskii, *XXVI s"ezd,* pp. 114ff.
59. *Pravda,* 27 February 1981.
60. Ibid., 25 February 1981.
61. Ibid., 26 February 1981.
62. Ibid.
63. Ibid., 27 February 1981.
64. Ibid., 25 February 1981.
65. Ibid.,
66. *XXVI s"ezd,* Vol. 1, pp. 251ff.
67. Ibid., p. 234.
68. Ibid., pp. 361ff.
69. Alice C. Gorlin, "Soviet Industry and Trade," p. 318.
70. *Pravda,* 17 November 1981.
71. Ibid., 18 November 1981.
72. Ibid.,
73. Olsson.
74. "Prodovol'stvennaia programma SSSR na period do 1990 goda i mery po ego realizatsii."
75. *Pravda,* 22 December 1982.
76. Ibid., 19 June 1983. At this meeting Iurii Andropov was appointed Chairman in the Presidium of the Supreme Soviet.
77. Ibid.
78. Ibid., 26 July 1983.
79. Ibid.
80. Ibid.
81. Cf. the beginning of Chapter 1, paragraph 3, and Bialer, p. 304.
82. *Pravda,* 22 July 1983.
83. Ibid., 7 August 1983.

7. Implementation and Results

1. Walter Williams, "Implementation Analysis and Assessment," p. 268.
2. Ibid., p. 273.
3. Ibid.
4. Evert Vedung, *Energipolitiska utvärderingar 1973-81,* p. 12.
5. Ibid., pp. 8ff.
6. Ibid., pp. 12ff.
7. Peter Rossi and Sonia Wright, "Evaluation Research: An Assessment of Theory, Practice, and Politics."
8. Cf. Dellenbrant, *Reformists and Traditionalists,* pp. 136ff.
9. Bialer, p. 304.
10. W. Brus, "The East European Economic Reforms: What Happened to Them?"
11. N. Baibakov, "Ekonomika obshchestva rozdennogo velikim oktiabriom," p. 14.
12. B. Shcherbitskii, "Kontrol i proverka ispolnenia—vazhneishaia funktsiia par-

tiinogo rukovodstva.''
13. *Pravda*, 9 December 1983 and, for instance, *Sovetskaia Latviia*, 10 December 1983.
14. Ibid.
15. *Pravda*, 23 January 1983 and 23 January 1984.
16. *USSR: Measures of Economic Growth and Development, 1950–80.*
17. Cf. A. G. Granberg, ''Regional Economic Interactions in the USSR,'' p. 335.
18. *Sovetskaia Estoniia*, 31 January 1984.
19. Lauschmann, p. 288.
20. Khorev, p. 11.
21. Zakumbaev, p. 4.
22. Dellenbrant, ''Soviet Social and Political Indicators,'' p. 54.
23. Granberg, ''Narodnokhoziaistvennaia effektivnost'.''
24. *Izvestiia*, 1 December 1982, *Nar. khoz. SSSR 1922–82*, p. 376.
25. Mozhin, p. 4.
26. *Nar. khoz. RSFSR 75*, pp. 328–330; *Nar. khoz. RSFSR 1970*, p. 10; *Nar. khoz. RSFSR 1975*, pp. 6–7. Data for 1982 are lacking.
27. *Materialy*, pp. 184ff. See also Chapter 6, above.
28. David A. Dyker, *The Process of Investment in the Soviet Union*, p. 28.
29. Nove, pp. 229ff.
30. ''Gosudarstvennyi biudzhet SSSR i biudzhety soiuznykh respublik, 1976–1980,'' p. 150.
31. Hutchings states that a republic is normally allocated subsidies when it must finance enterprises of all-union importance. Raymond Hutchings, *The Soviet Budget*, p. 44.
32. Cf. Igor Birman, *Secret Incomes of the Soviet State Budget*.
33. *Ekonomicheskaia gazeta*, 2 (1984).
34. *Nar. khoz. SSSR v 1982 godu*, p. 521.
35. Cf. Alastair McAuley, *Economic Welfare in the Soviet Union*, pp. 118ff., See also K. A. Novikov, ed., *Normativnye akty po ispol'zovaniiu trudovykh resursov*, pp. 738ff.
36. B. Moiseienko, ''O soderzhanii i tendentsiakh migratsionnoi politiki.''
37. *Materialy*, p. 104.
38. *Pravda*, 29 January 1984.
39. Dellenbrant, *Soviet Regional Policy*, p. 165. See also Olsson.
40.Riabushkin et al., *Regional'nye osobennosti vosproizvodstva i migratsii naseleniia v SSSR*, p. 167.
41. G. Baldwin, *Population Projections by Age and Sex*.
42. Cf. L. L. Rybakovskii, ''O migratsii naseleniia v SSSR.''
43. Iu. B. Bromlei and O. I. Shkaratan, ''Natsional'nye trudovye traditsii—vazhnii faktor intensifikatsii proizvodstva.''
44. Ibid., p. 38.
45. Ibid., p. 39.
46. Ibid., p. 40.
47. Iu. Bromlei, ''Etnicheskie protsessy v SSSR,'' p. 57.
48. It is interesting in this context to note the methodological instructions (*metodicheskie ukazaniia*) worked out for the five-year plans do not contain any formulations indicating that any consideration should be given to national traditions.
49. Michael Rywkin, ''The Russia-wide Soviet Federated Socialist Republic (RSFSR): Privileged or Underprivileged?''
50. Cf. Rutkevich.
51. Dellenbrant, *Soviet Regional Policy*.
52. Boris Meissner, ''The 26th Party Congress and Soviet Domestic Politics.''

53. Ralph Clem, "Economic Development of the Russian Homeland: Regional Growth in the Soviet Union."

54. Ibid.

55. *Nar. khoz. SSSR 1980*, p. 12.

56. Robert Lewis et al., *Nationality and Population Change in Russia and the USSR.*

57. M. N. Rosenko, "Rol' russkoi sotsialisticheskoi natsii v razvitii i ukreplenii internatsional'nogo edinstva sovetskogo naroda."

58. Iu. Shiriaev et al., *Osnovnye napravleniia sblizheniia sotsialisticheskikh stran*, p. 3.

59. Cf. Alec Nove and J. A. Newth, *The Soviet Middle East: A Model for Development?*

60. D. I. Ziuzin, "Prichiny nizkoi mobil'nosti korennogo naseleniia respublik srednei Azii.*"

61. Cf. Nove and Newth, pp. 105ff.

62. Spechler.

63. Khorev, p. 50.

64. A skeptical attitude toward industrial development in Siberia is also to be found in Soviet literary works. See Valentin Rasputin, "Proshchanie s Materoi."

65. T. I. Zaslavskaia et al., "Sotsial'nye problemy razvitii Sibiri," pp. 3ff. An unpublished article on economic reforms presumably written by Zaslavskaia was the object of a broad debate in the Western press in 1983 and 1984.

66. Cf. Allen Whiting, *Siberian Development and East Asia: Threat or Promise?*

8. Review and Summary

1. H. Smolar, "La planification comme processus d'apprentisage. Le cas soviétique."

2. B. P. Kurashvili, "Ob"ektivnye zakony gosudarstvennogo upravleniia."

3. P. Ignatovskii, "O politicheskom podkhode k ekonomike."

BIBLIOGRAPHY

Newspapers

Izvestiia

Pravda

Pravda Vostoka

Sovetskaia Belorussiia

Sovetskaia Estoniia

Sovetskaia Kirgiziia

Sovetskaia Latviia

Sovetskaia Moldaviia

Sovetskaia Rossiia

Turkmenskaia iskra

Zaria vostoka

Statistical Material

Narodnoe Khoziaistvo RSFSR v 1970 godu.

Narodnoe Khoziaistvo RSFSR v 1975 godu.

Narodnoe Khoziaistvo SSSR v 1960 godu.

Narodnoe Khoziaistvo SSSR v 1970 godu.

Narodnoe Khoziaistvo SSSR v 1979 godu.

Narodnoe Khoziaistvo SSSR v 1980 godu.

Narodnoe Khoziaistvo SSSR 1922–1982.

Narodnoe Khoziaistvo SSSR v 1982 godu.

SSSR i soiuznye respubliki v 1980 godu. Moscow: Finansy i statistika, 1981.

SSSR i soiuznye respubliki v 1981 godu. Moscow: Finansy i statistika, 1982.

SSSR i soiuznye respubliki v 1982 godu. Moscow: Finansy i statistika, 1983.

"Vsesoiuznaia perepis' naseleniia." *Vestnik statistiki* 2 (1980) and 1 (1981).

Other Sources and Literature

Ådahl, Andreas. *Sovjetförvaltning*. Uppsala: Research Center for Soviet and East European Studies, 1971 (mimeographed).

Afanasevskii, E. "Territorial'naia organizatsiia proizvodstva." *Voprosy Ekonomiki* 4 (1981).

Alaiev, E.B. and S.I. Khvatov. "Istoricheskii protsess vyravnivaniia urovnei ekonomicheskogo sotsial'nogo razvitiia soiuznykh respublik," *Izvestiia Akademii Nauk SSSR. Seriia Ekonomicheskaia* 6 (1982).

Alisov, N. V. "Spatial Aspects of the New Soviet Strategy of Intensification of Industrial Production." *Soviet Geography: Review and Translation* (January 1979).

Allakhverdiev, M. "Sovershenstvovanie struktury promyshlennogo proizvodstva Azerbaidzhana." *Voprosy Ekonomiki* 10 (1981).

Allison, Graham T. *Essence of Decision: Explaining the Cuban Crisis*. Boston: Little, Brown & Co. Inc., 1971.

Andropov, Iu. V. "Shestdesiat let SSSR." *Kommunist* 1 (1983).

Arendt, Hannah. *The Origins of Totalitarianism*. New York: Harcourt Brace Jovanovich, 1951.

Azarov, E. "Kogda sozdaiotsia territorial'no-proizvodstvennyi kompleks." *Sovet Narodov Deputatov* 2 (1983).

Back, Pär-Erik. "Regionalpolitik och beslutsnivå." *Politik* (Umeå University) 2 (1979).

Bachrach, Peter, and Morton Baratz. "Two Faces of Power." *American Political Science Review* 56 (1962).

Bachurin, A. "Problemy uluchsheniia ispol'zovania trudovykh resursov." *Planovoe Khoziaistvo* 1 (1982).

Bahry, Donna Lynn. "Republic Politics and Federal Budget Policy in the USSR." Ph.D. diss., University of Illinois, Urbana-Champaign, 1972.

Bahry, Donna Lynn and Nechemias, Carol, "Half-full or Half-empty? The Debate over Soviet Regional Equality." *Slavic Review* 3 (1981).

Baibakov, N. "Ekonomika obshchestva razhdennogo velikim oktiabriom." *Planovoe Khoziaistvo* 12 (1982).

Baldwin, Godfrey. *Population Projections by Age and Sex: For the Republics and Major Economic Regions*. Washington, D.C.: U.S. Department of Commerce, Foreign Demographic Analysis Division, 1979.

Bandera, V. N. and Z. L. Melnyk, eds. *The Soviet Economy in Regional Pespective*. New York: Praeger Publishers, 1973.

Bandman, Mark K. *Territorial'no-proizvodstvennye kompleksy*. Novosibirsk: Izdatel'stvo "Nauka," 1980.

Barabasheva, I. S. "Upravlenie territorial'no-proizvodstvennym kompleksam (TPK)." *Sovetskoe Gosudarstvo i Pravo* 5 (1980).

Barghoorn, Frederick C. *Soviet Russian Nationalism*. Westport, Conn.: Greenwood Press, 1976.

Bialer, S. *Stalin's Successors: Leadership, Stability, and Change in the Soviet Union*. Cambridge: Cambridge University Press, 1980.

Bielasiak, Jack. "Policy Choices and Regional Equality among the Soviet Republics." *Ameri-*

can Political Science Review 74:2 (June 1980).

Billon, S. A. "Centralization of Authority and Regional Management." In *The Soviet Economy in Regional Perspective*, edited by V. N. Bandera and Z. L. Melnik. New York: Praeger Publishers, 1973.

Birman, Igor. *Secret Incomes of the Soviet State Budget*. Dordrecht: Martinus Nijhoff, 1981.

Blunden, John, et al. *Regional Analysis and Development*. London: Harper & Row, 1973.

Brezhnev, Leonid I. *Leninskim kursom. Rechi i statii*. Vol. 5. Moscow: Politizdat, 1976.

Bromlei, Iu. B. and O. I Shkaratan. "National'nye trudovye traditsii—vazhnyi faktor intensifikatsii proizvodstva." *Sovetskoe Gosudarstvo i Pravo* 2 (1983).

Bromlei, Iu. B. "Etnicheskie protsessy v SSSR." *Kommunist* 5 (1983).

Brus, Wlodzimierz. "The East European Reforms: What Happened to Them?" *Soviet Studies* 31 (1979).

Carrère d'Encausse, Hélène, "Determinants and Parameters of Soviet Nationality Policy." In *Soviet Nationality Policies and Practices*, edited by J. R. Azrael. New York: Praeger Publishers, 1978.

Chistiakov, M. "Metodicheskie ukazaniia k sostavleniiu odinadtsatogo piatiletnego plana." *Voprosy Ekonomiki* 1 (1981).

Clem, Ralph. "Economic Development of the Russian Homeland: Regional Growth in the Soviet Union." In *Ethnic Russia in the USSR*, edited by Edward Allworth. New York: Pergamon Press, 1980.

Clout, Hugh. *Regional Development in Western Europe*. New York: Pergamon Press, 1980.

Dahl, Robert A. *Who Governs? Democracy and Power in an American City*. New Haven: Yale University Press, 1963.

de Souza, Peter. *The Structure of Territorial Production Complexes*. Göteborg: Kulturgeografiska institutionen, 1982.

Dellenbrant, Jan Åke. *Soviet Regional Policy: A Quantitative Inquiry into the Social and Political Development of the Soviet Republics*. Atlantic Highlands, N. J.: Humanities Press, 1980.

————. "Soviet Social and Political Indicators. Selected Statistical Data on the Soviet Republics." *Contributions to Soviet and East European Research* (Uppsala, Sweden) 4 (1976).

————. *Reformists and Traditionalists: A Study of Soviet Discussions about Economic Reform 1960–1965*. Stockholm: Rabén och Sjögren, 1972.

Dellenbrant, Jan Åke and Adam Perlowski. "Teknologisk utveckling i Sovietunionen." *FOA-rapport* (Stockholm) (September 1981).

Deutsch, Karl. "Social Mobilization and Political Development." *American Political Science Review* (September 1961).

Dewdney, J. C. "Patterns and Problems of Regionalization in the USSR." *University of Durham. Dept. of Geography Research Papers* 8 (1967).

Dienes, Leslie. "Investment Priorities in Soviet Regions." *Annals of the Association of American Geographers* 62 (1972).

Dyker, David A. *The Process of Investment in the Soviet Union*. Cambridge: Cambridge University Press, 1983.

Dzafarli, T. M., et al. "Nekotorye aspekty uskoreniia nauchno-tekhnicheskogo protsessa." *Sovetskoe Gosudarstvo i Pravo* 2 (1983).

Eidem, Rolf. *Planekonomi eller ramhushållning?* Stockholm: SNS, 1976.

Engels, Friedrich. *Herr Eugen Dührings Umwälzung der Wissenschaft* (Anti-Dühring). Berlin: Dietz Verlag, 1965.

Feshbach, Murray. "Regional Branch and Wage Differentials in the Soviet Union." *The Association for Comparative Economic Studies* 2:2 (1975).

Friedrich, Carl, and Zbigniew K. Brzezinski. *Totalitarian Dictatorship and Autocracy.* New York: Praeger Publishers, 1956.

Fuchs, Roland J., and G. J. Demko. "Geographic Inequality under Socialism." *Annals of the Association of American Geographers* (June 1979).

Gillula, James W. "The Economic Interdependence of Soviet Republics." In *Soviet Economy in a Time of Change.* Washington, D. C.: Joint Economic Committee, 1979.

Godlund, S. *Regional politik i plan och verklighet.* Göteborg: Sparfrämjandets Förlag, 1970.

Gorlin, Alice. "Soviet Industry and Trade." *Current History* (October 1982).

————. "The Soviet Economic Associations." *Soviet Studies* 1 (1974).

Gosudarstvennyi biudzhet SSSR i biudzhet soiuznykh respublik 1976–1980. Moscow: Finansy i Statistika Publishing House, 1982.

Granberg, A. G. "Narodnokhoziaistvennaia effektivnost' uskorennogo razvitiia proizvoditel'nykh sil Sibiri." *Planovoe Khoziaistvo* 5 (1981).

————. "Regional Economic Interaction in the USSR." In *Regional Development Modelling,* edited by Albegov, et al. Amsterdam: North Holland, 1982.

————. "Sibir v narodnokhoziaistvennom komplexe." *Ekonomika i Organizatsiia Promyshlennogo Proizvodstva (EKO)* (Novosibirsk) 4 (1980).

Hansen, Niles, ed. *Public Policy and Regional Economic Development: The Experience of Nine Western Countries.* Cambridge, Mass.: Ballinger, 1974.

Hernes, Gudmund. *Makt og Avmakt.* Bergen: Universitetsforlaget, 1975.

Hill, Ronald, and P. Frank. *The Soviet Communist Party.* London: Allen & Unwin, 1981.

Hirschman, Albert, O. *The Strategy of Economic Development.* New Haven: Yale University Press, 1981.

Horek, Stephan M., ed. *Guide to the Study of the Soviet Nationalities.* Littleton: Libraries Unlimited, Inc., 1982.

Hough, Jerry, and Merle Fainsod. *How the Soviet Union Is Governed.* Cambridge, Mass.: Harvard University Press, 1979.

Hunter, Floyd. *Community Power Structure. A Study of Decision Makers.* Garden City, N. Y.: Doubleday Publishing Co., 1963.

Hutchings, Raymond. *The Soviet Budget.* Albany: State University of New York Press, 1983.

Huzinec, George A. "A Reexamination of Soviet Industrial Location Theory." *Professional Geographer* 3 (1977).

Ignatovskii, P. "O politcheskom podkhode k ekonomike." *Kommunist* 12 (1983).

Isard, Walter. *Introduction to Regional Science.* Englewood Cliffs, N. J.: Prentice-Hall, Inc., 1975.

Iusupov, K. N. "Regional'nye mezhotraslevye kompleksy i ikh spetsializatsiia." *Izvestiia Akademiia Nauk SSSR. Seriia Ekon.* 1 (1979).

Katz, Z., et al. *Handbook of Major Soviet Nationalities.* New York: Free Press, 1975.

Kepbanov, E. A. "Rol' gosplana soiuznoi respubliki v obespechenie ego kompleksnogo razvitiia." *Sovetskoe Gosudarstvo i Pravo* 3 (1984).

Khorev, V. S. *Territorial'naia organizatsiia obshchestva: aktual'nye problemy regional'nogo upravleniia i planirovaniia v SSSR.* Moscow: Izdatel'stvo "Mysl'," 1981.

Khrushchev, A. T. *Geografiia promyshlennosti SSSR.* Moscow: Izdatel'stvo "Mysl'," 1979.

Khudaiberdiev, N. "Perspektivy ekonomiki Uzbekistana." *Planovoe Khoziaistvo* 8 (1981).

Knop, H., and A. Straszak, eds. *The Bratsk-Ilimsk Territorial Production Complex: A Field Study Report.* Laxemburg: IIASA, 1978.

Kochetkov, A., et al. "Upravlenie krupnymi proizvodstvenno-khoziaistvennymi kompleksami." *Voprosy Ekonomiki* 1 (1981).

Kolbasov, O. S., and A. I. Kazannik. "Okhrana prirody pri perebroske stoka severnykh i sibirskikh rek v iuzhnye raiony strany." *Sovetskoe Gosudarstvo i Pravo* 9 (1981).

Kopylov, N. "Novyi ekonomicheskii raion." *Ekonomicheskaia Gazeta* 11 (1983).

Koropeckyj, I. S. "Equalization of Regional Development in Socialist Countries: An Empirical Study." *Economic Development and Cultural Change* (October 1972).

————. "Industrial Location Policy in the USSR during the Postwar Period." In *Economic Performance and the Military Burden in the Soviet Union.* Washington, D. C.: Joint Economic Committee, 1970.

————. "The Development of Soviet Location Theory before the Second World War—I." *Soviet Studies* 19:1 (July 1967).

Kosolapov, R. I. "Klassovye i natsional'nye otnosheniia na etape razvitogo sotsializma." *Sotsiologicheskie Issledovaniia* 4 (1982).

Koval, N. S., ed. *Planirovanie narodnogo khoziaistva SSSR.* Moscow: Vysshaia Shkola, 1975.

KPSS v rezoliutsiiakh i resheniiakh s "ezdov, konferentsiii i plenumy TsK. Vol. 19. Moscow: Politizdat, 1972.

Kurashvili, B. P. "Ob "ektivnye zakony gosudarstvennogo upravleniia." *Sovetskoe Gosudarstvo i Pravo* 10 (1983).

Kvint, V. L. "Politologicheskie i pravovye aspekty regional'noi nauchno-tekhnicheskoi politiki." *Sovetskoe Gosudarstvo i Pravo* 4 (1983).

Lauschmann, Elisabeth. *Grundlagen einer Theorie der Regionalpolitik.* Hanover: Gebrüder Jänecke Verlag, 1973.

Levitt, Ruth. *Implementing Public Policy.* London: Croom Helm, 1980.

Lewis, Robert, R. Rowland, and R. Clem. *Nationality and Population Change in Russia and the USSR.* New York: Praeger Publishers, 1976.

Lewytzkyj, Borys, ed. *Who's Who in the Soviet Union.* Munich: K. G. Saur Verlag, 1984.

Londsdale, Richard E. "Regional Inequity and Soviet Concern for Rural and Small-town Industrialization." *Soviet Geography: Review and Translation* (October 1977).

Lorendahl, Bengt. *Nordisk Regionalekonomi.* Stockholm: Föreningarna Nordens Förbund, 1974.

Löwenhardt, John. *Decision Making in Soviet Politics.* London: Macmillan Publishers, 1981.

————. *The Soviet Politbureau.* Edinburgh: Canongate Publishing Ltd., 1982.

Maier, V. F. *Urovni zhizni naseleniia SSSR.* Moscow: Politizdat, 1977.

Makhkamov, K. "Formirovanie i razvitie iuzhno-tadzhikiskogo TPK." *Planovoe Khoziaistvo* 10 (1981).

Malinin, S. "Nushno respublike, vygodno strane." *Ekonomicheskaia Gazeta* 40 (1965).

Manjušis, I. "Sochetanie otraslevogo i territorial'nogo upravleniia." *Voprosy Ekonomiki* 4 (1983).

Manokhin, V. M. "S uchetom otraslevogo i territorial'nogo printsipov (St. 16 Konstitutsii SSSR)." *Sovetskoe Gosudarstvo i Pravo* 10 (1979).

Materialy XXVI s"ezda KPSS. Moscow: Politizdat, 1981.

McAuley, Alastair. *Economic Welfare in the Soviet Union. Poverty, Living Standards and Inequality.* Madison: University of Wisconsin Press, 1979.

Medvedev, V. "Narodnokhoziaistvennye kompleks i mezhnatsional'nye otnosheniia." *Kommunist* 17 (1982).

Meissner, Boris. "The 26th Party Congress and Soviet Domestic Politics." *Problems of Communism* (December 1980).

Metodicheskie ukazaniia k razrabotke gosudarstvennykh planov razvitiia narodnogo khoziaistva SSSR. Moscow: Izdatel'stvo "Ekonomika," 1974.

Meyer, Alfred G. *The Soviet Political System: An Interpretation.* New York: Random House Inc., 1965.

————. "USSR, Incorporated." *Slavic Review* (October 1966).

Mills, C. Wright. *The Power Elite.* New York: Oxford University Press, 1959.

Minakir, P. A. *Ekonomicheskoe razvitie regiona: programnyi podkhod.* Moscow: Izdatel'stvo "Nauka," 1983.

Mints, A. A. *Resursy, sreda, rasselenie.* Moscow: Izdatel'stvo "Nauka," 1977.

Moiseenko, B. "O soderzhaniii i tendentsiiakh migratsionnoi politiki." In *Demograficheskaia politika v SSSR.* Moscow: Finansy i Statistika Publishing House, 1983.

Mozhin, V. P. "Ratsional'noe razmeshchenie proizvoditel'nykh sil i sovershenstvovanie territorial'nykh proportsii." *Planovoe Khoziaistvo* 4 (1983).

"My gordy otchestvom svoim." *Kommunist* 2 (1983).

Myrdal, Gunnar. *Economic Theory and Underdeveloped Regions.* London: Duckworth & Co., 1957.

Nekrasov, N. N. *Regional'naia ekonomika: teoria, problemy, metody.* Moscow: Izdatel'stvo "Ekonomika," 1975.

Notkin, I., ed., *Proportsii vozproizvodstva v period razvitogo sotsializma.* Moscow: Izdatel'stvo "Nauka," 1976.

Nove, Alec. *The Soviet Economic System.* London: Allen & Unwin, 1977.

Nove, Alec, and J. A. Newth. *The Soviet Middle East: A Model for Development?* London: Allen & Unwin, 1976.

Novikov, K. A., ed., *Normativnye akty po izpol'zovaniiu trudovykh resursov.* Moscow: Izdatel'stvo "Iuridicheskaia Literatura," 1972.

"Ob uluchshenii planirovaniia i usileniii vozdeistviia khoziaistvennogo mekhanizma na povyshenie effektivnosti proizvodstva i kachestva raboty." *Planovoe Khoziaistvo* 9 (1979).

Obshchaia metodika razrabotki general'noi skhemy razmeshcheniia proizvoditel'nykh sil na 1970–1980 gg.. Moscow: Izdatel'stvo "Ekonomika," 1966.

Ohlsson, Lars. *Lokal förvaltning i Sovjetunionen. Sovjeterna: vision och verklighet.* Stockholm: Rabén och Sjögren, 1979.

Olsson, Mats-Olov. "De sovjetiska unionsrepublikernas nationalinkomst." *Bidrag till öststatsforskningen* 2 (1980).

"Otraslevoe i territorial 'noe upravlenie v SSSR i GDR." *Sovetskoe Gosudarstvo i Pravo* 5 (1979).

Pallot, Judith, and Denis Shaw. *Planning in the Soviet Union.* London: Croom Helm, 1981.

Pataridze, Z. "Ekonomika Sovetskoi Gruzii: dostizheniia i persepktivy." *Planovoe Khoziaistvo* 7 (1981).

Prodovol'stvennaia programma SSSR na period 1990 goda i mery po ego organizatsii. Moscow: Politizdat, 1982.

Programmy i ustavy KPSS. Moscow: Izdatel 'stvo "Politicheskaia Literatura," 1969.

Rappoport, Ann Littman. "Soviet Policies towards the Union Republics. A Compositional Analysis of 'National Integration.'" Ph.D. diss., Ohio State University, Columbus, 1978.

Rasputin, Valentin. "Proshchanie s Materoi." *Nash Sovremennik* 10-11 (1976).

Riabushkin, T. V., ed., *Regional'nye osobennosti vosproizvodstva i migratsii naseleniia v SSSR.* Moscow: Izdatel 'stvo "Nauka," 1981.

Rosenko, M. N. "Rol' russkoi sotsialisticheskoi natsii v razvitii i ukreplenii internatsional 'nogo edinstva sovetskogo naroda." *Istoria SSSR* 1 (1982).

Rossi, Peter, and Sonia Wright. "Evolution Research: An Assessment of Theory, Practice and Politics." *Evaluation Quarterly* 1 (1971).

Ruben, J. "Plan i initsiativa." *Planovoe Khoziaistvo* 5 (1982).

Rumer, B. "Soviet Investment Policy: Unresolved Problems." *Problems of Communism* (September-October 1982).

Rutkevich, N. M. "Sblizhenie natsional'nykh respublik i natsii SSSR po sotsial'no-klassovoi strukture." *Sotsiologicheskie Issledovanie* 2 (1981).

Rybakovskii, L. L. "O migratsii naseleniia v SSSR." *Sotsiologicheskie Issledovaniia* 4 (1981).

Rywkin, Michael. "The Russia-wide Soviet Federated Socialist Republic (RSFSR): Privileged or Underprivileged?" In *Ethnic Russia in the USSR,* edited by Edward Allworth. New York: Pergamon Press, 1980.

Saushkin, Iu. G. *Ekonomicheskaia geografiia: Istoriia, teoria, metody, praktika.* Moscow: Izdatel 'stvo "Mysl '," 1973.

Schroeder, Gertrude E. "Regional Differences in Incomes and Levels of Living in the USSR." *The Soviet Economy in Regional Perspective,* edited by V. N. Bandera and Z. L. Melnik. New York: Praeger Publishers, 1973.

————. "Regional Differences in Income in the 1970s." In *Regional Development in the USSR. Trends and Prospects.* Newtonville: Oriental Research Partners, 1979.

————. "Regional Living Standards." In *Economics of Soviet Regions,* edited by I. S. Koropeckyj and G. E. Schroeder. New York: Praeger Publishers, 1979.

Seers, D. et al., eds. *Underdeveloped Europe: Studies in Core-Periphery Relations.* Hassocks, England: The Harvester Press, 1979.

XXVI S"ezd Kommunisticheskoi partii Sovetskogo Soiuza. Stenographic report, I-III. Moscow: Politizdat, 1981.

Shabad, T. "Soviet Regional Policy and CMEA Integration." *Soviet Geography: Review and Translations* (April 1971).

Shabad, T. and V. L. Mote. *Gateway to Siberian Resources.* New York: John Wiley & Sons Inc., 1977.

Shcherbitskii, B. "Kontrol' i proverka ispolneniia—vazhneishnaia funktsiia partiinogo rukovodstva." *Kommunist* 10 (1983).

"Shestdesiat let SSSR. Doklad Iu. V. Andropova." *Kommunist* 1 (1983).

Shiriaev, Iu., et al. *Osnovnye napravleniia sblizheniia sotsialisticheskikh stran.* Moscow: Izdatel'stvo "Nauka," 1982.

Smolar, H. "La planification comme processus d'apprentissage. Le cas soviétique." *Revue d'études comparatives est-ouest* (September 1979).

Solomon, Peter H. Jr. *Soviet Criminologists and Criminal Policy.* New York: Columbia University Press, 1978.

Spechler, Martin C. "Regional Development in the USSR, 1958–1978." In *Soviet Economy in a Time of Change.* Washington, D. C.: Joint Economic Comittee, 1979.

Subotskii, Iu. V. "Otraslevaia sistema i ego tsentr upravleniia," *Sovetskoe Gosudarstvo i Pravo* 11 (1981).

Taderoshan, F. V. "Sovetskii narod—sotsial'naia osnova sovetskogo mnogonational'nogo obshchenarodnogo gosudarstva." *Sovetskoe Gosudarstvo i Pravo* 12 (1982).

Takezhanov, S. "Nekotorye voprosy otraslevogo planirovaniia v usloviiakh respubliki." *Planovoe Khoziaistvo* 2 (1981).

Telepko, L. N. *Urovni ekonomicheskogo razvitiia raionov SSSR (Voprosy ikh izmereniia i sblizheniia).* Moscow: Izdatel'stvo "Ekonomika," 1971.

Tsapkin, N. V. and P. S. Petrov. *Planirovanie narodnogo khoziaistva SSR.* Moscow: Izdatel'stvo "Mysl'," 1977.

Udovenko, V. G. "Razvitiiu mineral'no-syrevoi bazy Belorussii—bol'she vnimaniia!" *Promyshlennost' Belorussii* 3 (1967).

USSR: Measures of Economic Growth and Development. Washington, D. C.: Joint Economic Committee, 1982.

Vaino, Karl. "Problemy i perspektivy povysheniia effektivnosti proizvodstva v respublike." *Planovoe Khoziaistvo* 3 (1982).

Vasilev, V. G. "Razvitie poisko-razvedochnykh rabot na gaz v SSSR." *Gazovaia Promyshlennost'* 3 (1969).

Vedishchev, A. I. "Soizmerenie urovnei khoziastvennogo razvitiia ekonomicheskikh raionov SSSR." In *Ekonomicheskie problemy rasmeshcheniia proizvoditel'nykh sil SSSR.* Moscow: Izdatel'stvo "Nauka," 1969.

Vedung, Evert. "Energipolitiska utvärderingar 1973–81." *DFE Rapport* (Swedish Council for Energy Research) (Stockholm) 52 (1982).

Voloboi, P. and V. Poporkin. "O pokazateliakh khoziaistvennogo urovnia raionov i oblastei." *Ekonomika Sovetskogo Ukrainy* 19 (1968).

von Borcke, Astrid, and Gerhard Simon. *Neue Wege der Sowjetunion-Forschung: Beitrage zur Methoden und Theorie-Diskussion.* Baden-Baden: Nomos Verlaggesellschaft, 1980.

Weber, Alfred. *Über den Standort der Industrien.* Tübingen: J C B Mohr, 1909.

Whitehouse, D. and D. Kamerling. "Asiatic RSFSR." In *Economics of Soviet Regions*, edited by I. S. Koropeckyj and G. E. Schroeder. New York: Praeger Publishers, 1981.

Whiting, Allen S. *Siberian Development and East Asia: Threat or Promise?* Stanford: Stanford University Press, 1981.

Williams, Walter. "Implementation Analysis and Assessment." In *Social Program Implementation*, edited by W. Williams and R. Elmore. New York: Academic Press, 1978.

Williamson, J. G. "Regional Inequality and the Process of National Development." *Economic Development and Cultural Change* 4:2 (July 1965).

Zaikauskas, B. "Razvitie khoziaistvennogo mekhanizma v respublike." *Voprosy Ekonomiki* 12 (1981).

Zakumbaev, A. K. *Ekonomicheskoe razvitie soiuznykh respublik i raionov.* Alma-Ata: Izdatel'stvo "Nauka," 1977.

Zamakhin, A. "Na rel'sakh effektivnogo truda." *Sovety Narodov Deputatov* 3 (1983).

Zasedaniia verkhovnogo soveta SSSR, sedmogo sozyva (piataia sessiia). Stenographic report. Moscow: Politizdat, 1969.

Zaslavskaia, Tatiana I., et al. "Sotsial'nye problemy razvitiia Sibiri." *Izvestiia sibirskogo otdeleniia Akademii nauk SSSR. Seriia obshchestvennykh nauk.* 1 (1982).

Ziuzin, D. I. "Prichini nizkoi mobil'nosti korennogo naseleniia respublik srednei Azii." *Sotsiologicheskie Issledovania* 1 (1983).

BIOGRAPHICAL INDEX

Aganbegian, Abel, 9
Ådahl, Andreas, 9
Alaev, E. B., 60
Aliev, G., 118
Alisov, N. V., 88, 89, 90
Allakhverdiev, M., 91–92
Allison, Graham, 27
Andersson, Åke, 9
Andropov, Iurii, 8, 39, 83, 94, 126, 127–129, 135, 160, 182
Arendt, Hannah, 27
Åström, Lars-Martin, 8
Azarov, E., 79

Bahry, Donna Lynn, 52
Baibakov, Nikolai, 83, 120–121, 135
Bairamov, Dr. Dzhuma, 9
Baldwin, Godfrey, 159
Bandman, Mark, 9
Barabasheva, I. S., 79
Barghoorn, Frederick, 29
Barry, Donald, 29
Batyurin, A., 95, 96
Berglund, Sten, 9
Bialer, Seweryn, 10, 11, 14, 26, 96–97, 99, 134–135, 136
Bielasiak, Jack, 52
Bogomiakov, G. P., 119
Brezhnev, Leonid, I. 8, 36, 37, 39, 98, 103, 108, 109, 110, 111, 116, 117, 120, 131, 159, 180, 182
Bromlei, Iulian, 159–160
Brzezinski, Zbigniew, 27, 28, 29

Chentemirov, Minas, 144–145
Chernenko, K. Iu., 182
Clem, Ralph, 166
Conquest, Robert, 28

Dahl, Robert, 25
Demirtian, K., 118
Demko, George J., 50, 51
de Souza, Peter, 9
Dienes, Leslie, 87

Eltsin, B. N., 119
Engels, Friedrich, 40, 41, 42, 43

Fedirko, P. S., 119
Feigin, Ia. G., 44, 45–46
Fogelklou, Anders, 9
Friedrich, Carl, 27, 28
Fuchs, Roland J., 50, 51

Gapurov, M., 117
Gillula, James W., 52
Godlund, Sven, 18
Goldin, Grejnim, 8
Gorbachev, Mikhail S., 135, 183
Graham, Loren, 29
Granberg, Alexander G., 9. 89, 145
Griškevičius, Petras, 116
Grossu, S., 108, 118

Hagström, Ulla, 8
Hansen, Niles, 19
Hernes, Gudmund, 25

Hirschman, Albert O., 12
Hough, Jerry, 29
Hunter, Floyd, 25
Huntington, Samuel, 29

Ignatovskii, P., 181
Iivonen, Jyrki, 9
Isard, Walter, 21, 34

Juviler, Peter, 29

Khorev, B. S., 19, 174
Khrushchev, A. T., 44
Khrushchev, Nikita S., 72
Khudaiberdiev, N., 90, 91, 93, 106
Khvatov, S. I., 60
Kiselev, T. Ia., 108, 118
Klauson, V., 103
Koropeckyj, Ivan S., 31, 45, 49, 50, 51
Kosolapov, R. I., 39
Kunaev, D., 117
Kurashvili, B. P., 181

Lauschmann, Elisabeth, 18–19, 23, 143
Lenin, Nikolai, 36, 37–38, 40, 41, 42,
   43, 45, 126
Liashko, A. P., 118
Linden, Carl, 28

Makhamov, K., 91
Malinin, S., 87
Manjušis, I., 94
Manokhin, V. M., 83
Marx, Karl, 38, 40, 41, 43, 45, 47
Maslennikov, N. I., 145
Meyer, Alfred G., 26, 27, 29
Michnik, Stefan, 9
Mills, C. Wright, 25
Minakir, P. A., 33
Mints, Aleksei, 88, 90
Molin, Ewa, 8
Myrdal, Gunnar, 11–12, 177

Nekrasov, N. N., 20, 22
Nørgaard, Ole, 9
Notkin, A. I., 59

Olsson, Mats-Olov, 9

Pataridze, Z., 91
Perlowski, Adam, 8

Ploss, Sidney, 28
Rafto, Thorolf, 9
Rappoport, Ann Littmann, 51–52
Rashidov, Sh., 105, 106, 117
Rasulov, D., 117
Rosenko, M. N., 171–172
Rozenblat, Czeslaw, 9
Ruben, Iu., 104
Ruben, J., 94
Rutkevich, M. N., 59

Saushkin, Iu. G., 40
Schroeder, Gertrude E., 31, 47–49, 51,
   55
Shabad, Theodore, 90
Shcherbitskii, B., 135
Shevardnadze, Edvard, 108, 118
Shkaratan, O. I., 160
Solomentsev, M. S., 118, 119
Solomon, Peter, 28
Spechler, Martin C., 52, 174, 177
Stalin, Joseph, 42, 43–44, 99
Stewart, Philip, 29
Subotskii, Iu. V., 92
Susiluoto, Ilmari, 9

Takezhanov, S., 92
Tarschys, Daniel, 9
Tatu, Michel, 28
Telepko, L. N., 59
Tikhonov, Nikolai, 98, 108, 109, 111,
   116, 151, 182

Udovenko, V. G., 87
Usubaliev, T., 108, 117

Vaino, Karl, 93–94, 102, 103, 104, 116–
   117
Vedishchev, A. I., 21, 59
Veinger, Musja, 8
Voss, August, 104, 116

Wallin, Lena, 8
Weber, Alfred, 42, 43
Williamson, J. G., 57, 177

Zaikauskas, V., 94
Zakumbaev, A. K., 59, 60, 152
Zamakhin, A., 94
Zaslavskaia, Tatiana, 174–175

SUBJECT INDEX

Abasha region, 118
Academy of Sciences, 57–58, 68, 86, 89, 92–93, 100, 130
Administration: concerns, 75; problems and reforms, 81–84
Agriculture, 71; growth of, 32; output by republic, 113; workers' incomes, 48
Agriculture Ministry, 66
Agrogoroda, 4
All-Union Council of Ministers, 69–70
Altai krai, 168
Amur oblast, 168
Angara-Ienisei region, 79
Angara River, 78
Anti-Dühring, 40
Armenia: agricultural output, 113; capital investments in rubles, 146, 148; employed population, 156, 158; employment rate, 157; industrial development, 71; industrial development index, 60; industrial growth, 114, 115; industrial output, 113, 122, 137; leadership changes, 118; national income, 153, 154, 155; 1984 budget, 150; per capita national income, 56; population, 16, 156, 158, 164; population growth, 16; socioeconomic characteristics, 56; standard of living, 48
Ashkhabad, 9
Associations of enterprises, 74–75
ASSR. *See* Autonomous republic
Automotive Industry Ministry, 65
Autonomous republic (ASSR), 80–81;

government, 72–74
Aviation Industry Ministry, 65
Azerbaidzhan, 91; agricultural output, 113; capital investments in rubles, 146, 148; economic growth, 118; employed population, 156, 158; employment rate, 157; industrial development, 71, 96; industrial development index, 60; industrial growth, 92, 96, 114–115, 137; industrial output, 113, 122, 137; labor shortage, 95; national income, 153, 154, 155; 1984 budget, 150; per capita national income, 56; population, 72, 156, 158, 164; population growth, 16, 72; production potential, 15, religion, 71–72; socioeconomic characteristics, 56; socioeconomic development, 55, 56; standard of living, 49

Baikal-Amur Railway (BAM), 78, 79, 88, 110, 111, 113, 167, 169, 175, 182
Baltic republics, 147; capital investments in, 144, 146–147, 162, 164; consumption of goods and services, 49; criticism of union ministries, 94; economic policies, 95; as economic region, 73–74; employment problems, 107; and European bloc, 130; industrial development index, 59; industrial growth, 171; labor force shortage, 107; labor productivity, 59; labor shortage, 155; lack of developmental

interest in, 86; manufacturing in, 71; national income, 152; per capita investments, 146–147; population, 163; regional development, 8; regional policy changes, 93–94; socioeconomic development, 134, 161–162; standard of living, 48–49, 70; wage coefficients, 151

Bank of Sweden Tercentary Foundation, 9

Belgium, 11

Belorussia, 118, 127, 147; agricultural output, 113; agricultural output improvements, 108; capital investments in rubles, 146, 148; developmental planning, 86–87; economic experiments in, 128; as economic region, 73–74; employed population, 156, 158; employment rate, 157; and European bloc, 130; industrial development index, 60; industrial output, 114, 122, 137; industry in, 71; labor productivity, 59; national income, 153, 154, 155; 1984 budget, 150; oil extraction, 87; per capita national income, 56; population, 71, 156, 158, 164; population growth, 16; research and scientific institutions, 70; socioeconomic characteristics, 56; socioeconomic development, 161–162; standard of living, 48–49

Boguchany, 113

Bratsk-Ilimsk production complex, 167

Budgets: republic (1984), 150; transfers from union to republic, 149

Bundesinstitut für ostwissenschaftliche und internationale Studien, 9

Bureau of the Central Committee, 69

Bureaucracy, 95

Bureaucratic model, 26

Buriatia, 167, 168; capital investments, 169; population, 169

Capital investments, 24, 143–151; see also individual republic names

Caucasian republics, 90, 142, 147; agricultural growth, 121; capital investments in, 144, 145, 162, 164; economic policies, 95; as economic region, 73–74; industrial development in, 71–72, 92; industrial growth, 121; labor productivity, 59; population,

163; socioeconomic development, 134, 161–162; wage coefficients, 151

CC. See Central committee

Central Asia, 9, 13, 51, 52, 86, 90, 105–106, 111, 142, 147; agricultural growth, 121, blocs, 129–130, 178, 179; capital investments, 144, 145, 162, 164; distribution of resources, 13–14; economic development, 109; economic growth, 117; economic policies, 95; as economic region, 73–74; economy, 160; employment, 154; employment problems, 107, 110; equalization, 141–142; flow of resources in, 7–9; industrial development, 92, 95, 139; industrial development index, 59; industrial growth, 115, 121; industrial production, 112; industrial traditions, 172; labor productivity, 59; labor reserves, 155; labor resources, 121; labor shortage, 95; level of consumption, 5; location criteria, 173; macroregional analysis, 33–34; national income, 152; population, 163; population growth, 162–163; production development, 88; regional development, 8; social growth, 117; socioeconomic development, 55, 72, 134, 161–162; standard of living, 49; stage budget funding, 149; TPC development, 111; underemployment 96; underground economy, 173; wage coefficients, 151; water program, 68

Central Committee (CC), 30, 36, 63, 64, 69, 83, 98, 99, 101, 103, 106, 117, 118, 127, 180, 182; resolutions, 125–126

Central Council for Trade Unions, 127

Central Economic-Mathematical Institute, 68

Centralized economic decisionmaking, 12

Centralized planning system, 12

Central Russia: labor productivity, 59

Chemical Industry Ministry, 65, 91

Chemical and Petroleum Machine Building Industry Ministry, 65

China, 175

Chita oblast, 168

Christianity, 71–72

Civil Aviation Industry Ministry, 65

Class system, 38

CMEA countries, 49, 83, 89, 130, 172
Coal Industry Ministry, 66
Communications Equipment Industry Ministry, 65
Communications Ministry, 65
Communist Party, 36–37, 41, 53, 62, 64, 81, 85, 97, 116, 117, 131, 135, 145, 163, 171
Compensation theory, 53
Construction for the Far East and Trans-Baikal Area Industry Ministry, 65
Construction of Heavy Industry Enterprises Ministry, 66
Construction Materials Industry Ministry, 66
Construction Ministry, 66
Construction of Petroleum and Gass Industry Enterprises Industry Ministry, 65
Construction, Road and Municipal Machine Building Industry Ministry, 65
Consumption of goods and services, 49
Council of Ministers, 63, 64, 65, 67, 69, 80, 81, 91, 92, 94, 99, 100, 101, 107, 108, 117, 118–119, 120, 127, 182
Council for the Study of Productive Forces, 68
CPSU, 37, 105, 126
CPSU Congress, 102
Cuba, 27
Culture Ministry, 66
Czechoslovakia, 50

Defense, 49, 50; military planning, 175
Defense Industry Ministry, 65
Defense Ministry, 65
Department of Soviet and East European Studies, 9
Dictatorship, 27–28
Doctrine of equal development, 3
Dvoinoe podchinenie, 65

Eastern Siberia, 33; capital investments, 168; economic reforms, 135; industrial development index, 60; wage coefficients, 151
Economic Councils, 62, 82
Economic experiments, 126, 127–131
Economic Institute of the Academy of Sciences, 57–58
Economic Institute of the Gosplan of the TSSR, 9

Economic Institute of the Kazak Academy of Sciences, 59
Economic reform (1965), 74, 94, 98, 99–102, 104, 109–110, 112, 116
Economic reform (1973), 74, 75, 76, 99
Economics: location rules, 40–46; organizational planning and administration, 77, 78; Soviet policy, 14–15, 45; Soviet principles, 44
Economy: activity, 17; growth, 14, 50, 71; investments in, 12
Edinonachalie, 76
Edinstvo, 39
Edinyi narodno-khoziaistevnnyi kompleks, 39–40
Education, 20–21, 53, 54
Education Ministry, 66
18th Party Congress, 42
Ekonomika i Matematicheskie Metody, 31
Electrical Equipment Industry Ministry, 65
Electronics Industry Ministry, 65
11th Five-year Plan, 8, 37, 93, 98, 103, 104, 105, 108, 109, 111, 112, 120–125, 128, 129, 134, 136, 138, 142, 147, 152, 175, 178
"Elitists," 25
Employment, 12, 21, 24, 34, 96, 153–159; levels, 106; rate, 177
Enterprise, 76
Estonia, 93–94, 103, 108, 139, 163, 171; agricultural output, 113, capital investments in rubles, 146, 148; Communist Party in, 102–103, 116; Communist Party support, 102–103; development, 99, 104; economic development, 104–105, 142; economic situation, 103; employment population, 156, 158; employment rate, 157; future growth, 103–104; growth in capital investments, 125; growth in labor productivity in industry, 124; growth in national income, 140; industrial development index, 60; industrial growth, 114, 115, 121, 137; industrial output, 113, 122, 123, 137, 140; industrial production, 112; industry, 147; labor productivity, 140, 152; national income, 139, 140, 153, 154, 155; national income growth, 124; 1984 budget, 150; Party Congresses in, 102; per capita national in-

come, 56; population, 71, 72–73, 156, 158, 164; population decline, 71; population growth, 16; research and scientific institutions, 70; socioeconomic characteristics, 56; socioeconomic development, 134; standard of living, 48, 70, 165

Ethnic pluralism, 45

Europe, 33, 86, 129; capital invetments in, 144, 145, 162, 164; distribution of resources, 13–14; employment, 154; labor shortage, 95; population, 163; socioeconomic development, 161–162

European bloc, 130–131

European USSR, 87, 128–129; flow of resources in, 7–9; macroregional analysis, 33–34; regional development in, 8; standard of living, 48

Executive Committee, 79

Far East, 33; capital investments, 166, 168; distribution of resources, 13–14; economic importance, 100; industrial development index, 60; investment sharing, 166; labor shortage, 150; Soviet location theory, 42; wage coefficients, 151

Ferrous metallurgy ministry, 66

15th Party Congress, 41, 108

Filialy, 75

Finance Ministry, 66

Finland, 11

Fish Industry Ministry, 66

Five-year Plans, 37, 67, 69, 77, 89, 96, 98, 102, 107–108, 109

Food Industry Ministry, 66

Food program, 63, 125–126

Foreign Affairs Ministry, 66

Foreign Trade Ministry, 65, 67

Fruits and Vegetables Ministry, 66

Gas Industry Ministry, 65

General Machine Building Industry Ministry, 65

General Secretary, 28

Geographic Institute, 88

Geography: distribution of industry, 37; distribution of resources, 3–4; and regional differences, 50; sectoral barriers, 80, 83

Geology Ministry, 66

Georgia, 91, 108; agricultural development, 71; agricultural output, 113; capital investments in rubles, 146, 148; economic growth, 118; employed population, 156, 158; employment rate, 157; growth in industrial output, 137; industrial development, 71; industrial development index, 60; industrial growth, 114, 115; industrial output, 113, 122, 137; national income, 153, 154, 155; 1984 budget, 150; per capita national income, 56; population, 16, 156, 158, 164; population growth, 16; socioeconomic characteristics, 56; standard of living, 48

Germany, 28, 43, 50

GKNT. See State Committee for Science and Technology

Glavki, 74, 75

GOELRO. See State Commission for Electrification of Russia

Gosekonomkomissiia, 82–83

Gosplan, 21–22, 24, 68, 69, 73, 75, 80, 81, 82, 83, 86, 87, 88, 90, 91, 92, 95, 100, 102, 104, 116, 117, 118, 120, 135, 145

Gossnab, 5

Gosstroi, 106

Government, central state, 65

Great Britain, 11

Great Patriotic War, 43; see also World War II

Grundlagen einer Theorie der Regionalpolitik, 18

Health Ministry, 66

Heavy and Transport Machine Building Industry Ministry, 65

Helsinki, 9

Higher and Secondary Specialized Education Ministry, 66

House of Nationalities of the Supreme Soviet, 82–83

Hungary, 50, 99, 127

Iakutia, 79, 167, 168; capital investments, 169; economic development, 168; economic expansion, 170, 171; TPC formation, 113; population, 169; raw materials industry, 5; urbanization, 169

Ienisei River, 78

Immigrant laborers, 5
Immigration, 170
Income, 20–21, 51; distribution, 51; growth, 123, 124, 138
Industrial Construction Ministry, 66
Industrial output, 137; *see also* individual republic names
Industrialization, 20–21
Industry, 65–66, 71; development of, 41; geographic distribution, 37; growth of, 32; growth rates by republic, 122, 123; output by republic, 113, petroleum, 146
Installation and Special Construction Work Ministry, 66
Institute for Economics and Industrial Organization, 9, 68, 86, 89
Institute for State and Law, 92–93
Instrument Making, Automation Equipment and Control Systems Industry Ministry, 65
Internal Affairs Ministry, 66
Intersectoral commissions, 83
Intersectoral committee, 83
Investments, 12, 21, 34, 51, 128; distribution, 147; growth of, 14, 111; policy, 143; structure, 147
Irkutsk oblast, 168
Irrigation, 93
Irysh River, 93
Islam sect, 6, 72
Istoriia SSR, 171–172
Italy, 11
Izhdiventsy, 156
Izvestiia, 31

Japan, 169
Justice Ministry, 66

Kamtchatka oblast, 168
Kansk-Achinsk, 79
Kazak Academy of Sciences, 59
Kazakhstan, 91, 142, 171; agricultural output, 113; capital investments, 144, 146, 148, 162, 164, 165; Communist Party in, 117; development in, 92; as economic region, 73–74; employed population, 156, 158, employment rate, 157; energy production, 111; growth in industrial output, 137; industrial development index, 60; industrial growth, 115; industrial output,
113, 122, 137; investment distribution, 147; irrigation of, 93; national income, 56, 152, 153, 154, 155; 1984 budget, 150; per capita national income, 56, 152, 153, 154, 155; population, 16, 156, 158, 163, 164; population growth, 16; production development, 88; socioeconomic characteristics, 56; socioeconomic development, 134; standard of living, 48; TPC formation, 109, 149; wage coefficients, 151; water diversion project, 117
Kemerovska oblast, 168
Kennan Institute for Advanced Russian Studies, 9
KGB. *See* State security agency
Khabarovsk krai, 168
Kirghizia, 108, 117, 118, 147; agricultural output, 113; capital investments in rubles, 146, 148; employed population, 156, 158; employment rate, 157; growth in industrial output, 137; industrial development, 96; industrial development index, 60; industrial growth, 115; industrial output, 113, 122, 137; national income, 153, 154, 155; 1984 budget, 150; per capita national income, 56; population, 16, 156, 158, 164; population growth, 16; socioeconomic characteristics, 56; socioeconomic development, 72, 134; standard of living, 48; water diversion project, 117
Kombinaty, 75, 76
Kommunist, 39, 58, 135, 181
Kompleksno-tselevye programmy, 116
Krai, 80–81, 101, 119, 168; definition, 72; government, 72
Kraiplan, 72
Krasnoiarsk krai, 119, 168

Labor: distribution, 50; productivity growth by republic, 124; shortage of, 94, 95
Land Reclamation and Water Resources Ministry, 66
Latvia, 94, 104, 108, 139, 171; agricultural output, 113; capital investments in rubles, 146, 148; Communist Party in, 117; developmental plans, 99; economic development, 104–105, 142;

employed population, 156, 158; employment rate, 157; growth in capital investments, 125; growth in labor productivity in industry, 124; industrial development index, 60; industrial growth, 115, 121; industrial output, 113, 114, 122, 123, 137; industrial production, 112; labor productivity, 116; national income, 124, 153, 154, 155; 1984 budget, 150; per capita investments, 147; per capita national income, 56; population, 16, 156, 158, 164; population growth, 16; socioeconomic characteristics, 56; socioeconomic development, 134; standard of living, 48, 70

Leningrad, 59, 70

Light Industry Ministry, 66, 71

Lithuania, 127; agricultural output, 113; capital investments in rubles, 146, 148; Communist Party in, 116, 117; economic experiments, 128; employed population, 156, 158; employment rate, 157; growth in industrial output, 137; growth in national income, 140; industrial development index, 60; industrial growth, 71, 114, 137; industrialization in, 71; industrial output, 113, 122, 137, 146; labor productivity, 140; national income, 153, 154, 155; 1984 budget, 150; Party Congresses in, 102; per capital investments, 147; per capita national income, 56, 140, 153, 154, 155; population, 16, 156, 158, 164; population growth, 16; socioeconomic characteristics, 56; standard of living, 48, 70; transportation system, 94; and 23rd Congress, 104

Location criteria, 172–174

Location policy, 17

Location theory, 42, 173

Machine Building for Animal Husbandry and Fodder Production Industry Ministry, 65

Machine Building Industry Minstry, 65

Machine Building for Light and Food Industry and Household Appliances Industry Ministry, 65

Machine Tool and Tool Building Industry Ministry, 65

Magadan oblast, 168

Maritime Fleet Industry Ministry, 65

Material production, 76

Meat and Dairy Industry Ministry, 66

Medical Ministry, 65

Medium Machine Building Industry Ministry, 66

Mestnichestvo, 20, 181

Mezzogiorno, 11

Military, 175, 177; defense of, 45, 49, 50; and political principles, 44

Ministries: dual subordination, 65–67; republic, 69; union, 65–66, 86, 117; union-republic, 66–67; see also individual names

Ministry for the Building Materials Industry, 92

Ministry of Defense, 64

Ministry for the Electrical Equipment Industry, 127

Ministry for the Food Industry, 127

Ministry for Heavy and Transport Machine Building, 127, 136

Ministry for Light Industry, 127

Ministry for Local Industry, 127

Moldavia, 108, 121; agricultural output, 113; capital investments in rubles, 146, 148; economic assistance, 118, as economic region, 73–74; employed population, 156, 158; employment rate, 157; industrial development index, 60; industrial growth, 114, 121, 137; industrial output, 113, 122, 137; national income, 153, 154, 155; 1984 budget, 150; per capita national income, 56; population, 16, 71, 72–73, 156, 158, 164; population growth, 16; research and scientific institutions, 70; socioeconomic characteristics, 56; socioeconomic development, 161–162; standard of living, 48–49

Moscow, 68, 70, 92, 130, 173

Moscow University, 88

Moslem sect, 49, 72, 159

Narodnoe Khoziaistvo SSSR, 30–31

National income, 153, 154, 155

Nationality, 15; policy, 170; regional differences, 47; social principles, 44

National versus regional development, 160–161

Natural resources, 24, 50; uneven distri-

bution of, 41
1981 decree, 101–102
1983 reform. *See* Economic experiments
9th Five-year Plan, 37, 137
Nonferrous Metallurgy Ministry, 66
"North-south problem," 11–17
Norway, 25
Novosibirsk, 68, 86, 89, 130, 168

Ob"edineniia, 74–75, 99
Oblast, 79, 80–81, 101, 119, 120, 165, 167, 168; definition, 72; government, 72
Oblplan, 72
Ob River, 93
Occupational training, 59, 172
Omsk oblast, 168
One-year Plan, 69

Party Congress, 8, 20, 30, 42, 43, 63, 68, 69, 77, 87–88, 98, 102–109, 109–120, 121, 155, 173, 180; regional development, 125–131
Pavlodar oblast, 79
Peasants, 38; *see also* Class system
Perebroska, 93, 117
Persia, 6
Petroleum Industry Ministry, 66
Petroleum Refining and Petrochemical Industry Ministry, 66
Planovoe Khoziaistvo, 31, 181
"Pluralists," 25
Podmena, 62
Poland, 50
Policy: Soviet stages, 180
Politburo, 24, 26, 28, 29, 63, 64, 69, 105, 117, 135, 136
Politics: distribution of resource decisions, 176; distribution and spread of power, 26, 27–30; input, 132–133; outcome, 132–133; output, 132–133; "pluralists," 25; policy shift effects, 30; and regional policy, 24–25; regional policy decisionmaking process, 176; scientific "elite," 25; Soviet principles, 44–45
Population, 47, 145–146; capital investments and, 165; composition in autonomous republics, 169; decline of, 71; employed by region, 156, 158; growth, 15–17, 71, 72–73, 90, 106, 162–165; native by republic, 164; ru-

ral, 48; urban, 48; *see also* individual republic names
Power and Electrification Ministry, 66
Power and Machine Building Industry Ministry, 66
Pravda, 31
Predpriiatie, 76
Presidium, 65
Price system, 4
Primorsk krai, 168
Production of Mineral Fertilizers Industry Ministry, 66

Radio Industry Ministry, 66
Railways Ministry, 66
Raion, 118, 145, 150; definition, 72
Rastsvet, 38–39
Raw materials, 47
Reforms: concern, 74, 75, 76, 99; economic, 74, 94, 98, 99–102, 104, 109–110, 112, 116; economic experiments, 126, 127–131
Region: capital investments, 162, 164, 169; capital investments in rubles, 146, 148; demographic policy development, 110; differences in, 35–61; division of, 73; economic, 73–74; economic growth, 36; employed population, 156; population differences, 47, 156; population growth, 163; population growth compared, 16; standard of living, 48–49; *see also* Republic; individual region names
Regional development, 96–97; center versus periphery relationship, 12–17; climate differences, 10; controversy, 85–97; definition, 17–22; economic development, 32–33; economic policy, 14–15; nationality differences, 10; natural resources differences, 10; official Soviet view, 36–40; after the Party Congress, 125–131; strategies, 12, 95–97; regional dualism, 11–17; socioeconomic development, 10; Soviet versus Western findings, 57–61; Western studies, 47–61
Regional equalization, 50
Regional policy, 98–131, 170; aims and hypotheses, 23–30; cultural and national factors, 159–172; decisions, 128–129; definition, 17–22, 23, 132–134; development of Siberia, 20; ef-

fects, 151–154; employment, 154–159; evaluation, 30; goals, 19–20, 133; implementation methods, 30–34; implementation problems, 134–136; implementation and results, 19–21, 132–175; instruments, 143–151; location criteria, 172–175; means, 19–20; perspectives, 22; plan targets and fulfilment, 136–143; as a political issue, 24–25; research, 18; Soviet view, 18; statistical analysis, 32; textual analysis, 32; theoretical premises, 23–34

Republic Council of Ministers, 69

Republic Party Congress (1981), 102–109

Republic, 68–74, 92, 100; administrative level of, 68–74; agricultural output, 113; concerns, 75; equalization among, 128; growth in capital investments, 125; growth in indistrial output, 122, 123, 137; growth in labor productivity in industry, 124; growth in national income, 124; industrial development index, 59, 60; industrial output, 113; national income, 153, 154, 155; native population, 164; Party Congresses, 107; per capita national income, 56; see also Region; individual republic names

Research institutes, 68, 70, 100

Resolutions, 99

Resources: distribution, 13–14; geographic distribution, 3–4

Riga, 104

River reversal project, 96, 105–106, 129–130

RSFSR. See Russian Socialist Federated Soviet Republic

Russian Socialist Federated Soviet Republic (RSFSR), 33, 70, 98, 100, 108, 109, 118–119, 121, 126, 139; agricultural output, 113; capital investments in, 125, 144, 146, 148, 162, 164, 165, 166, 168; capital investments and distribution of population, 165; developmental plans, 99; distribution of resources, 13–14; economic development, 142, 166; economic regions, 73–74; employed population, 156, 158; employment rate, 157; growth in labor productivity in industry, 124; growth in national income, 140; in-

dustrial development index, 59, 60; industrial growth, 112; industrial output, 113, 122, 123, 137, 140; investments in, 85; labor productivity, 140; national income, 140, 152, 153, 154, 155; national income growth, 124; 1984 budget, 150; per capita investments, 147; per capita national income, 56; political activities, 69; population, 16, 72–73, 156, 158; population growth, 16; socioeconomic characteristics, 56; socioeconomic development, 134, 161–162; standard of living, 48, 49

Saian, 79, 80

Sakhalin oblast, 168

Sblizhenie, 5, 39, 170

Scandinavia, 5, 9

Secretariat, 29, 63, 64, 69

Sectoral barriers, 80, 83

Sectoral policy, 19

Security, 21

17th Party Congress, 42, 108

Shipbuilding Industry Ministry, 66

Siamon Foundation, 9

Sib-Aral Canal, 182

Siberia, 9, 13, 33, 42, 70, 111, 129; blocs, 130, 178; capital-intensive production, 143; capital investments, 145, 166; development, 20; developmental limitations, 88; developmental problems in, 86–90; development of TPCs, 111, 118–119; economic development, 79, 89, 109; economic importance, 100; energy production, 90, 111; flow of resources in, 7–9; growth of investments, 139; industrial development, 95, 96; industrial growth, 112–113; industrial investments, 4–5; industrialization, 96; intersectoral agencies in, 80; investment in, 85, 145; investment sharing, 166; labor shortage, 95, 150, 151; living conditions, 5; location criteria, 42, 73; macroregional analysis, 33–34; national income, 89; per capita investments, 147; projected investment, 120; regional development program, 8, 68; river diversion project, 182; social infrastructure, 119; Soviet location theory, 42, 173; standard of living, 110;

TPC development, 77, 111, 118–119; water diversion project, 93, 105–106, 117, 179; *see also* Eastern Siberia; Far East; Western Siberia
Siberian river water diversion project, 93, 105–106, 113, 117, 179
"Sibir" superprogram, 68, 70, 175
16th Party Congress, 42
Sliianie, 39
Socialism, 47; and production system, 40
Social wealth, 17
Socioeconomic development, 20–21, 30, 35, 55–57
Solidarity, 21
Sotsiologicheskie Issledovaniia, 31
Soviet Institute in Helsinki, 9
Soviet Regional Policy: A Quantitative Inquiry into the Social and Political Development of the Soviet Republics, 7, 30, 54, 55, 56, 146
Soviet Union: administration problems and reforms, 81–84; agricultural growth, 32; budget expenditures, 51; bureaucracy, 11, 84, 95; capital investments, 15, 143–151; capital investments in Asian RSFSR, 168; capital investments per capita, 164; capital investments by region, 162, 165, 166, 169; class system, 38; cultural traditional, 49, 159–172; declining growth rate, 14; declining economic growth, 13–14; distribution of power, 130–131; distribution of resources, 13–14; dual organization, 62; economic growth, 71; economic policy, 45, 128–129; employed population by region, 156; employment, 153–159; employment rate, 157; ethnic pluralism, 45; growth in capital investments by republic, 125; growth in industrial output by republic, 122, 123, 137; growth in labor productivity in industry by republic, 124; growth in national income, industrial output, and labor productivity in industry plan target and plan outcome, 138; growth in national income by republic, 124; industrial development index by republic, 59, 60; industrial growth, 32; industry development, 41; investments in rubles per capita by region, 146; labor productivity in central Russia, 59,

117; labor shortage, 103; laws, 43; location criteria, 42, 172–175; manpower, 7–9; nationalities, 47; national income, 51, 56, 152, 153, 154, 155; native population by republic, 164; natural resources, 7–9; organizational issues, 84; organizational overview, 77, 78; overview of regional development, 10–22; patterns, 43; per capita national income, 56; planning and administration, 61, 62–84; policymaking stages, 180; population composition in autonomous republics, 169; population by region, 16, 156, 163; population by republic, 164; principles, 43; regional development, 7–9, 85–97; regional differences, 7–9, 35–61, 176; regional policy views, 7–9, 18; religious differences, 47; republic budget (1984), 150; research validity, 32; rules of economic activity, 40–46; social economic complexity, 39–40; society, 131; socioeconomic characteristics by cluster, 56; socioeconomic development, 177; standard of living, 21–22; transfers from union to republic budgets, 149; wage coefficients for industry in economic raions, 151; Western studies of regional differences, 47–61
Sovnarkhoz reform, 24, 49–50, 57, 62, 73, 82, 83, 93, 99
Standard of living, 21–22, 48–49, 53, 70; housing, 60; measurement, 60–61
State Commission for Electrification of Russia (GOELRO), 73
State committees, 67
State Committee for Material and Technical Supply. *See* Gossnab
Stage Committee for Science and Technology (GKNT), 67
State Economic Commission, 82–83
State Planning Committee. *See* Gosplan
State security agency, 64
Supreme Soviet, 20, 65, 68, 69, 98, 101, 102, 120, 126, 145
Sverdlovsk oblast, 119
Sweden, 11, 17
Swedish 1980 Steel Mill Project, 5

Tadzhikistan, 117, 147; agricultural output, 113; capital investments in rubles, 146, 148; economic development, 91; employed population, 156, 158; employment rate, 157; growth in industrial output, 137; industrial development, 96; industrial development index, 60; industrial growth, 115; industrial output, 113, 122; labor productivity, 152; national income, 153, 154, 155; national traditions, 160; 1984 budget, 150; per capita national income, 56; population, 16, 156, 158, 164; population growth, 16; socioeconomic characteristics, 56; socioeconomic development, 55, 56, 72, 134; standard of living, 48; TPC formation, 109

10th Five-year plan, 14, 37, 104, 105, 108, 109, 111, 121, 137, 142, 148, 149

10th Party Congress, 41

Territorial production complex (TPC), 77–81, 100, 109, 167, 182; definition, 79; formation, 121; types, 77–81

Theory of surplus value, 4

Timber, Pulp and Paper, and Wood Processing Industry Ministry, 66

Tiumen', 119, 167, 168; intersectoral agencies in, 80

Tomsk oblast, 168

Totalitarian model, 27–28

TPC. See Territorial production complex

Tractor and Agricultural Machine Building Industry Ministry, 66

Trade Ministry, 66

Trans-Baikal, 65

Transport Construction Industry Ministry, 66

Trans-Siberian railroad, 88, 175

Tsarist Russia, 3, 12, 35, 36

Turkey, 6

Turkmenistan, 9, 67, 107, 108, 139, 147; agricultural output, 113; capital investments in rubles, 146, 148; developmental plans, 99; economic development, 142; economic situation, 107; employed population, 156, 158; employment rate, 157; growth in capital investments, 125; growth in labor productivity in industry, 124; growth in national income, 141; industrial development, 96; industrial develop-

ment index, 60; industrial growth, 115; industrial output, 113, 122, 123, 137, 141; irrigation of, 93; labor productivity, 141; national income, 152, 153, 154, 155; national income growth, 124; 1984 budget, 150; oil industry in, 107, 149; per capita national income, 56; population, 16, 156, 158, 164; population growth, 16; socioeconomic characteristics, 56; socioeconomic development, 134; standard of living, 48; underdevelopment of, 102; water diversion project, 117

Tuva, 167, 168; capital investments, 169; population, 169

12th Five-year Plan, 182

12th Party Congress, 41

20th Party Congress, 105

22nd Party Congress, 107

23rd Party Congress, 104

25th Party Congress, 109

26th Party Congress, 63, 93, 98, 102, 109–120, 122, 126, 130, 151, 159

Über den Standort der Industrien, 42

Ukraine, 118, 127, 135; agricultural output, 113; capital investments in rubles, 146, 148; developmental planning, 86–87; economic experiments, 128; as economic region, 73–74; employed population, 156, 158; employment rate, 157; and European bloc, 130; growth in industrial output, 137; industrial development index, 60; industrial output, 113, 114, 122; industry in, 45; labor productivity, 59; national income, 89, 153, 154, 155; 1984 budget, 150; per capita national income, 56; population, 16, 71, 164; population growth, 16; regional policy priorities, 87; research and scientific institutions, 70; socioeconomic characteristics, 56; socioeconomic development, 161–162; standard of living, 48–49

Unemployment: among women, 160

Union level, 63–69; associations, 75; ministries, 86, 94, 117; relationship with local Soviets, 101–102; TPC importance, 77–78

University of Illinois, Russian and East

European Center, 9
Uppsala University, Department of Soviet and Eastern European Studies, 9, 30
Ural mountains, 42, 86, 109; Soviet location theory, 42; TPC formation, 109; wage coefficients, 151
Urbanization, 20–21, 53, 54, 169
Ust-Ilimsk, 88
Uzbekistan, 9, 90, 108, 139, 147; agricultural output, 72, 83, 105, 113; capital investments in rubles, 146, 148; developmental plans, 99; economic development, 142; economic situation, 107; economy, 106; employed population, 156, 158; employment in, 106–107; employment rate, 157; growth in capital investments, 125; growth in industrial output, 137; growth in labor productivity in industry, 124; growth in national income, 141; industrial development, 96; industrial development index, 60; industrial growth, 115, 121; industrial output, 113, 122, 123, 137, 141; industrial production, 112; irrigation of, 93; labor productivity, 141; national income, 153, 154, 155; national income growth, 124; 1984 budget, 150; Party Congress in, 106; per capita national income, 56; population, 16, 90, 106, 156, 158, 164; population growth, 16, 90, 106; socioeconomic characteristics, 56; socioeconomic development, 72, 134; standard of living, 48; 20th Party Congress, 105; underdevelopment, 102; water diversion project, 117

Vedomstvennost', 20, 84, 90–95, 181
Vedomstvennye bar'ery, 80
Vestnik Statistiki, 31
Volga River, 59
Voprosy Ekonomiki, 31

Wage coefficients, 150–151
Wallenberg Foundation, 9
Water: building of power station, 88; diversion of Siberian rivers, 113, 117, 179; economic importance, 106; program in Central Asia, 68
"Weight indicators," 100
"Welfare colonialism," 52, 177
Western Europe: growth patterns, 114
Western Siberia, 33, 109; capital investments, 168; developmental programs, 110; industrial development index, 60; labor productivity, 59; TPC expansion, 113; wage coefficients, 151
Women: employed population, 156, 158; employment rate, 157, 177; unemployed, 160
Workers, 38; industrial, 48; *see also* Class system
World War II, 42, 43

Yugoslavia, 6, 49

ABOUT THE AUTHOR

Jan Åke Dellenbrant is Associate Professor of Soviet and East European Studies at Uppsala University, Uppsala, Sweden. During the 1985/
86 academic year he was Professor of National Security Affairs and
Soviet Area Studies Coordinator at the Naval Postgraduate School in
Monterey, California.

Dr. Dellenbrants's previous books in English include *Soviet Regional Policy: A Quantitative Inquiry into the Social and Political Development of the Soviet Republics* (1980) and *Reformists and Traditionalists:
A Study of Soviet Discussions about Economic Reform, 1960–65*
(1972). He is currently writing a book on the regional dimension of
Soviet foreign policy.